MANAGING REGULATORY REFORM

MANAGING REGULATORY REFORM

The Reagan Strategy and Its Impact

MARSHALL R. GOODMAN
MARGARET T. WRIGHTSON

PRAEGER

New York
Westport, Connecticut
London

891773

Library of Congress Cataloging-in-Publication Data

Goodman, Marshall R.
    Managing regulatory reform.

    Bibliography: p.
    Includes index.
    1. Trade regulation—United States.
2. United States—Politics and government—
1981-   . I. Wrightson, Margaret Tucker,
1950-   . II. Title.
HD3616.U47G67   1987   338.973   87-2436
ISBN 0-275-92472-5 (alk. paper)

Library of Congress Catalog Card Number: 87-2436
ISBN:0-275-92472-5

First published in 1987

Praeger Publishers, 1 Madison Ave., New York, NY 10010
A division of Greenwood Press, Inc.

Printed in the United States of America

∞

The paper used in this book complies with the Permanent
Paper Standard issued by the National Information Standards
Organization (Z39.48-1984).

10 9 8 7 6 5 4 3 2 1

To Our Families

CONTENTS

TABLES AND FIGURES

Tables

Figures

ACRONYMS

ACIR	United States Advisory Commission on Intergovernmental Relations
AEC	Atomic Energy Commission
AFDC	Aid to Families with Dependent Children
APA	Administrative Procedures Act (1972)
CAB	Civil Aeronautics Board
CBO	Congressional Budget Office
CDBG	Community Development Block Grant
CETA	Civilian Employment Treasury Act
CPSC	Consumer Product Safety Commission
CRGR	Committee to Review Generic Requirements
DFRA	Directory of Federal Regulatory Agencies
DOE	Department of Energy
EDA	Economic Development Administration
EDB	Ethylene Dibromide (pesticide)
EOP	Executive Office of the President
EPA	Environmental Protection Agency
ERDA	Energy Research and Development Administration
ETO	Ethylene Oxide (carcinogen)
FAA	Federal Aviation Administration
FCC	Federal Communications Commission
FDIC	Federal Deposit Insurance Corporation

FMC	Federal Maritime Commission
FIFRA	Federal Insecticide Fungicide and Rodenticide Act
FRC	Federal Regional Councils
FRD	Federal Regulatory Directory
FTC	Federal Trade Commission
GAO	General Accounting Office
HEW	Health, Education and Welfare Department
HHS	Department of Health and Human Services
HUD	Housing and Urban Development
ICC	Interstate Commerce Commission
JTPA	Job Training Partnership Act (of 1982)
LILCO	Long Island Lighting Company
NAAQS	National Ambient Air Quality Standards
NACO	National Association of County Officials
NASA	National Aeronautics and Space Administration
NCAQ	National Council on Air Quality
NEPA	National Environmental Policy Act
NGA	National Governors' Association
NHTSA	National Highway Traffic Safety Administration
NLC	National League of Cities
NRC	Nuclear Regulatory Commission
NTSB	National Transportation Safety Board
OBRA	Omnibus Budget Reconciliation Act (of 1981)
OIRA	Office of Information and Regulatory Affairs
OMB	Office of Management and Budget
OPEC	Organization of Petroleum Exporting Countries
OPM	Office of Personnel Management
OSHA	Occupational Safety and Health Administration
RARG	Regulatory Analysis Review Group
RCRA	Resource Conservation and Recovery Act
RIP	Regulatory and Information Policy
SDWA	Safe Drinking Water Act
SEC	Securities and Exchange Commission
SIPs	State Implementation Plans
SMCR	Surface Mining Conservation and Restoration
TMI	Three Mile Island
USCM	U.S. Conference of Mayors
USDA	U.S. Department of Agriculture

PREFACE

Ronald Reagan came to Washington in 1981 with a plan to limit the federal government's role in the federal system: The plan called for tax relief, budget relief, and regulatory relief. Old hands in Washington and experts on the presidency discounted Reagan's chances for success: The new president faced a divided Congress, an entrenched bureaucracy, and powerful interest groups—each contributing its share to an alliance that, over decades, had helped to build a powerful federal establishment.

The challenge was considerable for at the time of Reagan's inauguration the federal government's activities seemed boundless, cutting across all sectors of the economy, affecting the ways in which many public and private institutions were run, and reaching deeper than ever before into the activities of state and local governments. At the same time, however, the prospect of a radical redirection in federal domestic activities—even under the leadership of a highly popular president—was not greeted with unabashed enthusiasm for, since Franklin Roosevelt's New Deal in the 1930s, the federal government had been bestowing benefits—as well as imposing burdens—on all that were involved with it.

This book is about one aspect of President Reagan's vision, his regulatory relief plan: a plan to limit the federal role in regulatory matters by reducing burdens on business and industry through deregulation of social as well as economic regulatory programs, and by devolving regulatory authority for many of the programs comprising cooperative federalism to state and local governments. We will also have something to say about regulatory relief in the context of regulatory reform: what these two terms mean in theory and in practice, and how they have been related to one another during the past six years.

Because the Reagan administration pursued its regulatory relief policy via a management strategy rather than a legislative strategy, this book is about public administration as well as public policy. Understanding how the Reagan administration went about "managing" toward its regulatory goals as well as how successful it was in achieving its goals are of equal concern in this book. By conducting survey research, in-depth interviews, and by drawing on public and internal government documents, we seek to provide both a broad overview and a detailed assessment of the Reagan regulatory relief policy and the management strategy through which it was to be achieved. By these means, we endeavor to answer questions raised by earlier research on the Reagan regulatory experiment—questions about its efficacy and effectiveness—and to provide a context for future consideration of presidential regulatory administration.

We are both assistant professors at Georgetown University; from 1985 to 1987 Wrightson served as staff director of the United States Senate Subcommittee on Intergovernmental Relations, Committee on Governmental Affairs. In that capacity, she was principal aid to Senator Dave Durenberger (R-MN), who—as chairman of the intergovernmental subcommittee—oversees the Office of Information and Regulatory Affairs (OIRA) in the Office of Management and Budget. OIRA administers the president's regulatory planning and review programs established by executive orders 12291 and 12498 and is widely considered the nerve center of the Reagan regulatory management initiative.

While the views expressed in this book are the responsibility of the authors alone, we wish to thank Timothy Conlan, David Beam, Harold Seidman, Marver Bernstein, Michael Fix, and Frederic Andes for the advice they have given along the way and for the expertise they have generously shared with us in the past. We would also like to express our debt to one another. This book is the product of a three-year collaboration, each providing advice, insight, and encouragement to the other throughout this time.

Thanks also goes to the many research assistants who have contributed to this book, notably Rhonda Radliffe, Jeffrey Fortenberry, Paul Marshall, John Stanton, Anthony Aliamo, Carol Copp, Mark Warren, Susan Olszewski, Randy Gross and Shereen Beydoun. We are grateful for technical and editorial assistance from Susan Kalish.

Last, and perhaps most important, we wish to thank the many, unnamed Washington staffers—in OMB, in the executive branch and independent agencies, and on Capitol Hill—as well as those lobbyists and public-elected officials who took the time to share their insights with us.

Without all of these people, this book would not have been written. We are grateful to them.

MANAGING
REGULATORY
REFORM

1 INTRODUCTION

To those who were familiar with the size, range and strength of the many institutions that influence federal regulatory policy, none of Ronald Reagan's campaign promises seemed more quixotic than his pledge to roll back 20 years of regulatory buildup. Where regulation was concerned, the deck seemed stacked against any president. It was widely assumed that presidential efforts to affect significantly the content, targets, or growth of regulation could not prevail against the many powerful counter-factors that existed. The president would have to contend with a Congress reluctant to give up any of its accustomed use of regulatory powers to direct the course of public policy and with an extensive bureaucracy of specialized federal regulatory agencies, some formally independent of the executive branch. Presidential efforts would also be hemmed in by the watchdog efforts of a large establishment of interest groups and advocacy organizations headquartered in Washington, and by public opinion that, in many ways, favored a tough approach to federal regulation in environmental, consumer protection, health and safety and other areas.

Overall, it is fair to say that giving siege to the regulatory establishment that he inherited as president was a task worthy of the "Great Communicator" for it pitted him against nearly every component of government and type of organized interest in Washington. While Reagan's electoral victory had been formidable, the incoming administration faced a divided Congress, well-organized interest groups, and a bureaucracy whose vested interest lay with the status quo.

Yet six years after taking office, Ronald Reagan seems not only to have brought regulatory growth to a halt, but to have turned the regulators around and started marching them back down the hill. The Reagan administration achieved this degree of success by tackling the regulatory establishment in a new way—one quite different from the means adopted by any previous administration. Instead of working through Congress to change the statutes on which regulations are based—adopting what might be called a statutory strategy—the Reagan administration focused the bulk of its efforts on the agencies that administer regulatory activities. We have termed the set of activities that made up these efforts as Reagan's administrative or management strategy to achieving regulatory reform.

The purpose of this book is to describe the new approach that the Reagan administration developed to carry out its regulatory reform program, to evaluate the strengths and weaknesses of this approach, to investigate where it proved successful and where it failed, and to speculate on the permanency of the changes effected through this management strategy for regulatory reform.

REAGAN AND PREVIOUS PRESIDENTS

Ronald Reagan was not the first president to take regulatory reform as a serious policy concern. Presidents Ford and Carter both made some efforts to halt the rapid growth of regulatory activities that marked the 1960s and 1970s. But Reagan's efforts went much farther than those of his predecessors. For one thing, regulatory reform was for Reagan part of a broader campaign to return government to its pre–New Deal roots. As Reagan saw it, less government (with the exception of defense) was the answer to a sluggish economy and strained intergovernmental relations. For Reagan, deregulation went along with a set of deeply held policy goals, including lower taxes, less federal involvement in state and local affairs, fewer domestic programs, and fewer bureaucrats with less money to run the programs that remained. Another factor that makes Reagan's regulatory reform efforts different from those of his predecessors is that Reagan carried the goal of deregulation into many areas of social regulation, such as the environment, consumer protection, and civil rights.

But the most striking difference between Reagan and previous presidents was the approach toward regulatory reform that his administration adopted. Presidents Ford and Carter followed the familiar path of working through Congress to change the statutes on which regulations are based. Thus, building on efforts begun during the Ford administration, Carter succeeded in passing a number of important regulatory initiatives in the areas of transportation and utility regulation. Reagan, in contrast, chose to travel the untried route of attempting to bring the regulatory bureaucracy under centralized White House control through a management strategy. Indeed, as administration spokespersons admit, very few of the successes of the Reagan administration's deregulatory efforts have come through working with Congress. While until 1986 Congress had passed almost no new regulatory statutes, neither had there been much legislative deregulation. In 1983, Christopher DeMuth, then administrator of the Office of Information and Regulatory Affairs (OIRA) of the Office of Management and Budget (OMB), described the administration's legislative successes as "disappointingly few" (DeMuth 1983). In 1986, despite a number of legislative opportunities, the record remains the same. With few exceptions, the accomplishments that have been achieved have been feats of administration, not legislation.

In the seriousness with which it has taken the issue of regulation, the Reagan presidency is unprecedented. Most past chief executives interceded in regulatory affairs only rarely and with little enthusiasm. In sharp contrast, under Reagan, executive office intervention in regulatory affairs has been vigorous and sustained. As Vice President George Bush expressed it when he unveiled the centrally planned and OMB–approved comprehensive Regulatory Program of the United States for 1985–1986, the first document of its kind in the history of the country: "This is ... the culmination of five years of efforts to put people, plans, and procedures in place to implement the President's regulatory policies." The new centralized approach to regulatory planning, Bush stated, "was the final link in a chain of actions by which the Reagan Administration has succeeded where past ones had failed" (Bush 1985, p. 1).

WHAT IS REGULATORY REFORM?

While Reagan administration spokespersons—and many journalists and scholars as well—have used the terms regulatory reform, and regulatory relief, deregulation, and even devolution somewhat interchangeably, there are important differences in their meanings. It is important to clarify these differences in meaning, for the way we define and use these terms has a great influence upon how we understand the goals of Reagan administration actions in the regulatory arena and also upon how we ultimately judge the success of these efforts.

Let us establish definitions for these crucial terms. Deregulation means the withdrawal of government from private sector affairs. Devolution means the withdrawal of the federal government from state and local government affairs. Regulatory relief means less regulation, reducing costs of administration and compliance. Deregulation and devolution are two of the most direct avenues to obtain regulatory relief.

In contrast, the term regulatory reform properly refers to adopting a more rational regulatory policy. Instead of being mainly preoccupied with questions of the costs of regulation, an authentic regulatory reform program would seek a more reasonable balance between competing values, being concerned with equity and effectiveness as well as with efficiency. A regulatory reform program might also concern itself with eliminating conflicting or confusing regulations, with enhancing the capacity of regulatory institutions to carry out regulatory statutes, and with working toward better partnerships with states and localities in the regulatory responsibilities they administer jointly.

It is evident, then, that the goals of regulatory relief and regulatory reform are not necessarily the same and may even be to some extent in conflict with one another. Regulatory relief could certainly be one result of regulatory reform, but simply lowering the regulatory costs of industry or government or withdrawing from the affairs of regulated entities are not tantamount to achieving true regulatory reform. The single-minded pursuit of reducing regulatory costs and national involvement in regulatory policies could lead to a regulatory policy that would be less rational, equitable, or effective. In such a case, regulatory relief would not merely be an inadequate strategy toward achieving regulatory reform, it would be a counterproductive one.

As we examine the enormous efforts of the Reagan administration in the regulatory arena, then, we must evaluate these efforts from two points of view: as regulatory relief efforts and regulatory reform efforts. It seems evident that administration efforts have generally tilted toward a regulatory relief approach. Occasional administration protests to the contrary notwithstanding, the Reagan regulatory change philosophy has been manifestly deregulatory and devolutionary. The language of the campaign and the transition period—"regulatory ventilation," "regulatory relief," "overregulation," "regulatory burdens"—all translated into a philosophy of maximum governmental restraint. As a public relations gambit, the administration's choice of slogans might have been wiser. As Murray Weidenbaum candidly admitted, "In retrospect, use of the term *regulatory relief* (as with the term *deregulation* in an earlier Administration) may have set the wrong tone for the effort. *Reform* may have predicated a more neutral approach to changes in the regulatory system" (Weidenbaum 1984, p. 17).

MANAGING TOWARD REGULATORY REFORM

To achieve his regulatory relief objectives, the president centralized power and decision making in the executive office of the president (EOP). The Office of Management and Budget (OMB) became the nerve center of domestic policy. Regulatory administration was politicized as suspect bureaucrats were swept out and replaced by conservative loyalists. When necessary, the president turned his own impressive powers of persuasion to wavering members of Congress. When that didn't work, he took his case directly to the American people, challenging them to pressure their senators and congressmen on the president's behalf. As two astute observers characterized it, "[H]e adopted the strategy of Wilson and Roosevelt to pursue the objectives of Coolidge and Harding" (Salamon and Abramsom 1984, p. 41).

One key to understanding the president's apparent preference for a management strategy over a statutory strategy is to look at how the important goal of regulatory relief stacked up against other broad policy goals of the Reagan administration. Although certainly a major goal for the administration, making changes in the regulatory system ranked far below the president's two highest domestic policy priorities: budget cuts and tax reform. The first of these goals dominated Reagan's first term in office; the latter—having culminated in large tax cuts in the first term—also dominated during the second. Apparently, the administration made an early decision to focus its efforts with regard to Congress on these two top priorities.

Looking at the situation from this perspective, it is clear why the Reagan administration did not make all-out efforts to achieve changes in several important regulatory statutes that, as it happened, were due to come up for renewal during Reagan's first term of office. Although the administration made some efforts—which were largely unsuccessful in the face of strong congressional opposition—to weaken some environmental statutes in 1981 and 1982, these efforts certainly did not compare with the administration's all-out campaign to pass the Omnibus Budget Reconciliation Act in 1981 or the Tax Reform Act of 1986. The generally successful campaign of Reagan's first term to cut federal spending in domestic programs did have significant dampening effects on regulatory activity, of course. But cutting spending is a management strategy, not a statutory strategy.

The decision not to pursue statutory reform followed from two additional considerations: the most dramatic opportunities to achieve regulatory reform had been seized by earlier presidents, and a number of members of the transition team were not inclined toward a modest agenda of social or intergovernmental regulatory reform. Reagan's predecessors had already achieved some notable triumphs by deregulating airlines, trucking, telecommunications, and gas. Thus, the incoming administration, determined to do something about regulation, faced the far more difficult task of tackling highly popular social regulatory programs. The commitment of Reagan advisors to making radical advances toward social deregulation and intergovernmental devolution compounded the problems posed by a legislative strategy.

In retrospect, it seems clear that the die was cast even before Reagan took his oath of office: the administration would manage its way toward its regulatory goals. White House advisors and OMB officials built a strategy consisting of five components: 1) a reexamination of existing rules with the intention to rescind or modify as many as possible; 2) a mandated slowdown in the issuance of new regulations; 3) a substantial relaxation in the enforcement of existing regulations; 4) the appointment of political loyalists that shared the president's anti-regulatory views; and 5) significant cuts in the operating budgets of regulatory agencies and regulatory programs administered by states and localities.

This was clearly an administrative strategy—a management strategy. It was based on the hope that the president could effectively harness his powers as chief executive and sweep past those who might oppose him in Congress and in the many interest and advocacy groups that have traditionally championed a strong regulatory policy.

EVALUATING THE MANAGEMENT STRATEGY

In the past six years, much has been written about the president's initiatives in particular regulatory programs. As important as these regulatory policies and the changes in them are, these are not the only issues that should concern us about the Reagan reform efforts. Equally important are the institutional issues—the administrative process through which the president and his staff sought to realize their policy objectives. While all recent presidents have tried to improve regulatory policy management, nearly all of Reagan's predecessors relied on legislative initiatives—persuading Congress to pass new statutes to alter regulatory policies.

In contrast to the steps taken by the Ford or Carter administrations to reduce paperwork or otherwise rationalize regulatory management, Reagan's strategy was adopted largely to substitute for statutory reform, not to augment it. While the administration floated a number of legislative proposals and passed a few of them, by and large the Reagan regulatory program has been one of management reform—the first concerted such presidential effort. As such, it offers an opportunity to compare statutory and management approaches to regulatory reform.

Traditionally, the legislative process provides diverse and competing interests opportunities to participate. Pluralism in policy formulation promotes the resolution of conflicts that are likely to arise during implementation. A related advantage is that coalitions brought together to secure passage of the legislation can continue to provide important support during implementation. Moreover, the imprimatur of Congress gives agencies and other implementors important flexibility, flowing from the knowledge that their actions are less susceptible to legal or political challenge. Finally, statutory reform is durable. Because they are not easily overturned, statutes generally outlast particular congresses and administrations. This promotes greater policy continuity and some argue that it increases compliance, since those who are subject to regulations recognize that the new rules, fixed in law, are there to stay.

From a presidential viewpoint, the principal disadvantage of the statutory approach is that legislative change takes time and effort. Moreover, because passing legislation depends to a great extent on coalition building and consensus, deregulatory policies proposed by a president will almost certainly not emerge from Congress without being significantly altered, raising the unpleasant specter of watered down, compromised outcomes. In addition, statutory reform may involve important opportunity costs. Part of its price may be lost chances to advance other, even more important presidential priorities. This sense of opportunity cost was clearly of concern to the Reagan White House. By applying administrative powers to the task of regulatory reform, the president was able to reserve legislation for other priorities. It is significant that while tax and budget policies could not be achieved without legislation, regulatory policy was susceptible to a management strategy; by bringing the regulatory establishment to a halt or slowing it down, deregulation and devolution could be achieved de facto.

Further, in sharp contrast to the legislative approach to regulatory reform, the principal advantage offered by management reform is its potential for swift implementation. Bypassing other branches of government, a president may be able quickly to institute changes without much interference. On the management route, there is less need to compromise. Finally, to the extent that actions are portrayed as procedural—relying on the language of good government—efficiency, effectiveness, coordination—management may be at least to some degree portrayed as nonsubstantive and nonpartisan.

These advantages notwithstanding, the management strategy does pose significant problems to those using it. First, administrative reforms that are not built on a broad consensus may meet resistance in the form of noncompliance, legal challenge, and political resistance. Bureaucracies tied to past agency practices may oppose change in the name of fulfilling their statutory missions. Moreover, in a federal system of government, if state and local officials are excluded from the formulation of policies that they must eventually administer, they may resist the new rules, taking any number of actions to thwart them. Finally, management reforms can be dangerously short-lived. Ironically, an incoming administration can turn the same management techniques used to deregulate, to reregulate.

Overall, the Reagan regulatory reform initiative raises a number of questions regarding the extent, the effectiveness, and the appropriateness of the management strategy. First, there is a set of questions concerning what actually happened when the Administration set out to transfer its vision of regulatory reform to reality. How broadly was the management strategy applied to the sprawling and extremely diverse federal regulatory bureaucracy? To what extent did Administration efforts actually reach the various executive branch agencies, the independent regulatory agencies, the social regulatory agencies, or the economic regulatory agencies? Were some components of the management strategy more widely used than others?

There are also many important questions dealing with effectiveness of the strategy. How effective has the management strategy been—measured against both the president's own standard of regulatory relief and our standard of regulatory reform? How does the performance of Reagan's approach compare with the approaches employed by previous presidents? Were some of the five components of the management strategy more effective than others? Was there a difference in effectiveness among different policy areas or types of regulatory agencies? How about long-term effectiveness of administration efforts? How resilient have they proved over the six years that Reagan has been in office? How durable are these changes likely to be as future administrations with different views of regulation come along?

Finally, there is a set of questions concerning the appropriateness of the management strategy, such as: have the administration's actions constituted true regulatory reform, or merely regulatory relief benefiting a narrow set of business and industry interests at the expense of the general public? Have the attempts to achieve centralized control of the regulatory bureaucracy resulted in a more rational management system, or merely snarled the functioning of the regulatory agencies to such an extent that regulatory relief has come about as a side-effect of organizational paralysis?

Questions such as these concerning the appropriateness of the administration's actions have been raised by many observers (Verkuil 1982; Tolchin and Tolchin 1983; The Alliance for Justice 1983; Eads and Fix 1984a; OMB Watch 1985a). In general, these concerns are not the focus of our research, which instead centers on the process of the Reagan initiatives. However, two basic questions underlie these types of concerns and our research as well: To what extent can a president alter the way public policy is made so as to exclude competing interests? And, what are the consequences of such exclusion for our democratic institutions?

This chapter has provided a brief overview of the purposes of this book and some definitions of the concepts it will explore. Chapter 2 provides a history of presidential involvement in the management of federal economic and social regulatory policy. We first examine the growth of federal regulatory activity through the Progressive Era, the New Deal period, and the period of social regulatory growth in the 1960s to the 1970s that led to the backlash against regulation that, in turn, set the stage for the regulatory relief efforts of the Reagan administration. We then describe the beginnings and the progress of Reagan's overall regulatory reform program. In Chapter 3, we attempt to view the Reagan regulatory reform campaign from the agency perspective. We present the results of an extensive survey of career staff and political appointees in a broad range of regulatory agencies carried out in 1984 and 1985 after the Reagan initiatives were well established. Data from our survey shed much light on questions of the impact of administration efforts and how these efforts have been perceived by agency staff responsible for implementing them.

Chapters 4, 5, and 6 present three detailed case studies of the application, success, and limitations of the management strategy in specific policy areas. Chapter 4 deals with intergovernmental relations; Chapter 5 deals with environmental protection; and Chapter 6 deals with nuclear licensing. These three policy areas offer a range of settings in which to observe the management strategy at work. The case study of intergovernmental relations shows how the management strategy performed in a complex field that cuts across a wide range of policy areas, a field beset by a multitude of governmental and extra-governmental institutional constraints on federal initiatives. The case study of environmental protection shows the management strategy at work in an executive branch agency, the Environmental Protection Agency, in which all components of the strategy could be applied. The case study of nuclear licensing demonstrates how the administration applied the management strategy to an independent agency, the Nuclear Regulatory Commission.

In our concluding chapter we again return to the broad questions raised in this introductory chapter. We review the insights that our interviews and case studies provide concerning the extent, the effectiveness, and the appropriateness of the management approach to regulatory reform. We then evaluate the degree of success achieved by the Reagan administration, noting the roles played by Congress, the bureaucracy, the courts, public opinion, the media, and interest groups in mitigating the impact of the management strategy. Finally, we speculate about the lessons of our findings for presidential administration and offer some advice to future presidents who might endeavor to follow in the Reagan administration's managerial footsteps.

2 PRESIDENTS AND THE MANAGEMENT OF REGULATORY POLICY

In order to understand the Reagan regulatory experiment, we must first look backwards, and place administration actions in the context of regulatory history. This chapter reviews the history of federal regulation since the creation of the Interstate Commerce Commission a century ago, and traces presidential involvement in regulatory administration. We review the steady rise of regulation through the twentieth century, paying particular attention to the peak period of regulatory growth. We then look at the rise of antiregulation sentiment in the mid–1970s, and see how this movement found political expression in the Reagan administration. We also sketch the broad outlines of Reagan's regulatory relief initiatives, comparing these strategies with those of earlier presidents. In the chapters that follow, we will carry out more detailed analyses of events in various policy areas.

THE RISING TIDE OF REGULATION

Contrary to recent antiregulation rhetoric, federal regulation did not spring full-blown onto an unprepared economy in the 1970s. The first major federal regulatory statute was the Interstate Commerce Act, enacted a century ago in 1887. Most historical accounts tie regulatory growth to three broad periods of political reform: the Progressive era at the turn of the century, the New Deal era of the 1930s, and the liberal political period of the 1960s and thereafter. Moreover, some new regulatory statutes were enacted during the relative calm between these periods. As Figures 2.1 and 2.2 show, these apparent waves of regulatory

Figure 2.1
Growth of Regulatory Agencies

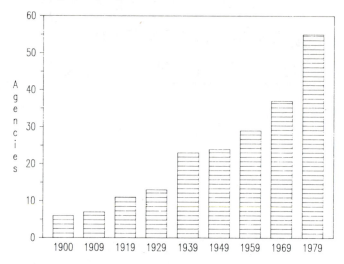

Source: Penoyer, 1981.

Figure 2.2
Major Regulatory Adoptions: A Decade-by-Decade Comparison

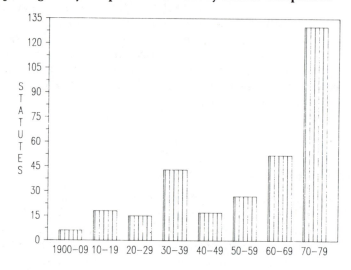

Source: Penoyer, 1981.

activity actually resembled crests, each higher than the last, all coming on a rising tide of regulatory activity (McCraw 1980).

Altogether, between 1900 and 1980, 131 regulatory statutes were enacted, and the number of regulatory agencies increased from six to 56 (Penoyer 1981). Of these 56 agencies, 30 were created during the three peak growth periods. As might be expected, the cumulative increase in numbers of agencies and statutes reflected a substantial expansion in the scope and influence of regulatory activity. Thus, by the time of Ronald Reagan's election in 1980 most, if not all, sectors of the economy were subject to some form of federal regulation.

Regulatory Means and Objectives

Before explaining the growth of federal regulation, we must first address two basic questions: What is regulation? and Why does the government regulate?

One standard definition states that a regulation is a rule or order having the force of law. Stone (1982) has amended this definition to add the crucial point that such rules or orders are typically backed by different kinds of sanctions or punishments, for example: monetary fines, federal preemption of program responsibilities, loss of social or economic privileges, and criminal penalties. Of course, regulations, together with the sanctions that accompany them, exist to implement laws—generally, but not always, in the form of regulatory statutes. Over the years, regulatory statutes have been passed, and regulations have been written, to fulfill constitutional promises as interpreted by presidents, legislatures, and the courts.

Scholars have categorized government regulation in various ways. For example, Ripley and Franklin (1984) subdivided regulation into two categories according to purpose: protective regulation, which safeguards the rights of citizens; and competitive regulation, which protects the economic interests of certain businesses and industries against foreign, sometimes domestic, competition. Other scholars emphasize differences among the mechanisms of regulation. For example, Kneese and Schultze (1975) drew a fundamental distinction between two means of regulatory intervention: command-control, which dictates behavior, and market-based, which manipulates incentives.

Theorists disagree about the extent to which the federal government should use regulation to control the behavior of individuals, corporations, or state and local governments, but they nearly all agree that regulatory powers and the sanctions that give them teeth are generally considered to be—along with the powers to tax and spend—basic tools of any government. This book focuses on a period when the political consensus was changing, from one that favored a growing reliance on regulation to realize increasingly broad interpretations of social and individual rights, to one that favored a more limited role for government. It is a period in which regulation, itself, has been heavily criticized but also one in which support for many of the goals of regulation has remained strong.

Both recent criticism of regulations and the Reagan administration regulatory relief efforts should be interpreted in the light of a long history of regulation. For nearly 100 years, regulatory powers have been put to work by presidents of different parties and by many congresses to achieve a wide variety of benefits for U.S. business and industry, as well as for the general public and minority people. Over the years, regulatory policies have protected fledgling industries; secured freedom from slavery; promoted fair housing and voting rights; and protected us from impure foods, polluted air and water, and toxic wastes. Indeed, as Meier (1985) has pointed out, proponents of deregulation have often overstated the case against federal regulation and spread myths that it is always expensive, intrusive, inefficient, and ineffective. Clearly these are oversimplifications. There is nothing inherently evil about federal regulatory power. Regulation has a long history. Rationally applied, it is fundamental to viable government. In summary, regulation is one of a number of fundamental powers the federal government has to protect constitutional rights and attain statutory objectives. In this sense, regulation is as old as the Constitution and as new as the most recent federal court ruling or agency guidance. It is important to understand how basic regulation is with respect to the operations of government even as we explore what happened when one president set out to change the regulatory status quo.

Regulatory Growth: The Tide and the Crests

There is no single explanation for the long-term rise in regulatory activity over the past 100 years. Many of the independent agencies created during the Progressive and New Deal periods were congressional responses to industrialization or technological innovations, such as aviation, pharmaceutics, nuclear energy, and mass communications (Cushman 1949; Redford 1952; Bernstein 1955; McCraw 1980). These changes, in turn, precipitated the development of a range of troublesome social, environmental, and public health problems. Because many of these effects were concentrated in the nation's burgeoning urban areas, however, rural-dominated state legislatures were reluctant to take action, leaving a regulatory vacuum eventually filled by the federal government (ACIR 1981).

While such historical trends in technology, in the nation's economy, and in our federal system of government help to explain the long-term steady rise in federal regulation, they tell us less about the peak growth periods. Many of the statutes passed during each period of regulatory expansion were the products of political factors, including public opinion, media interest, the pressures of specific interest groups, and the activities of congressional and executive branch policy entrepreneurs. As studies of the formation of individual regulatory policies show, well-publicized natural disasters often have played a supporting role (Wilson 1980).

The passage of the Interstate Commerce Act in 1887 was the culmination of 20 years of agitation by farmers, merchants, and middlemen who blamed the decline in agriculture prices on monopolistic rate setting by large railroads. Over time, a great deal of regulation was enacted in response to the demands of business and industry groups (Ripley and Franklin 1984). Human tragedies, graphically portrayed by muckraking journalists of the Progressive period, contributed heavily to the passage of the Pure Food and Drug Act of 1906, as did the policy entrepreneurship of a single executive branch official, Harvey Wiley, then chief chemist of the Department of Agriculture (Nadel 1971). Similarly, much of the explosion in economic regulation during the 1930s was the result of the political style of Franklin Roosevelt—his response to the Great Depression (McCraw 1980). Media coverage, interest group activity, and pressure from key Agriculture Department officials were again powerful forces contributing to the passage of the Food, Drug and Cosmetic Act of 1938. Here again, political pressure was given a helping hand by a well-publicized disaster: the deaths of 100 people that resulted from the inclusion of a toxic solvent, diethylene glycol, in an untested sulpha drug marketed by the Massingil Company (Meier 1985).

The New Social Regulation of the 1960s and 1970s

While the Progressive and New Deal eras and the 1960s to 1970s period are similar in many ways, the differences between them should not be underestimated. It is the differences in the kind of regulation enacted in the late 1960s and 1970s—the amount and scope of new regulation added, as well as differences in regulatory administration—that help to explain why the political climate for regulatory reform improved dramatically in the late 1970s.

The New Social Regulation. During the 1960s and early 1970s, the face of federal regulation was transformed by an unprecedented amount of social regulation. The range of newly regulated activities was remarkably broad, cutting across all sectors of the economy, touching the way many public and private institutions were run, and reaching deeper than ever before into the activities of state and local governments. The tools of federal regulation were applied to many previously untried issues during

Table 2.1
Major Regulatory Enactments of the Progressive and New Deal Periods

Date of Enactment	Title of Legislation	Subject of Regulation
1887	Interstate Commerce Act	railroad rates
1890	Sherman Antitrust Act	anti-trust
1902	Newlands Reclamation Act	irrigation and reclamation
1906	Pure Food and Drugs Act	food and drug purity
1906	Hepburn Act	railroad rates
1913	Federal Reserve Act	banking and finance
1913	Clayton Act	anti-trust
1914	Federal Trade Commission Act	anti-trust and unfair business practices
1920	Federal Power Commission Act	public utilities
1933	Agriculture Adjustment Act	agricultural production
1933	Tennessee Valley Authority Act	electric power
1933	Securities Act	stocks and bonds
1933	Glass-Steagall Banking Act	banking, insurance
1934	Securities and Exchange Act	stock exchange
1934	Communications Act	radio and telegraphic communications
1935	Motor Carrier Act	trucking rates
1935	Wagner Act	labor relations
1935	Public Utility Holding Company Act	anti-trust
1935	Rural Electrification Act	electric power
1938	Civil Aeronautics Act	air transportation

Source: Compiled by author.

this period, including civil rights, consumer protection, environmental protection, workplace safety, truth in lending, fair packaging and labeling, transportation safety, fair housing, and equal employment. To be sure, some of these new social regulatory initiatives were rooted in the muckraking of the Progressive period or the aspirations of the New Deal (Conlan 1985; Meier 1985). However, as Table 2.1 shows, until the 1960s the most important federal regulatory activities directed prices, entry, exit, and services provided in the marketplace. In previous periods, federal regulation directed economic activity; it was not designed to shape the societal consequences of economic activity and public policy.

Regulatory Growth. In the 1960s and early 1970s, social regulation expanded the range of federal involvement in the private sector and interstate and local affairs while more traditional forms of economic
regulation also continued to grow. As a result, regulatory expansion after
1960 substantially out-paced that during either of the two earlier periods.
Of the nearly 400 regulatory statutes and amendments enacted since
1900, nearly half were passed after 1960. Furthermore, many of the new
statutes required the creation of new agencies or the extension of existing
ones. Of the 56 regulatory agencies created since 1900, nearly half were
added since 1960. Budget outlays for regulatory administration reflected
these changes. In the last decade alone, federal regulatory expenditures
have tripled in constant dollars, from just under $1 billion to over $3 billion. Staff growth in regulatory agencies reflects a similar increase, from
about 30,000 full-time employees in 1970 to nearly 90,000 in 1980. The
expansion of agency rule-making activity is reflected in the increase in
size of the *Federal Register*, which more than quadrupled between 1970
and 1980, growing from 20,000 pages to nearly 90,000 pages in length.

Changing Regulatory Administration. Along with this expansion of regulatory reach and intensification of regulatory activity, significant
changes occurred in the administration of regulation. The federal government ceased to rely exclusively on independent commissions for administrative support and began to turn, instead, to executive branch
agencies.

This change broke a nearly 100-year precedent: since its creation in
1887, the Interstate Commerce Commission (ICC) had served as the
model for virtually all regulatory administrative activity (Fisher 1981).
The ICC, as we will explain in more detail later, was set up as an independent agency, to carry out the policies inherent in the legislation
passed by Congress. Nearly all of the New Deal regulatory programs
were administered by newly created independent commissions: the Federal Home Loan Bank Board in 1932, the Federal Deposit Insurance
Corporation (FDIC) in 1933, the Federal Communications Commission
(FCC) and the Securities and Exchange Commission (SEC) in 1934, the
National Labor Relations Board (NLRB) in 1935, the Federal Maritime
Commission (FMC) in 1936, and the Civil Aeronautics Board (CAB) in
1938. Similarly, in the 1940s and 1950s, the national response to technology spawned by the war effort was to create two more independent
commissions: the Atomic Energy Commission to regulate the young
nuclear industry and the Federal Aviation Administration (FAA) to control air traffic, license pilots, and inspect airplanes. In the 1960s and
early 1970s, six similarly structured independent commissions were
added: the Equal Employment Opportunity Commission (1964), the
States Postal Service Board (1970), the Consumer Product Safety Commission (1972), the Nuclear Regulatory Commission (1974), the Com-

modity Futures Trading Commission (1974), and the Federal Energy
Regulatory Commission (1977).

In addition to these traditionally structured independent commissions,
a number of the most important new regulatory programs of the 1960s
and 1970s period were housed in agencies reporting directly to the
president. These included the National Highway Traffic Safety Administration (NHTSA 1969), the Environmental Protection Agency (EPA
1971), and the Occupational Safety and Health Administration (OSHA
1974). Each of these agencies is headed by a single administrator, selected
by the president and serving at his discretion. Also during this period,
the federal grant-in-aid system was increasingly brought into service as
a mechanism of federal control. Regulations attached to federal grants
dealt with issues ranging from employment practices to wheelchair access
to historic preservation. As a result, the regulatory responsibilities of all
existing executive branch agencies, as well as the newly created Department of Education (1977) and the Energy Department (1978) were expanded across the board. The net effect of these changes was that, while
a substantial amount of regulation continued to be administered by independent agencies, regulatory responsibility was increasingly falling
within the political and administrative sphere of the executive branch.

The New Regulatory Politics of the 1960s and 1970s

What accounts for the tremendous increase in federal regulatory activity? Many of the social problems attacked by federal regulators in this
period were not new; neither was environmental damage resulting from
industrial and technological growth. For an explanation, we have to look
to the political mood of the country during this time. It seems that at
least as important as the need for regulation was the emergence of
demand for it. By 1960, public attitudes had clearly shifted from one
of laissez-faire to a "get tough" attitude toward business and industry,
and even toward state and local governments that were viewed as contributing to social and environmental problems (Bardach and Kagan
1982; Ball 1984). Changed attitudes were reflected in the behavior of a
range of actors including presidents, opinion leaders, interest groups,
and especially Congress.

Activist Presidents. Insofar as the presidential role is concerned, the
seeds of the regulatory activism of the 1960s and 1970s were planted
during the New Deal which, among other things, greatly strengthened
the presidency as an institution. A perceived lack of leadership on the
part of Congress, the Hoover administration, and state governments in
the face of ominous economic signals, was thought to have contributed
heavily to the depth of the depression triggered by the stock market
failure in 1929. The activism of Franklin Roosevelt, the sharply accel-

erated national involvement in the economy, as well as a change in the balance of power between the nation and the states, helped to end the Great Depression.

After the war, public opinion profoundly shifted in favor of an activist federal government. There was a growing conviction that the national government could and should play an important role improving the daily lives of its citizens; and in the eyes of many, the president had the principal responsibility for national leadership. Nearly all modern presidents have carried on this tradition, strengthening the role of the federal government in the economy and in domestic affairs. Not surprisingly, they have made use of federal regulatory power to carry out these efforts.

Congressional Entrepreneurs. Until the 1960s, presidential domestic initiatives were often thwarted by a Congress that functioned as a graveyard of presidential legislative proposals. In the 1960s and 1970s period, this pattern changed. Not only did Congress look more favorably on presidential policy initiatives—including executive regulatory proposals—it produced considerable initiatives of its own. Indeed, a number of major studies of contemporary regulation identify Congress as the principal agent of regulatory growth (Halperin 1976; McCraw 1980; Wilson 1980; Malbin 1981; ACIR 1981).

Some examples document the extent of congressional leadership concerning the regulatory enactments of the 1960s and 1970s. While President Lyndon Johnson shepherded the Civil Rights Act of 1964 through Congress in the wake of President John Kennedy's assassination, he received a great deal of help from Senator Hubert Humphrey (D-MN), then majority whip. One of the principal regulatory features of this legislation is the requirement that no person be denied the benefits of federally assisted programs on the basis of race, color, or national origin. Subsequent to passage of this act, other far-reaching applications of its regulatory features have been enacted: Title IX of the Education Amendments of 1972, which prohibits discrimination against women in educational institutions receiving federal aid; Section 504 of the Rehabilitation Act of 1973, which prohibits discrimination against handicapped people; and the Age Discrimination Act of 1975, which protects the rights of the aged in federally assisted programs. In each case, the legislation modelled on Title VI was authored and championed by a member of Congress, with relatively little involvement by the White House. Title IX was the product of efforts by Congresswoman Edith Green (D-OR) and Senator Birch Bayh (D-IN). Section 504 of the Rehabilitation Act was conceived and championed by Congressman Charles Vanik (D-OH) and Senator Humphrey. The Age Discrimination Act was a congressional idea advocated by a bipartisan coalition. President Richard Nixon signed the sex and handicapped discrimination acts without comment, after having vetoed the latter twice. President Gerald Ford signed the Education Act, but only with a great deal of reluctance about its regulatory character (Conlan 1985). Legislative histories show that a great many environmental policies were also congressionally inspired. Indeed, President Nixon's advocacy of environmental programs developed only after Senator Edmund Muskie (D-ME)—the leader on environmental statutes—was nominated as the Democratic candidate for vice-president in 1968. A 1980 congressional study of the growth of federal regulation during this period concluded that—although some important regulatory programs resulted from presidential initiatives—the chief source of regulatory growth had not been Presidents Kennedy, Johnson, Nixon, Ford, nor Carter. The source of most regulatory growth, the study stated, "was not the executive branch at all, but Congress, and the legion of congressional staff members on the lookout for issues through which their principals—particular congressmen and senators—could attain visibility and national prominence" (McCraw 1980).

Changes in the way Congress operates may underlie the turnabout. The growing congressional regulatory role, ACIR (1984, p. 15) believes:

was the direct result of a refashioning of Congress as an institution beginning in the 1960's and continuing into the 1970's. As a result of two periods of sweeping reform, an institution dominated by a small coterie of aging, conservative and strong willed committee chairmen was transformed into one of more equal, independent and liberal members.

The trend toward congressional democratization was strengthened by such factors as the erosion of traditional norms of seniority; the growth of professional staff; the elimination of parliamentary and other rules which protected legislative minorities; the proliferation of subcommittees; and by the decline in party loyalty (Dodd and Oppenheimer 1977; Mann and Ornstein 1981). These changes, in turn, translated into new opportunities for members to develop and promote their own legislative initiatives. As Michael Malbin (1981, p. 1) noted, the legislative fever that first struck a few liberal Democrats proved contagious.

[T]he changes first permitted liberal Democrats to find problems for government to address. After a while they came also to be used by new-style conservative Republicans who were equally eager to pursue their own legislative ideas. Congressional structures were adapted to serve self-promoting, individualistic legislative styles.

The Media and Public Support for Regulation. Spectacular disasters and the crises that flame up from smoldering social problems are the beat of thousands of reporters and broadcasters; such events are constantly discussed in public affairs and news broadcasts, and in newspapers, magazines, and scholarly and trade journals. If tragic incidents can be tied to regulatory failures or other mistakes of government, they become that much more newsworthy. While media attention alone cannot move government, well-publicized crises do affect public opinion, which in turn influences elected officials, inspiring government investigations and perhaps legislative and regulatory initiatives.

In a recent example, the January 1986 explosion of the space shuttle *Challenger* prompted an immediate, well-publicized federal investigation, which is likely to result in stepped-up regulation of the operations of the National Aeronautics and Space Administration (NASA). Sometimes media concern can move industry to action, as when the manufacturers of Tylenol decided to substitute caplets (coated tablets) for traditional capsule packaging after a series of lethal tampering incidents. But media attention can move government to regulation if industry fails to act. For example, the Gerber company did little in response to news reports of glass shards found in several jars of baby food in Maryland in 1986; the state of Maryland stepped in almost immediately, however, and ordered all Gerber products off the shelves until the source of the problem could be identified. Even more recently, the accident in the Soviet Union at the Chernobyl nuclear power plant prompted immediate federal investigations into a number of similarly designed plants in the United States.

The public has come to expect that, in a television age, reporting on such incidents will be carried into the nation's living rooms through live coverage, follow-up coverage, and news analyses. Such coverage accelerated dramatically in the 1960s. Graphic media coverage of the Birmingham riots in 1962 shocked the American public. Moreover, few observers could remain unmoved by the image of chemically induced fires burning on the Cuyahoga River in Cleveland in 1969, or the sight of countless waterfowl mired in oil from tanker spills such as the one that occurred off the Santa Barbara coast in 1970. Equally compelling were news accounts of cancer deaths tied to leaking chemical dump sites and media portrayals of the dilemma of residents of communities such as Love Canal who could neither live in nor sell their houses after discovering toxic chemical wastes in their soil and drinking water.

Television was not the only medium through which such messages were sent: a number of books and studies played a part in arousing public opinion and sparking federal regulatory actions during the period. Two landmark efforts were Rachel Carson's *Silent Spring* (1962), which detailed the ecological consequences of pesticides and other forms of environmental pollution, and Ralph Nader's *Unsafe at Any Speed* (1965), which criticized existing federal regulation of the automobile industry.

During this period, print and television journalism, as well as scientific research, chronicled the visible evidence of social problems and of economic market failures. During this same period, opinion polls reflected

growing public concern about social and environmental regulatory problems. There is little doubt this public sentiment played a major role in
public willingness to accept the new social regulatory programs (Sundquist 1962; Kelman 1980; McCraw 1980; Wilson 1980; Meier 1985).

The public mood and media attention also fostered a climate conducive to the development of a new type of special interest groups that
championed a wide variety of particular social causes. As ACIR (1984,
p. 69) noted,

In the past interest groups could only be sustained if they had a mass membership
or business sponsorship. In contrast, many of today's public interest lobbies
survive on foundation and governmental grants and volunteer support. Although populist in character and rhetoric, some have very small memberships.
Others have developed large followings through the use of computerized direct-
mail fund-raising drives. Neither form tends to represent old-style economic
interest of business, labor, or agriculture. Yet such groups have had a major
influence on the environmental, consumer and safety regulations of the contemporary era.

The growth of such advocacy organizations during and after the 1960s
was remarkable, increasing from a few dozen in 1960 to hundreds by
1980. As a number of studies of regulatory politics have shown, these
groups were often very effective, articulating the concerns of their constituencies, carrying on lawsuits to clarify what public policies should be,
testifying before Congress, contributing to the design of relevant legislation, and keeping a watchdog's eye on the activities of regulatory
agencies.

The 1960s and 1970s also saw an upsurge in recourse to the courts
to ensure the rights of such groups as women, minorities, and the handicapped; to protect the environment; to gain a better deal for consumers;
and to achieve social change in other areas. Thus, the judicial branch
of government became drawn into regulatory activity to some extent as
well—enforcing and interpreting regulatory statutes.

Regulation, then, is a basic governmental function with substantial
historical roots in this country. Even so, the most recent period of regulatory growth marks a substantial departure from earlier periods. Regulatory growth in the 1960s and 1970s far outpaced the crests of
regulatory activity that characterized the Progressive and New Deal eras.
The tool of regulation was applied to new goals and new forms of administration were adopted to administer many of the new regulatory programs. The politics of regulatory policy-making also changed in
important ways as members of Congress assumed leadership formerly
wielded by the president, aligning themselves with a growing political
constituency for regulatory initiatives in many areas.

Both the executive and legislative branches of government have a part in the development of regulatory policies, as the preceding discussion has shown. And, both Congress and the president have a stake in the implementation of regulatory programs. The following section explains the process by which regulatory policy is implemented and looks at the complex play of power between these two branches of government that results from this process.

CONGRESS, THE PRESIDENT, AND REGULATORY ADMINISTRATION

When it comes to regulation, the power to execute policy is in many ways the power to make policy. The tendency of Congress to pass economic and social regulatory statutes broad in coverage and wide in administrative latitude has led to a significant devolution of policy-making responsibility to administrators of the regulatory agencies. Bureaucratic discretion, however, opens opportunities for the executive branch to influence the course of public policy after legislation has been passed. Congress tries to safeguard its interest through oversight; and, the president, for his part, may attempt to influence regulatory policy and administration through his power to take care that the laws be faithfully executed. Until recently, however, neither the chief executive nor the Congress has managed to exert effective control over the regulatory bureaucracy.

Congress and Regulatory Administration

Until recent years, Congress was generally content to protect its prerogatives by establishing independent regulatory agencies, thus insulating regulatory activities from routine executive branch management. This precedent was set during the legislative debates preceding the final passage of the Interstate Commerce Act of 1887. At that time, two possible forms of regulatory administration were vigorously debated in Congress. One school of thought urged Congress to empower the Justice Department to enforce a specific railroad policy to be enunciated by Congress itself. Such a solution would follow classical management theory calling for hierarchical lines of command as well as maintaining the traditional roles of the legislature and executive laid out in the constitution. The progressives in Congress, in contrast, favored creating a new type of regulatory administration in the form of a commission to set specific policies concerning the railroads under a general regulatory charter, in much the same way the states had regulated the railroads before the federal government intervened.

At the time, critics argued that an independent commission would be sluggish, subject to undue influence by the regulated industry, and politically unaccountable. Supporters of the commission approach argued that a conventional hierarchical management structure would not work because regulating the railroads necessitated broad powers and a wide mandate to match the complexity of the task. Lawmaking power—together with judicial responsibilities to arbitrate conflicting interests among the railroads, to defend public and private interests, and to provide expert opinion to the courts—required a particular structure of administration that would best be provided through a specialized commission independent of the executive branch. Ideally, such a structure would meld the virtues of expertness, group deliberation, and impartiality (Redford 1952). The progressive reformers of the day believed that none of these virtues would be found in the executive branch which they considered to be mired in special interest and patronage politics and undependable for making policy beneficial to the general public. The railroad companies sided with those favoring a commission, regarding it as the lesser of the two evils, while a number of powerful legislators joined forces with the progressives to preserve their oversight role.

In the end, conventional management wisdom fell victim to an unlikely political coalition consisting of progressive reformers, representatives from the railroads, and key members of Congress. The result was an altogether new form of federal bureaucratic administration created more by happenstance than constitutional logic, one that Fisher (1981) likened to no man's land—exercising legislative, executive, and judicial powers. Congressional advocates for regulatory commissions generally disagree, justifying this form of regulatory administration in constitutional terms and characterizing commissions as arms of the legislature.

While such characterizations were a bold stroke—summoning up the separation of powers doctrine—Congress was not content to rely on constitutional semantics alone to protect its regulatory sway. It took more pragmatic action by staggering the terms of the commissioners to insulate them from presidential transitions. Moreover, congressional statutes forbid a president from removing a commissioner except for serious cause. Finally, Congress placed restrictions on the number of commissioners who may belong to the same political party.

Overall, while Congress at the turn of the century found it necessary and convenient to pass off much of the burden of regulatory policymaking, it had no desire to allow the executive to expand to fill the regulatory vacuum. While independent commissions solved this problem, they created a second. If Congress was not going to spell out detailed regulatory policies in the statutes, other means would have to be sought to ensure that commission policy-making might reflect congressional will.

Congress has several traditional tools of oversight that would seem to be helpful in guiding the actions of regulatory agencies. Congress has the power to confirm Presidential appointments, to authorize appro-priations, to conduct investigations, and to undertake casework. Yet, with respect to regulatory activities, the legislature has used these tra-ditional tools of oversight sparingly and without a great deal of success (Ogul 1976). For example, Robinson (1978, p. 180–181) characterized FCC oversight hearings more as "ritual" than an effective management process:

It is not uncommon for the seven FCC Commissioners, accompanied by twenty or more top staff members to appear before a subcommittee of one—the chair-man. Although other members may join the chairman intermittently during these sessions, only the presence of television cameras compels more than a few members to attend oversight hearings—and televised news coverage of such hearings is rare. Another problem is that those members who do attend often are not prepared adequately to exercise their oversight function.... Thus, agency members and their staff come to hearings armed with documents and materials that may have taken several man-months to prepare, to be confronted all too often with trivial questions about the closing of a telegraph office in a Congressman's district or the latest "equal time" case or programming complaint. The frequent result is a mixture of misdirected questions, bland or evasive responses, and some degree of posturing, all punctuated with occasional quar-relsome debate. After several hours of such maneuvers, the Congressmen and agency members retire to their respective lairs to resume their previous tasks. The record of the session is then assembled and shipped to the Government Printing Office to be put in a suitable printed form for burial in appropriate libraries and archives.

In the 1970s congressional dissatisfaction with traditional oversight tools was reflected in the increased use of the legislative veto through which Congress reserves the right to overrule agency rules. Over 85 statutes with legislative veto provisions were enacted in that decade, 33 in the Ninety-sixth Congress alone (Norton 1981).

The value of the veto as a tool of oversight is a matter of some con-troversy. Some scholars argue that it increases staff level decision-making at the expense of elected officials and the public by encouraging behind-the-scenes alliances between congressional and bureaucratic staff before rules are even promulgated. Others believe that it preserves the ability of Congress to legislate broadly without fear of giving the bureaucracy the proverbial keys to the store (Scalia 1979; Shafer and Thurber 1981; Sundquist 1981).

Congress has consistently argued that the legislative veto is constitu-tional in that agency rule making is a legislative act. On the other hand, all recent presidents have opposed it. In 1983, in a seven-to-two decision, the Supreme Court sided with the president (*Immigration and Naturali-zation Service* v. *Chadha* 462 U.S. 919) finding the veto unconstitutional because it put the legislature in the business of executing the laws. Because Congress has increasingly relied on the legislative veto for oversight, the discretion of the regulatory bureaucracy has been enhanced as a result of the *Chadha* decision. This, in turn, has improved the president's opportunities at the expense of Congress.

Presidential Regulatory Management: Early Initiatives

Presidents have long recognized that the exercise of management oversight of bureaucratic regulatory activity offers an important opportunity for putting the presidential stamp on regulatory policy. The President's Committee on Administrative Management—the Brownlow Commission—stated this formally in 1937.

Yet, as suggested earlier in this chapter, a president intent on influencing regulatory administration must contend with not one but two forms of regulatory administration: executive branch agencies and the independent commissions. Conventional wisdom has suggested that presidents are likely to have the least success influencing commissions because of their ties to Congress.

Independent Commissions. Presidents have never fully subscribed to the "arm of Congress" view of independent commissions, however. From time to time, most modern presidents have intervened in regulatory administration. President Wilson worked to place a stipulation in the act creating the FTC that the president had power to order the commission to make investigations. There is no doubt that Wilson believed that as president he was entitled to impress his policies on independent commissions and to expect conformity to those policies (Cushman 1949, p. 681).

Presidents have a number of means by which to influence independent regulatory commissions. The most important ones are the powers to appoint members, to designate chairmen, and to approve agency budgets, paper work collection requests, and legislative proposals.

Empirical research suggests that presidents have made little systematic use of these powers to shape regulatory administration until very recently. For example, Robinson (1978) found that presidents have never used appointments to control communications policy; instead, he wrote, the potential has been "frittered away, largely through presidential indifference." In research on OMB activities, Hibbing (1985) found that while the budget office has had power over commission budgets for over 40 years, it rarely has exercised that power until the 1980s. OMB activities with respect to legislative clearance and paperwork have followed much the same pattern. OMB has possessed these powers for some time, but did not fully exploit them until Reagan.

With some accuracy, Fisher (1981) has characterized the regulatory commissions as stepchildren of both Congress and the president, with precious little attention paid by either. Indeed, until Reagan became president, the struggle for influence was largely defensive, with each side seeking to prevent the other from exercising control, yet neither wanting to do so consistently itself (Fisher 1981, p. 157).

Executive Branch Agencies. It would certainly appear that the president, as chief of the executive branch, is on firmer ground in attempts to influence the actions of executive agency regulatory administration. Presidents can appoint and remove department secretaries at any time. They control about 2000 political appointments outside the reach of the Civil Service. Since 1978, presidents have had the power to direct personnel policy through the Office of Personnel Management (OPM). With the help of OMB, the president prepares the federal budget, approves all proposed legislation, and controls the amount and flow of federal paper work. Moreover, since Nixon instituted the Quality of Life Review for environmental regulations coming out of EPA, the executive has monitored all executive branch agency rule making.

Taken together, the chief executive has at hand an impressive array of tools. Yet the testimony of those who have served past presidents, those who specialize in public administration, and those with a stake in the outcomes, indicates that no president had made a concerted effort to bring this formidable array of management powers to bear on regulatory policy. None, that is, until Reagan (Hall 1961; Bruff 1979; Fisher 1981; Ball 1984). For the most part, when they have sought to reform or redirect these policies, past presidents have relied on legislation, not administration. While scholars disagree about the extent to which various forces dominate regulatory administration, few, if any, identify the president as the prime mover. The conventional wisdom has long been that the president "is the political actor least likely to intervene" (Meier 1985, p. 25).

In one sense, this is surprising. To the extent that the regulatory bureaucracy is where the policy action is, we might have expected past presidents to focus some concerted effort there. However, until Gerald Ford began to investigate concerns about the inflationary impact of cumulative layers of federal regulation, presidents intervened only sporadically. One reason is that until the mid–1960s most regulatory policies were administered by independent regulatory commissions, not executive branch agencies. Thus, regulatory administration was not within the day-to-day purview of the president's staff. A second reason is that until the 1970s regulation was regarded as a relatively arcane, noncontroversial, and even respected part of the federal bureaucratic establishment. To be sure, academics and political insiders worried that the system was growing increasingly inefficient and unaccountable. But as long as criticism remained confined to these narrow circles, presidents were largely content to stand on the sidelines, apparently following the maxim, "If it ain't broke, don't fix it." Moreover, presidents who did make forays into the civil service and expertise-laden environment of regulatory agencies did not always come back winners. Later in this chapter we will have more to say in this regard, looking at the Nixon, Ford, and Carter experiences. Thus, when Reagan took office in 1981, the potential for presidential influence of regulatory administration was still an open question.

THE RISE OF ANTIREGULATION SENTIMENT

In the late 1960s and 1970s the conditions which led presidents to ignore regulatory administration were changing. First, because the new social regulation enacted during this period was assigned to executive branch agencies, opportunities for presidential influence were greater. Moreover, the 1970s were years of unprecedented activity among newly created regulatory agencies—including the EPA, the Department of Education, OSHA, the National Highway and Transportation Safety Administration (NHTSA), and the Consumer Product Safety Commission (CPSC)—thanks to the sweeping congressional mandates that had created them. Second, federal grant-in-aid programs, most of which were administered by executive branch agencies, had taken on an increasingly regulatory character, as the number of conditions of aid and crosscutting requirements multiplied (Mitnick 1980; Wilson 1980; Beam 1981; Kettl 1983). As a result, by the mid–1970s regulatory administration was no longer of minor import and certainly not noncontroversial.

Not surprisingly, the circle of critics widened. Business interests that had tolerated, even welcomed, economic regulation were decidedly less enthusiastic about the advent and growth of social regulation.

Some of the complaints of business and industry were strengthened substantially by academic research, principally that of economists. Economic researchers speculated that regulation had significantly contributed to recent declines in economic productivity. According to two former members of President Carter's Council of Economic Advisors, upwards of 25 percent of recent declines in U.S. productivity could be explained by government regulation (Litan and Nordhaus 1983). According to Murray Weidenbaum, by 1980 the administrative costs of regulation alone exceeded $100 billion annually (Weidenbaum and DeFina 1978). These rising costs were attributed not only to the amount of new regulation, but also to the manner in which all regulation was being implemented. The heart of the economists' critique was that many regulatory policies flew in the face of the laws of economics. They argued that, if economic principles were applied to regulatory decisions, inflation would fall, and productivity would go up.

While economic critiques of regulatory policy originated in the 1940s, by the early 1970s they had blossomed into a full-scale, Washington-based academic movement. A Ford Foundation grant of nearly $2 million to The Brookings Institution produced dozens of books and monographs, over 50 scholarly articles, and nearly 40 doctoral dissertations on the subject of overregulation—all promising greater government efficiency and enhanced national productivity through regulatory reform (Derthick and Quirk 1985). The first target of such research was economic regulation. In some cases, scholars argued that the entire rationale and structure of federal control of the marketplace was flawed. Government involvement, they argued, forced industries to act in ways that undercut management efficiency and reduced productivity. Regulations often failed to solve the problems they were designed to solve and even created unanticipated new problems. Furthermore, some regulations were judged to be overly protective of the industries they were supposed to regulate, creating artificial barriers to competition that might bring better products and services into the marketplace. Various economists thus urged the deregulation of many industries, including air transportation, trucking, and telecommunications. Free market competition, these economists argued, offered better assurance of reasonable rates and adequate service than government rules and standards. Few other scholars disagreed. Having reviewed some 150 scholarly articles, Joskow and Noll (1981) concluded that while economists are often accused of being unable to agree on anything, there was unanimous professional agreement that price and entry in several multi-form markets is inefficient and ought to be eliminated.

Soon thereafter, by the mid–1970s, researchers began to question social regulatory policies in many areas, including pollution, auto regulations, housing, consumer protection, employment opportunity, and health care. In regard to social issues, however, few researchers challenged the need for federal regulation; rather, they focused on the methods. Drawing on economic analysis, they argued for the application of economic criteria to regulatory decision making and for regulatory solutions that emphasized market-type incentives.

Researchers raised concerns about the costs and effectiveness of such social regulation. They argued that the costs of regulation exceeded the benefits, producing a state of overregulation. They also pointed out that many existing regulatory strategies were ineffective, especially those contained in environmental statutes. Overall, given the wide range of social problems to solve and the scarcity of resources to solve them, economists argued for priority setting, for streamlined implementation, and for settling for overall efficiency rather than complete equity in the social regulatory arena.

As a result of economic research, by the mid–1970s the term *regulatory reform* took on a new meaning. No longer was regulatory reform equated solely with modifying the relationship between the president and the independent agencies, the primary usage of the term as recently, for example, as the reform mandate of the Ash Commission during the Nixon administration. Nor did the term imply a get-tough attitude with business and industry, as when it had been applied to social initiatives during the 1960s and early 1970s (Bardach and Kagan 1982). Instead, regulatory reform became a code word for proposals to cut back excessive or inappropriate government regulation. In an era of scarce resources, the protective treatment many industries were receiving from government regulators, as well as many formerly sacrosanct social regulatory programs, came into question as research uncovered their high costs to consumers and taxpayers.

Economics and Regulatory Policy: The White House View

Declining public opinion and economic debate appear not to have been lost on recent presidents. Ford was concerned about regulatory costs. In his presidential campaign Carter criticized the regulatory bureaucracy, as did Reagan. Indeed, the 1976 and 1980 presidential elections can be viewed, in part, as reflections of antigovernment public attitudes. As candidates, both Carter and Reagan had strongly criticized the federal establishment, and both came to power believing they had a mandate to do something about it.

*Ford and Carter Administrative Efforts.*While the Reagan administration will be remembered for its efforts to manage regulatory reform, the Ford and Carter administrations are likely to be remembered at least in part for legislative reforms they achieved in economic regulation.

As discussed earlier in this chapter, economic deregulation had become a fashionable issue in Washington in the late 1970s. This issue had political support from liberals such as Senator Ted Kennedy (D-MA) and conservatives such as Gerald Ford. The virtues of economic deregulation were espoused by economists as well as political scientists, even the American Bar Association. Public opinion supported deregulation, so, too, key special interest lobbyists such as Ralph Nader. In short, as one old political hand put it, deregulation had become "a new kind of religion."

In response to this powerful political consensus, both Ford and Carter advanced deregulatory economic reforms. Ford established the Domestic Council Review Group on Regulatory Reform in the White House, and a great deal of legislative groundwork was laid there during his short tenure in the oval office. Ford's efforts bore fruit under Carter as the following statutes were enacted: the Railroad Revitalization and Reform Act (1976), the Airline Deregulation Act (1978), the Natural Gas Policy

Act (1980), the Motor Carrier Act (1980), the Depository Institutions Deregulation and Monetary Control Act (1980), and the Staggers Act (1980), which deregulated railroad transportation.

In addition to their legislative reform efforts, both the Ford and Carter administrations continued the presidential regulatory review program initiated by Nixon. The goals of these programs can be summarized as the timely, systematic, and continuous evaluation of regulatory objectives; their likely effectiveness; and the relevance of prior justifications for regulatory policies and programs. Following such guidelines, each president from Ford on has imposed some form of systematic review and analysis of executive agency regulations.

Executive Regulatory Review under Ford. As part of the "Whip Inflation Now" campaign, Ford introduced the Inflation Impact Statement (IIS) program, establishing a largely decentralized process whereby executive branch agencies would undertake economic analyses of their regulatory proposals. The program was established by Executive Order 11821: due to expire in 1976, it was continued by Executive Order 11949 and given a new name, the Economic Impact Statement program (EIS).

The OMB director who was granted administrative responsibility for the EIS program, instead exercised his discretion to delegate that authority, assigning it to the newly formed Council on Wage and Price Stability (CWPS). The creators of the EIS program hoped that agency economic analysis, if subjected to modest oversight by an arm of the executive office of the president, would result in more efficient regulations. This process, in turn, it was hoped, would reduce the social cost of regulation.

To fulfill the requirements of the executive order, each agency was to assess whether its regulatory proposals were likely to have a major impact on the economy. In practice, the rule of thumb was to classify any proposal with estimated costs in excess of $100 million annually as having a major impact. If a proposal crossed this threshold, the agency was required to prepare an EIS on it. Such EIS documents were certified by the agency head and published in the *Federal Register*.

Each EIS was to include an analysis of the principal and—where practical—secondary costs and benefits. Comparisons of the costs and benefits of alternative approaches were also required. The Wage Council reviewed each EIS and had the power to approve, or critique and return it. If unsatisfied with agency responses to its criticisms, the council could use its legislatively based authority to submit a formal statement to the relevant regulatory proceeding, or possibly a congressional hearing. If these formal powers proved inadequate, the council could (and sometimes did) bring its case to the press.

The tools of the Council on Wage and Price Stability were primarily exhortatory, however, and often proved ineffective. Expressing his frustration, a former council staff member commented: "[N]either CWPS nor OMB had the authority to delay implementation of or require changes in a regulatory decision, and an agency need not even acknowledge CWPS criticism, much less react to it." Overall, most impact statements submitted by agencies were of poor quality: cost estimates were dubious, benefits estimates were incomplete, and consideration of alternatives often nonexistent. Yet, in defense of agency analysts, it might be noted that the state of the art of cost-benefit analysis was not well advanced in the mid–1970s. In addition, the timing of most impact statement preparations—coming after proposals had been approved at the decision-making level within the agency—typically meant that such analyses were used only to justify a regulatory approach already taken. Speaking about his tenure as assistant director of CWPS, James Miller argued that impact statements should have been used as "input at the proposal formulation stage, since that is the time when information on costs, benefits, and alternatives is most likely to affect the ultimate decision" (Miller 1981, p. 18). Finally, the EIS process was weakened when OMB decided to delegate much of the program's oversight authority to CWPS—a fledgling agency among much more established and powerful line agencies.

Carter Administration Efforts. Problems experienced by the Ford administration led the Carter administration to strengthen and expand the regulatory review and oversight process. Executive Order 12044, issued in March 1978, was designed to correct previous quality and timing problems and to improve and increase presidential oversight.

The new program departed from the earlier one in a number of ways. For analyses, the concept of "major impact" was replaced with "significant impact," presumably so that agencies could weigh noneconomic but still significant impacts in their decisions. Similarly, the cost-benefit language was softened so that rules might be judged by other than economic criteria. To increase presidential control, the Regulatory Analysis Review Group (RARG) was created in the executive office of the president and given both oversight and independent review functions. Under the Carter program, analyses and RARG comments had to be made public, and RARG approval was required before the proposal could be published in the *Federal Register*. Apart from its oversight responsibilities concerning new regulations, RARG each year also analyzed 10 to 20 existing rules. The White House Economic Policy Group—composed of the OMB director, the chairman of the Council of Economic Advisors (CEA), and the secretaries of Commerce, Treasury, and Labor—undertook to play a coordinating function in the development of regulatory policy generally. This body attempted to promote uniform agency interpretations of regulatory policies and to coordinate agency implementation in areas of shared responsibilities. In addition, it was given responsibility for resolving disputes between RARG and agencies.

An added feature of the Carter program was Section 4 of Executive Order 12044, which for the first time applied some form of sunset measure to regulation. The order set forth goals such as efficacy and cost-control, and required agencies periodically to review their existing regulations in light of these goals.

Judgments of the Carter regulatory program are mixed. Most experts feel that the Carter administration built on the Ford experience, and that the Carter program achieved more impact on regulatory decision-making. Observers attribute Carter's moderate success to strengthened central oversight; the increased attention given to regulatory policy-making; the expansion of the program to existing rules; and to a growing recognition by policymakers that regulatory activity was "getting out of control."

One factor inhibiting progress was that despite RARG and CWPS efforts to improve agency analytical skills, by the end of the Carter administration very few agencies were good at regulatory analysis, and some did not yet understand what it meant. OMB required agencies to carry out analyses within their existing staff. Moreover, both the Carter program and its predecessor permitted agencies to determine the format for reviews, doing little to set standards by which to judge them.

In summary, the Ford and Carter programs shared a number of problems that reduced their effectiveness. Their continuing difficulties set the stage for further strengthening of the review process by Reagan, whose program can most accurately be viewed as the latest version of an evolving strategy for presidential oversight of agency regulation. On the other hand, both previous administrations can take credit for a large number of reforms, all built on strong consensus that economic deregulation was an idea whose time had come.

Before turning to the Reagan regulatory relief initiatives, it is worth asking why neither Ford nor Carter undertook to reform social regulation. Insofar as legislative efforts are concerned, the answers are fairly straightforward. For one thing, no major social regulatory statutes needed reauthorization during their terms of office. More important, outside certain academic economic circles, there was little support for undoing social regulatory programs. Although deregulation might have been a new religion in Washington, there was substantial variation among disciples regarding what it meant and where it should be applied. As a 1975 congressional Democratic Policy Statement read, "We note, however, that while 'regulatory' reform is a cliché whose time has come, one person's regulatory reform is another's environmental, consumer rip-off, unconscionable cancer risk, or return to the robber-baronies of yesteryear" (Derthick and Quirk 1985, p. 173).

It should also be noted that, deregulatory rhetoric aside, Carter signed into law several important new social regulatory statutes, including the Resource Conservation and Recovery Act (1976), the Surface Mining

Control and Reclamation Act (1977), the Marine Protection Research and Sanctuaries Act Amendments of (1977), the National Energy Conservation Policy Act (1978), the Natural Gas Policy Act (1978), and the Public Utilities Regulatory Policies Act (1978). What is more, Carter supported or acquiesced to the promulgation of dozens of executive agency rules implementing environmental and civil rights statutes, including costly new regulations in the areas of bilingual education, handicapped access to public transit, protection of the water supply, and hazardous waste.

We must conclude that the Carter administration demonstrated an ambivalence toward social regulatory reform. The president himself often pursued contradictory policies. While there is no doubt that Carter's antibureaucratic, antiregulatory sentiments were real, it is also true that when faced with competing values, he often chose to regulate as a means of meeting his commitments to civil rights, the environment, or to other social issues. This policy preference was reflected in his support for the vast increases in the federal government's regulatory role in block grants that were enacted during the Ford administration (Dommel et al. 1983). Also, Carter political appointees often clashed over the necessity for regulation; indeed, White House staff and agency heads generally differed dramatically on the subject. Thus, while RARG sought to curb agency regulatory inclinations, its recommendations were strongly resisted by agency heads, in most cases successfully (Eads and Fix 1984a).

Thus, while social regulatory change found support during the Ford and Carter administrations, it was limited support. For all the reasons described, much more reform activity had happened on the economic than on the social regulatory front by the end of 1979. All that was about to change. The inauguration of Ronald Reagan—a man who had long advocated limiting the federal government's domestic activities and freeing the market from government regulation—raised the expectation of academic experts, politicians and the general public alike, that a new era of regulatory reform had begun.

THE EMERGENCE OF A MANAGEMENT STRATEGY

The placement of major portions of the regulatory establishment within the executive branch and an increasingly antiregulation political climate do not sufficiently explain changes that have taken place since the Reagan administration took power; nor do they explain Reagan's emphasis on administration rather than legislation. The answers to these questions may be found in Reagan's policy agenda, his leadership style, his strong belief in limited government and an unfettered market, and his willingness to put the latter two to the test.

One of Ronald Reagan's main themes during the 1980 campaign was that national regulatory programs were out of control. Excessive regulation, he argued, was inhibiting the economy and undermining social progress. Early in his administration, Reagan stated: "During the presidential campaign, I promised quick and decisive action. Since taking office, I have made regulatory relief a top priority. It is one of the cornerstones of my economic recovery program" (White House, February 19, 1981).

Reagan's Regulatory Reform Goals

Common sense suggests that if we are accurately to gauge the success and effectiveness of Reagan's regulatory policy, we must have a clear idea of what the policy was intended to have accomplished. Unfortunately, however, presidential public statements of the goals of any policy are not always clear and can rarely be taken at face value. Unclear and even conflicting policy goals are often found in legislation as well, and are not the result of mere happenstance. Ambiguity in statutes result from congressional coalition building, serve as a way to build in needed administrative flexibility, or simply reflect congressional rhetoric. Presidents are equally likely to build in plenty of room for interpretation in their policy statements. Executive branch pronouncements can also be the product of bureaucratic bargaining, or nothing more than an occasion for political rhetoric.

The stated goals of the Reagan regulatory program were often described in very sweeping terms. Regulatory reform was never an end in itself, rather, it was promoted as a cornerstone of the economic recovery program. Economic recovery—considered the first order of business for the new administration—would come from a swift, major regulatory ventilation; substantial reductions in domestic program funding; cuts in income tax rates and indexing; and a stable monetary policy. Inclusion of regulatory reforms in the administration's most prominent domestic policy initiative guaranteed a high degree of visibility and public attention; these, in turn, were occasions for political rhetoric. For example, regulations were described as "tentacles" which were "strangling the economy." What is more, the benefits of regulatory relief were often oversold. For example, the president claimed that lifting regulatory burdens would move the nation "surely and predictably toward a balanced budget" (Congressional Quarterly 1981, p. 19-E).

Given the high priority the administration attached to regulatory relief, it is not surprising to find that the program and its goals were embodied in major presidential messages in the first year of the administration, including: the president's Report to the Nation on the Economy; the president's Economic Address before a joint session of Congress, the president's Annual Budget Message to the Congress, and the State of the Union Address. Overall, the goals of the Reagan regulatory reform program that can be gleaned from these presidential messages and other administration policy statements are the following:

1. to eliminate ineffective and burdensome regulations;
2. to postpone hundreds of regulations that have not yet been implemented;
3. to develop a centralized system that will provide for effective and coordinated management of the regulatory process; and
4. to eliminate and simplify regulations affecting state and local governments that are burdensome, unnecessary, and counterproductive.

These regulatory reform goals were predicated on a four-part rationale: that prior executive oversight of regulatory decisions were inadequate and needed to be repatterned after the expenditure process; that a number of existing statutes were not conducive to efficient regulation because they directed regulators to ignore costs; that regulations had excessively relied on command/control techniques rather than less restrictive approaches; and, finally, that in areas where the marketplace could reasonably be expected to fulfill the regulatory purpose, the presumption should be against regulating.

Both the goals and the rationale that supported them had been formulated well in advance of the president's inauguration. Indeed, their intellectual roots lie in the same academic circles that provided leadership for Carter's economic deregulation efforts. Several prominent conservative economists were recruited to head up the post-election transition, including Murray Weidenbaum and James Miller. It was Weidenbaum—the source of often-quoted statistics on the costs of regulation—who headed up the task force on regulation and later became the first chairman of the Council of Economic Advisors. It was Miller—a strong advocate and theoretician of cost-benefit analysis—who developed and implemented the plan to greatly strengthen the executive office of the president's regulatory oversight function and to move it from the White House to a permanent home in OMB.

The transition team also included task forces on the environment and most other areas of social regulation. While Miller was planning a centralized attack on agency regulations through OMB, advisors on these various transition task forces were seeking ways to alter the statutes that provided much of the basis for social regulation.

We cannot provide a full report of all the transition task forces' efforts here, but the case of environmental regulation is instructive. As Vig and Kraft (1984, p. 38) reported, in the fall of 1980 Reagan appointed a task force on environmental policy led by Dan Lufkin, former head of the Connecticut Department of Environmental Protection. The task force also included two former EPA administrators, William Ruckelshaus and

Russell Train. The official report produced by this task force called for moderate reforms of a number of key environmental statutes but did not advocate cutting back environmental efforts on a wholesale basis. At the same time, a parallel, but unofficial, task force report—which called for radical cutbacks in federal environmental regulation—was being prepared under the auspices of the Heritage Foundation (Vig and Kraft 1984). In the opinion of Russell Peterson, head of the Council on Environmental Quality under both Nixon and Ford, the Lufkin committee included some of the nation's most respected and influential Republican environmentalists, while the Heritage group consisted of the most conservative ideological critics. In the end, ideology won out. Only three copies of the Lufkin report were ever made, while the Heritage report was widely circulated among the transition staff.

An important question for our research has been this: Given the president's strong view on the evils of regulation, and the fact that a number of key environmental statutes were up for reauthorization, why didn't the administration move forcefully to push a social regulatory reform agenda on Capitol Hill? A number of factors suggested such a legislative strategy. The president had a strong mandate for reform in the Republican platform. Further, Carter had proved that presidential leadership could successfully get reforms through Congress in the area of economic regulation. Also, even among advocates of social regulation, some unhappiness existed as to its effectiveness and the tradeoffs necessitated by some policies.

There are several reasons why the administration decided early not to go the route of statutory reform. First, as mentioned earlier, while the public believed that the federal government should be reduced, there was no consensus as to how the government should reduce the burdens of regulation without sacrificing the social goals which continued to enjoy strong public support. Political support in Congress for much of the president's regulatory relief agenda was simply not strong enough. Two key environmental statutes, the Clean Air Act and the Clean Water Act, came up for reauthorization in the early years of the first term. But, as Chapter 5 shows, Reagan would not compromise, and Congress was deeply divided. Consequently, the reauthorizations of these two statutes were not the occasions for deregulation. Second, many of these programs were being implemented through complex intergovernmental partnerships. As Chapter 4 shows, state and local governments did not back the kind of wholesale deregulation of social regulatory statutes that was advocated by the conservative ideologues appointed to key posts in the new administration. Third, many political appointees, notably Ann Burford (chief administrator of EPA) and James Watt (secretary of Interior), favored executive branch deregulation rather than legislative modifications of federal statutes. Finally, the president's decision to embrace supply-side economics elevated tax and budget policy to top prominence in the new administration. Overall, the president was about to embark on the most ambitious plan for changing the tax structure and federal spending priorities since the New Deal. This effort would leave little time to campaign personally for legislative proposals which—in any event—would most likely divert congressional attention from other, higher priorities. Given OMB Director David Stockman's budget agenda and Stockman's political style, which featured a strong preference for cutting the budgets of agencies rather than modifying programs, it is not surprising that administrative efforts centered on OMB. Nor is it surprising that OMB's administrative efforts would rise in importance, while the recommendations of moderate Republicans for statutory reform of key social regulatory programs would fall by the wayside.

By the time of Reagan's inauguration, the die was cast. Recognizing the obstacles to a legislative strategy, and having set priorities which left little room for a legislative assault on regulation, the administration turned to a new type of strategy—a management strategy—that bypassed Congress and its allies among civil rights, labor, consumer, environmental, and women's groups.

Components of the Management Strategy

Eads and Fix (1984a) have usefully summarized the administrative strategy as consisting of the following elements:

1. a re-examination of existing rules, with an emphasis toward providing regulatory relief;
2. a mandated slowdown in the issuance of major new regulations;
3. a substantial relaxation (presumably within the limits of existing law) of efforts to enforce existing rules;
4. significant cuts in the operating budgets of regulatory agencies; and
5. the appointment of agency and commission heads and top level political appointees committed to regulatory relief.

The strategy assumed that the president's power to manage the executive branch directly along with the best use of his powers over independent agencies would effectively circumvent the other branches of government and outside opponents. Thus, a number of substantial and sweeping regulatory reforms could quickly be put into place. "If Congress would not cooperate . . . then the policy would be pursued by depriving agencies of resources and putting loyal ideologues in charge of them who would implement the rules and regulations in a different way" (Vig and Kraft 1984, p. 101). In hindsight, it appears that the keys to success of the Reagan administration were careful regulatory appointments and centralized administration under the leadership of OMB, for it was through them that the other elements of the strategy took shape.

Political Appointments. It would be difficult to overstate the importance the administration placed on careful appointments to executive agencies and independent commissions. Six months before the 1980 presidential election, Reagan advisors began to develop a system for identifying likely candidates to fill the nearly 2000 non–civil service positions subject to presidential appointment. By the time of the transition, the identification process was in full swing, guided by Edwin Meese, then counselor to the president, and E. Pendleton James, the designate for director of White House personnel. According to one member of the White House kitchen cabinet, appointments turned on three basic criteria: First, was the candidate a "Reagan man?" Next, was the candidate a Republican? Finally, was the candidate a conservative? According to Newland (1983), of these three criteria, conservative ideology was the most important.

Most observers agree that the Reagan strategy marked a fundamental departure from the staffing approach employed by previous modern presidents. According to a New York *Times* editorial (July 3, 1981), it was nothing short of a revolution in attitude involving the appointment of officials who in previous administrations might have been ruled out by concern over possible lack of qualifications, or conflict of interest, or open hostility to the mission of agencies they now lead.

Scholarly research supports this conclusion. For example, Newland (1983) found that Reagan appointees had substantially less experience than appointees of previous presidents. Newland's study of 150 middle-level management appointees indicates that nearly 60 percent of sub–cabinet level officers, nearly 80 percent of below sub–cabinet officers, and almost all of the independent branch agency appointees had no previous experience in the executive branch. Indeed, the aim in many agencies with responsibility for social, environmental, and individual rights concerns was to staff them with people eager to challenge the ideological and programmatic status quo (Nathan 1983, p. 74).

To maintain ideological purity and political loyalty of its appointees, the administration made certain that initial contacts were with White House, not agency, staff; and it stepped up the frequency of routine contacts and briefings between the White House and the executive agencies.

Finally, having made its selections, the administration moved to enhance the power of political appointees at the expense of the career service. Reductions in force (RIF) were used to removed, transfer, or demote old-time civil servants deemed uncooperative or ideologically suspect. Sometimes, as in the case of the Office of Surface Mining in the Interior Department and the research and enforcement divisions at EPA, appointees reorganized offices so frequently that career bureaucrats found it difficult, if not impossible, to perform their accustomed responsibilities.

OMB Oversight. The centerpiece of the administration's efforts was a vastly expanded regulatory clearance and oversight function for OMB. OMB's enhanced role was by no means unprecedented; as described earlier in this chapter, both Ford and Carter had imposed regulatory review and analysis on executive branch agencies to make agency regulatory decision making more rational and to reduce unnecessary regulatory burdens. The Reagan administration restructured and intensified these efforts, establishing more systematic oversight of agency procedures by OMB. The regulatory review process was housed in the Office of Information and Regulatory Affairs (OIRA) created by the Paperwork Reduction Act of 1980 as an office of OMB. At this time the OIRA staff was created by consolidating the Office of Regulatory and Information Policy (RIP) within OMB (45 staff positions), the Office of Government Programs and Regulations (previously part of the Council on Wage and Price Stability—20 staff positions), and the Office of Statistical Policy (previously part of the Commerce Department—25 staff positions).

The regulatory review process itself was not provided for in the Paperwork Act. It was created by Executive Order 12291, issued in February 1981. Regulatory review was intended to "reduce the burdens of existing and future regulations, increase agency accountability for regulatory actions, provide for presidential oversight of the regulatory process, minimize the duplication and conflict of regulations, and insure well-reasoned regulations" (White House, February 19, 1981). The following regulatory standards were to be applied to all regulatory decisions:

1. Administrative decisions shall be based on adequate information concerning the need for and consequences of proposed government action;
2. Regulatory activity shall not be undertaken unless the potential benefits to society from the regulation outweigh the potential costs to society;
3. Regulatory objectives shall be chosen to maximize the net benefits to society;
4. Among alternative approaches to any given regulatory objectives, the alternative involving the least net cost to society will be chosen; and
5. Agencies shall set regulatory priorities with the aim of maximizing the aggregate net benefits to society, taking into account the condition of the particular industries affected by the regulation, the condition of the national economy, and other regulatory actions contemplated for the future (Miller 1981, p. 44).

Insofar as presidential oversight is concerned, Executive Order 12291 established an approach very different from past review systems, which were decentralized and largely advisory in nature. The order consolidated all coordination and implementation authority in the OMB director, and through him, in OIRA. Viewed from a historical perspective, we might compare OMB's new acquisition of regulatory authority to its acquisition of control over agency budget decisions in 1921, or over agency legislative proposals in the 1930s. Yet, this dramatic transfer of power was not made through the usual tug and haul of bureaucratic bargaining. According to one account,

It was February 17, less than a month after the Reagan Administration took office, when the Office of Management and Budget called in top attorneys of the executive branch regulatory agencies to have a look at the President's new executive order on regulatory policy, an order that had been in preparation for weeks. Seated around the table in a second floor office in the Executive Office Building next door to the White House, the attorneys began to read, several taking out pens to note changes they wanted to make or parts they found objectionable. Not until the last page—where they saw President Reagan's signature—did they realize this was not the draft of a proposed order. It was the last word. (ACIR 1984, p. 168).

The director of OMB has many powers under the new system. The director has the authority to: prescribe criteria for determining major rules; order that any rule or set of related rules be treated as major rules; order an agency not to publish a notice of proposed rule making (NPRM) until OMB review is completed; order an agency not to publish a final rule or a regulatory impact analysis (RIA) until the agency has responded to OMB's views regarding the rule or RIA; issue uniform standards for developing RIAs; require an agency to obtain and evaluate additional data relevant to the regulation from any appropriate source; require inter-agency consultation to minimize or to eliminate rules identified as duplicative, overlapping, or conflicting; waive the RIA or other requirements for proposed or existing major rules; and require agencies to review current effective rules and prepare RIAs for major rules in accordance with schedules established by the director.

OMB's powers are not unrestrained, however. Appeals from the director's decisions may be taken to the appropriate cabinet council or to the president. According to the executive order, the director may not require any action that displaces an agency's responsibility under law or that conflicts with any procedural requirements of the Administrative Procedure Act or other applicable statute. The agency's response as well as OMB's negative comments are to be included in the rule-making file. Finally, the order does not give OMB direct authority over the substance of agency rules, and it does not expressly forbid an agency from publishing a proposed or final rule.

In the six years the regulatory review and oversight process has been in place, it has been the subject of a great deal of controversy. Indeed, when we discussed the review process with staff of OIRA, other OMB staff, agency staff, interest groups, and congressional members and staff, it seemed as though no two groups were talking about the same operation. Critics characterize OIRA powers as close to dictatorial. The OIRA administrator is regularly referred to as the regulatory czar, and the review process is likened to "the eye of the needle" or "the black hole."

OIRA officials, on the other hand, characterize their role as highly constrained by the size of the task, statutory language, and judicial interpretation. One top level OIRA official we interviewed described OIRA's role as that of a "watch puppy." From his point of view, OMB's powers under Executive Order 12291 are barely adequate to the task of rationalizing regulatory administration. And while OMB Director James Miller once characterized his leadership of OIRA in 1981 as that of the "toughest kid on the block," the Department of Justice—which has been responsible for defending the review process in court—has steadfastly maintained that the presidential review of agency rules is wholly advisory, an opinion echoed by each of OIRA's four administrators.

The view from Capitol Hill is different. Some in Congress see the OIRA process as nothing short of an unlawful invasion of congressional powers. Increasingly, even moderates object to what they perceive to be OMB's heavy-handedness, secrecy, and its bias favoring business and industry. Some congressional critics argue that the threat of OIRA intervention works more like a roadblock than a quality control process. Instead of improving a regulation by weeding out ill-advised proposals, they claim, OIRA oversight has had a debilitating effect on all rule making.

Outside government, the reaction to OMB's increased regulatory review is mixed, but the opposing forces are more vocal. Business groups that have benefited from this new process have welcomed OMB's attention. But once the initial enthusiasm for the Reagan regulatory campaign died down, so did business interest in regulatory review. By 1985, when Senate staff were searching for a business representative to speak on behalf of the administration at an OIRA oversight hearing, they were turned down by the Business Roundtable, the Chamber of Commerce, and the National Association of Manufacturers. All declined to testify on the grounds that they had insufficient institutional knowledge of OIRA activities to participate.

On the other hand, environmental and other interest groups that strongly oppose the process are well organized and persistent. In general, they argue that OIRA's major function is political: expediting actions that advance the president's agenda and stalling the rest (OMB Watch 1985). The charges—as we gleaned them from congressional testimony and other documents—range from inappropriate contacts with industry which are off the rule-making record to claims that OMB plays the role of "enforcer" by bullying and strong-arming agency personnel.

Whatever one's reactions to regulatory review, those feelings are bound to be magnified by the latest addition to the strategy: regulatory planning. This new process—initiated in 1985 with the issuance of Executive Order 12498—gives OMB a much earlier entrance into particular regulatory administrative activities. The idea of getting a head start for OMB as it attempts to shape agency rule making was originated by Miller on the basis of his CWPS experience. The process itself, however, is the brainchild of Reagan's second OIRA administrator, Christopher DeMuth, and was implemented by the third OIRA administrator, Douglas Ginzberg. According to Ginzberg, the idea of regulatory planning is to use more effectively the discretion that the president and his top policy makers in the regulatory arena are allowed in the statutes.

Regulatory planning brings administration policy to bear on decisions much earlier in the process by extending OIRA's involvement to include "significant prerule-making activities." Among such prerule-making initiatives are: actions taken to consider whether to initiate rule-making procedures; requests for public comment; and the development of documents that may influence, anticipate, or could lead to the commencement of significant rulemaking proceedings (OMB Bulletin 85–9 1985).

In addition, the order requires agencies to submit draft regulatory programs to OMB each year. The process thus holds agencies to a sort of regulatory contract with OMB, specifying the regulatory actions they will take in any given year. According to OMB's guidance to the agencies, the draft program must outline how agency regulatory policies, goals, and objectives are consistent with the administration's regulatory principles as stated in Executive Order 12291; and it should include a discussion of the most important regulatory actions it will take over the next year. Draft programs must highlight significant regulatory actions the agency will take to revise or rescind existing rules.

According to OIRA officials we interviewed, the purpose of the new regulatory program is to ensure that each proposed significant regulatory action is well thought out in itself and consistent with the priorities of other agencies and of the president. Equally important from the administration's view is the fact that this process increases the control of top management at the expense of lower echelon agency staff by forcing incipient rules to percolate up through the organization. It is also clear, however, that the program is intended to place limits on agency regulatory activity. OMB guidance states that once the administration's overall regulatory program for the year is completed, the agency head shall refrain from taking action not included in the program until OMB reviews such action. Only emergency situations and judicial deadlines are excepted. The presumption seems to be that most such reviews would result in OMB's returning the proposal for reconsideration.

Together, regulatory planning and review provide the president with a systematic management tool, one that parallels the budget process. That is, it provides OMB a means of negotiating with agencies over regulatory policy in much the same way the budget provides a context for negotiating agency expenditure policy. Unquestionably there is one important difference, however: while the budget is submitted to the legislature for approval, the regulatory negotiation and approval process remains within the executive branch.

Since the new regulatory planning process is internal and not subject to the public participation requirements of the Administrative Procedure Act or congressional review, it has generated a great deal of criticism from advocacy groups that fear their access to regulatory policy-making has been effectively foreclosed. For example, a 1985 OMB Watch report, entitled "OMB Control of Rulemaking: The End of Public Access," charged that the new program violates the basic constitutional principle that the president's role is to enforce the laws, not make them. According to such critics, the president's staff now can intervene quietly and at an early date in nearly any agency activity, superseding the discretion that Congress traditionally has delegated to federal agencies. Moreover, they argue, the new regulatory planning process procedures undermine the protections for public participation contained in the Administrative Procedure Act by providing a license for arbitrary and capricious OMB actions, long before public participation even begins.

The criticism from Capitol Hill and interest groups leaves the White House and OIRA staff largely undaunted. When interviewed in the fall of 1985 and again in the fall of 1986, top OIRA officials continued to discount the criticisms, attributing them to the "sour grapes" of special interests rather than the legitimate concerns of the larger public interest. Not only do they deny the criticism that the process gives OMB inappropriate powers and leverage, they also argue that, once in place, the planning and review programs will give Congress and the public early warning about planned agency initiatives. OIRA staff argue that the new process is consistent with public disclosure and will strengthen the oversight capabilities of Congress and the public. The delay between the effective date of the 1986 Regulatory Program and its publication—four months— suggests otherwise, however, Finally, insofar as social regulation is concerned, administration spokespersons and OIRA staff continue to deny that their intention is to reduce regulatory activities per se. Instead, they assert that they are improving regulatory performance and inserting a modicum of economic sense into the process. Speaking for the administration, Edwin Meese (1983, p. 191) stated:

The purpose of regulatory reform is not to decrease our ability to provide for clean air or clean water or better safety; the purpose is to take regulations that have developed over the years, some of which were historical accidents, some of which were designed to meet a specific need for which conditions have changed, some of which were in response to particular pressure groups and probably weren't needed in the first place, and to look at the entire scheme of regulations, which I think all of us have to agree has kind of grown like Topsy over the years, and to try to get it into a reasonable pattern of regulation necessary to preserve health and safety, and to carry out the necessary and appropriate functions of the federal government in the most expeditious, and streamlined way. In a nutshell that is what regulatory reform is all about.

SUMMARY AND CONCLUSIONS

This chapter has traced the development of federal regulation, and it has provided an overview of congressional and presidential responses to regulatory growth. In 100 years regulation grew from a small and relatively noncontroversial part of the federal bureaucratic establishment to a large and controversial function.

Nonetheless, past presidents and congresses paid little attention to regulatory growth, and even less to regulatory administration. The outcome was that by 1975 there were very few aspects of private sector activity that were not regulated in some way, and there was a great deal of intergovernmental regulation as well.

In the mid–1970s, as criticism of regulation and the system that produced it mounted, most experts agreed that federal regulatory policy needed an overhaul. Overregulation was widely blamed for a declining economy and great tensions in cooperative federalism. In particular, evidence mounted that much economic regulation had outlived its usefulness and was contributing to higher prices in transportation, telecommunications, and transported products. Consequently, a swell of bipartisan support for economic deregulation resulted in the passage of a number of important deregulatory statutes during the Carter administration.

Carter concentrated on economic regulation, leaving the Reagan administration to face the difficult problem of social and intergovernmental regulatory reform. Because the Reagan administration wished to clear the way for major tax and budget legislative initiatives, and because it hoped to advance regulatory changes certain to be controversial, the administration adopted a management regulatory reform strategy. The strategy was designed to bypass a Congress that was reluctant to modify social regulatory statutes, interest groups that supported the regulatory status quo, and state and local officials who regarded administration regulatory proposals as little more than a Trojan horse, masking a federal intent to withdraw from social, economic development, and environmental programs.

While the Reagan administration's management strategy was built on the legacy of recent presidential efforts to enhance executive office oversight of regulatory administration, it was substantially stronger and more centralized. In addition, unlike the efforts of earlier presidents, Reagan emphasized a careful, ideologically oriented choice of political appointments. In practice, the strategy has worked to redress the problems of social and intergovernmental regulation by reducing the amount of existing regulation and curbing growth. Because there is little public consensus about what benefits might accrue from social and intergovernmental regulatory reform and little if any congressional or interest group support for abandoning social regulatory goals, the administration's program has been highly controversial, and a number of efforts have been undertaken to prevent it from succeeding.

These efforts have not deterred the administration. To the greatest possible extent during the past six years, the administration has stayed the management course in its struggle for regulatory relief. It continues to bank on the belief that administrative manipulation can be used as a substitute for legislation when the latter seems unlikely to produce the desired results.

Whether that belief has been justified, how it has been implemented, and what its consequences have been are the subjects of subsequent chapters of this book. The following important questions about the Reagan management strategy will be addressed: To what degree have the administration's regulatory goals been adopted by both the independent and executive regulatory agencies? Was the adoption of these goals due to administration actions, or have other forces and actors played a role in shaping regulatory reform agendas? How did the performance of the management approach to regulatory change compare to the statutory approach used by other administrations? How successful have the different elements of the Reagan management strategy been in reducing the level of governmental regulation? Finally, if the strategy has been successful, measured against the administration's objective of regulatory relief, how has it measured up in terms of the broader problems of regulatory reform? Specifically, what have been the institutional consequences; and is the regulatory policy system more able to manage regulation as a result? Insofar as future reform is concerned, what is the Reagan legacy likely to be?

3 REINING IN THE REGULATORY BUREAUCRACY

In the preceding chapter we reviewed the history of the federal regulatory bureaucracy to date: its beginnings; its period of great expansion; and recent presidential attempts to restrain its growth, culminating in Reagan's major regulatory reform efforts. We described the overall goals and strategies of the Reagan administration in regards to regulatory relief, and showed how those efforts were perceived by Congress and by various groups outside of government.

But, how did the regulatory agencies themselves view these initiatives? Did personnel in the regulatory agencies agree with the need for thoroughgoing regulatory reform? To what extent did they adopt the regulatory reform goals of the president as their own? How did they view the specific types of strategies employed by the administration to implement these goals? How did they respond to these strategies? In framing their responses, to what extent were the agencies influenced by the reactions of Congress and other institutions of government or the pressures exerted by interest groups outside of government? Finally, from the agency perspective, did Reagan's regulatory reform efforts really work? Did administration efforts indeed touch every part of the regulatory bureaucracy? How effective have these reform efforts been across different agencies? Have some of the components of the president's strategy had more significant effects than others?

This chapter attempts to look at the Reagan regulatory reform program from the agency perspective. With 91 existing federal agencies, offices, and bureaus engaged in regulatory activities, it is inescapably a complicated perspective, but one that is essential to achieving a balanced picture of administration efforts. To investigate how regulatory agencies viewed these efforts, we surveyed 171 of the key personnel participating in regulatory reform in many different types of agencies. The survey contained a broad range of questions concerning regulatory reform goals and activities. The survey carried out in 1984 and 1985 was directed to top political appointees and managerial-level career personnel in 19 independent regulatory agencies and 36 executive branch agencies. Large and well-known agencies, such as the Federal Trade Commission, Interstate Commerce Commission, and the Environmental Protection Agency, as well as smaller, lesser-known agencies, such as the Federal Energy Regulatory Commission and the Commodity Futures Trading Commission were included in the sample. As many as 28 (or 70 percent) of the agencies were primarily engaged in social regulation, the remainder in economic regulation. Here we borrow the helpful definition developed by Eads and Fix. Hence, *social regulation* refers to the "set of federal programs that use regulatory techniques to achieve broad social goals. . . . *Economic regulation* refers to the programs that attempt to control prices, conditions of market entry and exit, and conditions of service, usually in specific industries considered to be 'affected with the public interest' " (Eads and Fix 1984, p. 12, emphasis added). The managers we surveyed ranged from mid-level project managers (GS 15) to agency and department heads (GS 18). Twenty-seven (or about 18 percent) of them were Reagan appointees, while 86 (or about 50 percent) were career personnel, many with more than ten years of government service. More detailed information concerning our research methodology and survey instrument can be found in Appendix 1.

SETTING REGULATORY REFORM GOALS

What Are the Items on the Agency Regulatory Reform Agenda?

As previously discussed, a primary goal of Reagan's regulatory reform program was to stimulate economic growth by mitigating the regulatory burdens of business and industry. This goal was to be achieved through a comprehensive administrative strategy including eliminating ineffective and burdensome rules, slowing down the development of new rules, and relaxing efforts to enforce existing rules. However, defining goal strategies is one thing, getting 91 separate regulatory bureaucracies in 56 agencies to accept the goals and implement the strategies is a completely different matter. Indeed, scholars have tended to view the task of getting bureaucracies to adopt goals and methods that have not been part of agencies' past missions or standard operating procedures as difficult at best. Writing a half-decade before the Reagan efforts to reform the regulatory bureaucracy began, Tugwell pessimistically states:

The management of a bureaucracy comprising perhaps thousands of careerists will be, at best, nominal; the agency heads will inevitably outmaneuver a politician-secretary. Presidential orders transmitted through such channels become more mysteriously changed to suit the bureaucracy's preferences. Policies persist from one Administration to another remarkably unchanged. Resistance to change is also reinforced by the alliance between bureaucrats and the appropriate Congressmen. Altogether, it requires a most sophisticated and determined President to effect any changes at all. (Tugwell 1974, p. 101)

Reagan certainly appears to have the determination to which Tugwell referred. In the 1980 presidential campaign in particular, Reagan waged a vigorous anti-Washington campaign, made harsh judgments concerning the federal government's inability to solve the nation's economic and social problems, and promised decisive action to control and redirect the federal bureaucracy. These feelings are summed up nicely in an aphorism from his 1982 inaugural address: "[G]overnment is not the solution to our problem. Government is the problem" (Reagan 1981, p. 11-E). Thereafter, as described here in Chapter 2, Reagan made concerted efforts to direct bureaucratic activities from the White House through a carefully developed network of political appointees.

However, while the strong determination to rein in the federal bureaucracy no doubt existed, it seemed questionable whether it was a realistically attainable goal. Could such a wide-ranging and comprehensive attack on Washington's regulatory bureaucracy really be expected to succeed, especially when other presidential attempts to make even marginal changes in the regulatory bureaucracy had failed? Indeed, there were several reasons to believe the bureaucracy would easily resist administration efforts at any radical change. First, as explained previously, presidents have historically held only limited control over much of the regulatory bureaucracy. Many agencies were independent of presidential control—with commissioners whose terms in office would not expire for several years into Reagan's presidency. Also, many of the regulatory bureaucracies within the executive branch had developed strong and influential relationships with a multitude of congressional subcommittee members and powerful interest groups outside of government. Reagan's ultraconservative ideological bent seemed in conflict with the attitudes and beliefs of many career bureaucratic officials who were deeply committed to the agencies' missions. Given that research findings clearly indicate that the personal beliefs and attitudes of career bureaucrats are likely to have great impact in agendas and policy preferences of their agencies (Downs 1967; Kelman 1980), it seemed likely that the president's program would encounter stiff opposition from the career bureaucracy, who would resist any major deviations from past policies and practices.

Given all these factors working against change, the first question that arises is the extent to which administration efforts actually penetrated the built-in defenses endemic to all bureaucracies. We were particularly interested in examining the extent to which the president's regulatory reform agenda had filtered down to bureaucratic officials and been formally adopted as official agency goals. Survey participants were thus asked to name the major regulatory reform goals that their agency was actively pursuing.

Given the large number of different policy goals the Reagan administration had established in this area, it was not surprising to find that the amount of variation among goals cited by survey respondents was quite high. Indeed, no less than 34 distinct regulatory reform goals were mentioned. These goals ranged from imposing less costs on the regulated community, to increasing consumer welfare, to updating regulations to keep pace with modern technology, to completely abolishing the agency.

Goals that were most frequently cited by agency officials as being central to agency regulatory reform efforts included:

- Less cost to the regulated community   (13%)
- Less paperwork burden on government and industry   (11%)
- Opening markets to foster greater competition   (10%)
- Getting government off industry's back   (9%)
- Getting rid of unnecessary regulations   (8%)
- Streamlining regulations so as to avoid duplication of efforts   (6%)
- Greater responsiveness to the public   (4%)
- Returning power to the states   (4%)
- Budget Stabilization   (3%)
- Update regulations to keep pace with technology   (3%)

These responses make it clear that the administration's regulatory reform message had indeed filtered down to the regulatory bureaucracy. The four most frequently mentioned goals reflect the administration's free market orientation, its proclivity toward smaller government, and efficacy of stimulating economic growth through the removal of government regulations on industry. What is also clear from these responses is that those surveyed regarded industry and not the general public as both the key element of the public concerned with regulatory reform and its main audience and beneficiary. Only 4 percent of those questioned mentioned the general public as a direct beneficiary of the reform activities. While several other goals were mentioned that clearly had a public orientation—such as increasing consumer welfare through the lowering of prices, and making regulations easier for the general public to understand—these responses combined made up less than 10 percent of all responses.

Despite the disparity in cited goals, we were able to place these goals into three distinct (although not necessarily mutually exclusive) categories: 1) those that had a very clear and direct economic orientation, such as opening markets to provide for greater competition and product diversity, privatization of government services, and "getting government off industry's back" in order to promote greater business and industrial growth; (2) those that had a clear *administrative–political* orientation such as streamlining regulations or reducing duplication of efforts, making agency personnel more efficient, reducing regulatory staff, speeding up the regulatory process and reducing procedural delays, modernizing agency technology, and reducing overall agency spending; and (3) those that had a clear public orientation, such as increasing consumer welfare. By far, the greatest number of responses fell into the economic category which accounted for 55 percent of the total, followed by administrative–political goals (35%) and goals oriented towards the general public (10%). Our survey responses thus indicate that economic goals were of primary importance in the eyes of the regulatory bureaucracy as they looked at regulatory reform issues. Administrative and political goals, while clearly secondary, still seemed to be important considerations to survey respondents, however. Goals oriented towards the general public apparently played a much lesser role. These findings are consistent with the administration's desire to make regulatory reform play a central part in the president's overall economic recovery program and the anti–big government ideological bent of the administration.

Surprisingly little variation occurred in the responses of officials from different types of agencies with regard to regulatory reform goals, as Table 3.1 shows. We grouped the responses according to whether respondents represented an independent versus an executive branch agency and according to whether the agency was primarily involved in economic or social regulation. As might be expected, officials of agencies with primary responsibility for economic regulation gave the most weight to economic goals; 61 percent of the goals cited by these officials were economic goals. Officials of independent agencies seemed to give slightly more weight to economic goals than did those from executive branch agencies (58% versus 53% of the goals cited were economic goals). Officials from social regulatory agencies and executive branch agencies cited administrative–political goals somewhat more often than those from other types of agencies (38% for social regulatory agencies and 37% for executive branch agencies). There was extremely little variation among types of agencies in the relatively low frequency with which public-oriented regulatory reform goals were mentioned. In addition, we found virtually no difference in the types of regulatory goals mentioned

Table 3.1
**Distribution of Types of Regulatory Reform Goals Cited by Officials in
Different Types of Agencies (in percent)**

| | | Type of Goal | |
Type of Agency (N*)	Economic	Administrative/ Political	Public
By organizational affiliation			
Independent agency (130)	58	30	12
Executive branch (281)	53	37	10
By type of mission			
Economic regulation (99)	61	26	13
Social regulation (312)	52	38	10
All agencies (411)	55	35	10

*N refers to the number of times goal was mentioned by all respondents representing
this type of agency.

Source: Compiled by author.

by Reagan appointees versus career bureaucrats, and federal versus regional officials.

What Factors Influence Agency Reform Goals?

Why did agencies adopt the particular set of regulatory reform goals
that they did? Was it simply a matter of following current presidential
directives, had these goals been adopted earlier under the Carter administration, or had they developed outside the government from industry
or bureaucratic pressures? To shed light on this question, respondents
were asked to describe the main impetus for the regulatory goal change
now important to their agencies. There was great diversity in their answers. While many cited Reagan administration directives, others identified Carter administration carryover, public pressure, industry
demands, congressional statutes and pressure, economic conditions, and
changes in the marketplace.

While the range of responses was wide, four factors emerged as most
important: presidential directives, especially as expressed in Executive
Order 12291 (26%); the leadership and policy beliefs of a recent administration appointee (16%); OMB oversight and intervention (14%); and
industry demands (11%). This list leaves little doubt that, according to
the perspectives of agency officials, the Reagan administration played a

very strong role in shaping agency regulatory reform goals and most agency staff cite elements of the management strategy as the reasons.

We grouped all responses into the following categories: internal agency, presidential, and other external factors. Internal agency factors included any impetus for change that seemed to have emerged from within an agency, suggesting that an agency's regulatory reform agenda was inner-directed. Presidential factors included any manifestation of presidential influence as embodied in (for example, E. O. 12291 and E. O. 12498), and recommendations developed by the Bush Task Force on Regulatory Relief. Other external factors include new statutes mandating change, demands of interest groups and other forms of public pressure, the influence of academic analyses, congressional oversight, and economic forces.

The agenda-setting factors mentioned by respondents did not always fall neatly into these categories for coding purposes. The most difficult to categorize were apparently internal factors that had been precipitated or otherwise influenced by the Reagan administration or other external factors. For example, Reagan appointees played a major leadership role in regulatory agenda setting. In this case, while changes that occurred emerged from within, credit for them also goes to the president, via his appointment powers. Nonetheless, since not all political appointees played an equally aggressive leadership role when it came to regulatory reform, we coded these responses as internal factors.

Based on this system of categorization, 44 percent of all responses were found to be internal agency factors, 31 percent presidential factors, and 25 percent "other" kinds of outside factors (see Table 3.2). As might be expected, the greatest evidence of presidential influence was found in the executive branch agencies (41% of responses from officials in this type of agency cited presidential factors). Almost as many responses (40%) from executive branch agencies cited internal agency factors as influential, however. The independent agencies, by contrast, reported a much lesser influence from presidential factors (only 14%)—while giving much weight to both internal agency factors (47%) and a variety of external factors (39%) notably statutory deregulation and industry demands.

Regulatory reform goals at agencies primarily concerned with economic regulation seemed most influenced by internal agency factors (40%) and external factors other than presidential (38%). By contrast, presidential factors were more frequently cited as influential in agencies primarily concerned with social regulation. Those surveyed at these agencies cited presidential factors in 35 percent of the responses and internal agency factors in 44 percent of the responses. This finding may reflect the great importance that President Reagan placed on changing business as usual in the social regulatory agencies. Over and above the

Table 3.2
Factors Influencing Adoption of Regulatory Goals (in percent)

Type of Agency (N*)	Type of Factor		
	Internal Agency	Presidential	Other External
By organizational affiliation			
Independent agency (79)	47	14	39
Executive branch (160)	40	41	19
By type of mission			
Economic regulation (60)	40	22	38
Social regulation (181)	44	35	21
Respondents from all agencies (248)	44	31	25

*N refers to the number of times goal was mentioned by all respondents representing this type of agency.

Source: Compiled by author.

variation in response among different types of agencies, it seemed evident from this data that—at least from the agency point of view—recent regulatory reform initiatives have developed from many diverse forces.

It would thus certainly be an oversimplification to say that Ronald Reagan alone was responsible for reform goals adopted by the regulatory agencies during his administration. While the president was definitely a major actor in bringing about a new emphasis and immediacy toward regulatory reform efforts, many factors apparently shaped agency agendas. In many cases, regulatory reform efforts were already ongoing. For instance, consider the following: when respondents were asked to compare approaches towards regulatory reform taken both by the Carter and Reagan administrations, more than two-thirds (68%) stated that the approaches were either identical or highly similar in emphasis and goals. Typical comments include: "They have been very similar in approach in that both have been generally pro-competitive and with similar goals"; "Identical regulatory reform approaches—a seamless garment"; "the processes are basically the same, i.e., analyze the impacts of the alternatives prior to choosing the appropriate actions"; "Similarities exist in their use of regulatory analysis techniques, favoring of deregulation, and interest in techniques other than 'command and control' regulation."

At least from the point of view of many agency officials, then, the regulatory reform goals of President Reagan were neither as new nor as intrusive as might have been thought, given some of the rhetoric of administration spokespersons. Apparently internal, presidential and other outside factors all play a role in shaping agency regulatory agendas. The mixture and effect of these factors may vary among different regulatory agencies and policy areas, but the fact remains that—in the eyes of agency personnel—it has been a combination of factors that accounted for recent regulatory change, rather than merely presidential initiatives. This point was observed throughout the remarks of respondents. A comment by one Food and Drug Administration official we interviewed is typical:

The regulatory program of this agency has an unusual amount of support from the regulated industries as well as the general public. The work we do is seen as a public good. Change occurs not so much from 'regulatory reform' as from technological advances, completion of programs, and initiation of new efforts.

As further proof that there exists a widespread belief that regulatory reform developed out of a mix of several factors, we found no variance in the responses of political appointees versus career bureaucrats. One might have expected that political appointees would have given a greater share of the credit for recent regulatory initiatives to the person who appointed them—President Reagan. However, we found that both sets of actors cited presidential initiatives (as well as internal and other external factors) with the same frequency.

Who Formulates Regulatory Reform Goals?

Given the diversity in regulatory reform goals as well as the range of factors that lead to their development, we were interested in examining the extent to which various government and nongovernment actors participated in formulating the new regulatory directions that emerged in the 1980s. There are, of course, methodological difficulties in making such investigations across a field of such diverse organizations as the 91 federal regulatory agencies, offices and bureaus. Nonetheless, analysts have been able to identify the principal actors and their relationships, at least on a general level. Key participants in regulatory formulation have tended to be the executive and centralized federal bureaucracy, Congress, the courts, the regulated interests, intervenors, state government officials, and various other outside voices, such as public interest groups, think tanks, academics, and journalists (Ripley and Franklin 1984; Meier 1985).

We asked surveyed officials to rate the degree of influence in for-

Table 3.3
How Agency Officials Rank the Degree of Influence of Various Groups in
the Formulation of Agency Reform Goals (in percent)

| Type of Group | Percentage Rating Formulation Role as Significant to Moderate | | | | |
	Organizational Affiliation Independent Executive		*By Type of Mission* Economic Social		All Agencies
Executive appointees	90	88	89	88	89
Career agency personnel	94	81	92	84	86
Interest groups	76	76	87	73	76
Office of Management and Budget	27	76	39	67	61
U.S. Senate	67	40	70	42	50
U.S. Congress	64	42	63	45	49
U.S. Senate staff	52	32	58	32	39
U.S. House staff	55	33	56	35	40
Other government Departments	45	31	55	29	36
State elected officials	12	22	14	20	19

Source: Compiled by author.

mulating agency goals of the following groups: executive administrative
agency appointees, career bureaucratic officials, OMB staff, other departments and agencies, federal and state legislators, congressional staff,
interest groups, and others. The influence of such groups was characterized as significant; moderate; minimal; or nonexistent. Responses are
shown in Table 3.3.

   The two groups that are seen as playing by far the greatest role in
formulating regulatory reforms are executive administrative appointees
and career agency administrative personnel, with 89 percent and 86
percent of the entire sample respectively rating their role as either significant or moderate. There was not much variation in these responses
across the different agency categories.

   One of the most interesting findings—from the view of agencies—is
that interest groups and OMB apparently play a markedly more influential role in shaping regulatory initiatives than does Congress. More
than three-fourths (76%) of respondents identified interest groups as
significantly or moderately involved in agency regulatory activities and
61 percent ranked the influence of OMB as significant or moderate. This
compares with approximately 45 percent for federal legislators and their
staffs. (As we shall see in later chapters, this observation seems to be
only partly correct. While our case studies and interviews of congres-

sional staff confirm a marked decrease in informal congressional-agency interactions, overall they do not indicate that Congress was uninvolved in regulatory policy formulation or administration.) There was some variation in the degree to which interest groups were reported to be influential. In particular, officials of economic regulatory agencies tended to rank the influence of interest groups higher than respondents in other types of agencies. It would be a mistake to conclude, however, that such influence is all on one side. Respondents reported that their agency's reform activities often brought out the interest groups on all sides of an issue. Indeed, most of the respondents reported high involvement from interest groups that supported regulatory reform on some issues, and argued against it on others. As one Food and Drug Administration official surveyed stated,

Regulatory reform is a nice concept like apple pie and motherhood. Everyone supports reform as long as it supports their position. Where a regulation serves as a barrier to new competition, the regulation is supported by the existing interest no matter how burdensome. Consumer and other special interest groups believe that regulatory reform is "deregulation" and a lessening of protection.

Most of the people we interviewed believed their agencies' response to interest group demands was balanced and to some extent, countervailing influences cancelled each other out. In the words of one respondent: "We generally assume that we are correct if both industry representatives and organized 'consumer advocates' are yelling at the same pitch." Only a small percentage (6%) contended that interest groups had disproportionate access to their agency. However, a very few of those interviewed viewed the access that interest groups had to their agency as disproportionate. There did seem to be some feeling, however, that interest group pressure as brought to bear through the executive office or OMB might have had excessive influence on the regulatory reform agenda. As one EPA official surveyed commented,

Here, it was perceived that industry brought wish lists to OMB and the White House and that is how the agenda was formulated. In some instances, "reforms" which were rammed through were in direct violation of either existing statutes or judicial case law (e.g., repealing regulations without going through the Administrative Procedure Act type procedures). We spent a fair amount of time litigating (and losing) cases which were the result of OMB directives.

Similarly, the Bush Task Force was also frequently mentioned by respondents as a way of putting pressure on the agency to act favorably to industry's regulatory demands. Indeed, such use of the Task Force by industries was encouraged by C. Boyden Gray, the counsel for the

Presidential Task Force on Regulatory Relief, before the U.S. Chamber of Commerce:

If you go to the agency first, don't be too pessimistic if they can't solve the problem there. If they don't, that's what the task force is for. We had an example of that not too long ago but the people were not being completely candid with their own top people or the task force. We told the lawyers representing the individual companies and the trade associations involved to come back to us if they had a problem.

Two weeks later they showed up and I asked if they had a problem. They said they did, and we made a couple of phone calls and straightened it out, alerted the top people at the agency that there was a little hanky-panky going on at the bottom of the agency, and it was cleared up very rapidly, so the system does work if you use it as sort of an appeal. You can act as a double-check on the agency that you might encounter problems with. (Gray 1981, p. 53).

While Reagan officials have down-played this advocacy role in the wake of bad publicity that followed revelations such as those reported by Gray, we found no survey evidence that this kind of interaction is on the decline, raising the following question: Given a great deal of administrative access and support, why didn't industry and business groups play an even more pervasive role in the regulatory process? According to respondents, it was not lack of resources, or being out-lobbied by pro-regulation forces. It was conflict from within. For reasons we will explore in later chapters, industry and business officials were deeply divided over whether the Reagan regulatory experiment was in their best interest. Consequently, while some argued for regulatory changes, others argued against them.

According to respondents, industry infighting caught the administration off guard. As one EPA official pointed out,

The Administration belatedly learned that there was no one 'industry position.' For example, there is an industry which profits from waste disposal as well as one which generates waste; it is more pro-industry to ease or to tighten the restrictions on waste disposal? Another example: for air regulations impacting small refiners, is it more 'pro-industry' to favor (by repeal) those who avoided compliance, if to do so imposes severe economic disadvantages on those who complied with the regulations when they were promulgated? Thus, the Administration's early efforts at pleasing industry were quite crude.

Our survey instrument was not designed to measure directly such "second-hand" influence of interest groups on the regulatory process, but responses to open-ended questions seem to have identified them as significant.

The role of OMB in regulatory reform has been one of the most controversial elements of administration efforts. As we have seen, the influence of OMB on the formulation of regulatory reform within the agency was ranked higher than that of Congress by surveyed agency officials. There was a great deal of variation, however, in the way officials representing different types of agencies ranked the influence of OMB. In general, OMB influence was perceived as greater by officials in the social as opposed to economic regulatory agencies and executive branch as opposed to independent agencies. Only 27 percent of those surveyed in the independent agencies and 39 percent in the economic regulatory agencies ranked OMB influence as significant or moderate. By contrast, 67 percent of the respondents in the social regulatory agencies and 76 percent of those in the executive branch agencies felt this way. Some researchers have suggested that OMB is not only the most dominant actor in executive branch administration, but in the independent regulatory agency administration as well (Brigman 1981; Fisher 1981). Our findings qualify this conclusion. According to our data, while OMB has influenced the formulation of independent regulatory agencies' regulatory policies, the budget office is by no means omnipresent.

In addition, our data confirms findings from earlier research that OMB has concentrated its efforts on social regulation. While OMB's role in the social regulatory agencies was rated as moderate or significant by 67 percent of those surveyed, only 39 percent rated it that high for economic regulatory agencies. Several explanations may account for this phenomenon. First, most economic regulation is administered by independent commissions which, according to our respondents, have enjoyed greater freedom from direct intervention by the executive office of the president. From the administration's view, less direct involvement may be required. For one thing, Congress passed numerous important deregulatory statutes during the Carter years. For another, the natural Reagan constituency within the business community has objected far more to social than economic regulation. Thus, there may have been less of a need for OMB to play a strong activist role. Moreover, as Table 3.3 indicates, according to our respondents, Congress has been more involved in economic than social regulatory issues. (These findings—valid in 1984–1985—would no doubt be qualified in 1987 in light of important environmental statutes passed at the close of the 99th Congress. We discuss this point more fully in Chapter 7.)

In the first years of the administration's regulatory relief program, critics of Executive Order 12291 feared that it would give OMB the power to delay the regulatory process to serve its own ends (House, Committee on Energy and Commerce 1982b, pp. 103). OMB officials and administrative spokespersons had vociferously argued that this would never happen. As James C. Miller III, then executive director of the Presidential Task Force on Regulatory Relief, stated before a House subcommittee,

The last thing we want to do is have our review process be characterized as trying to block the regulations, so we give very expeditious treatment to these proposals when they come over. Nine days I think is a very short time period compared with the months and sometimes years it takes to draft the original regulation. Besides that, I think that the process that the President has instituted here of providing some discipline on the agencies probably will speed up—the net effect will be to speed up—the regulatory decision-making process rather than slow it down. (House, Committee on Energy and Commerce 1982b, p. 67)

Responses to our survey by agency officials, however, support the contention that OMB did in fact use the review process as an "administrative black hole." When asked to identify the major factors that have either helped or hurt regulatory reform efforts in their agencies, respondents identified OMB as a frequent *impediment*. It is clear from their responses that many believe OMB's efforts were often counterproductive. As one official complained,

OMB's review process has impeded effectiveness. Ideologue's at OMB require excessive analysis and documentation even when rule changes are cost saving. They want *maximum* cost reduction, not *satisfactory* cost reduction.

In particular, regulatory officials expressed much concern over the quality of OMB regulatory reform reviews. Almost without exception, there seemed to be great doubts among the career bureaucracy over OMB's ability (specifically that of OIRA) to conduct RIA reviews as mandated by E. O. 12291. As a director of Regulatory Economics in an executive branch agency charged, "Economic analyses [as called for by E. O. 12291] tend to be fairy tales with regard to costs, benefits, and market competence."

In comparison with executive appointees, career personnel, interest groups, and OMB, other sorts of actors—congressional representatives and their staffs, other government departments, and state elected officials—were seen as relatively less influential over the regulatory reform process. Only about half of those interviewed ranked congressional influences as significant or moderate, although, as previously mentioned, congressional influence was perceived as significantly stronger among the officials representing independent agencies and economic regulatory agencies.

A similar pattern held for the influence of other government departments. Only slightly more than one-third of respondents perceived these groups as significant or moderate in influence; such influences were ranked relatively higher by respondents representing independent and economic regulatory agencies. In addition, in a separate open-ended question which asked what linkages with other agencies or political officials had been developed as a direct result of reform efforts, 23 percent responded by saying "none."

Although one of Reagan's stated goals was to shift regulatory responsibility for many programs to the states, state officials played almost no role in the development of these proposals. Only 19 percent of the respondents rated state officials as playing a significant or moderate role in the formulation of regulatory reforms.

PUTTING REGULATORY REFORM INTO PLACE

Administrative Strategies Versus Statutory Strategies

As set out in the beginning of this book, there are numerous advantages and disadvantages to both statutory and administrative regulatory reform strategies. Responses to our survey of agency officials provide clear evidence of the preference of administrative strategies over statutory means. By the beginning of Reagan's second term, the administration's regulatory management program was in place across the board and well understood by executive and independent regulatory agency staff. In addition, most bureaucrats believed that a great deal of regulatory change had been accomplished through the use of what we have characterized as the management or administrative strategy. As explained earlier, the Reagan administrative regulatory relief strategy consisted of five components: (1) a re-examination of existing rules; (2) a mandated slowdown in the issuance of major new regulations; (3) a relaxation of efforts to enforce existing rules; (4) significant cuts in agencies operating budgets; and (5) the appointment of new personnel. When asked to rate the extent to which regulatory reform had been introduced through administrative means (high; moderate; slight; not at all), 87 percent of the surveyed officials responded that their use was either high or moderate (see Table 3.4). Only 10 percent characterized these efforts as slight, with the remaining 3 percent saying there had been no administrative reform efforts at all. In contrast, efforts aimed at statutory reform were perceived as far fewer. Forty-two percent of those surveyed characterized the usage of statutory reform strategies in their agency as either high or moderate, compared with 22 percent saying it had been slight, and 36 percent saying there had been no efforts whatsoever.

Both independent and executive regulatory agencies were making heavy use of administrative reform—88 percent of the independents and 86 percent of the executive agencies indicated that they were making high to moderate use. A more noticeable difference was observed be-

Table 3.4
Agency Officials' Perceptions of Effectiveness of Administrative versus Statutory Strategies in Advancing Regulatory Reform

| | Percentage Ranking Strategy as: | | | | | |
| | Statutory Strategies | | | Administrative Strategies | | |
	High or Moderate	Slight	Not at All	High or Moderate	Slight	Not at All
By organizational affiliation						
Independent agency	50	21	29	88	10	2
Executive branch	38	22	40	86	10	4
By type of mission						
Economic regulation	64	21	15	100	0	0
Social regulation	35	22	43	81	13	6
All agencies	42	22	36	87	10	3

Source: Compiled by author.

tween economic and social regulatory agencies. Economic regulatory agencies apparently used administrative measures to change policy much more than social regulators used them: 100 percent of the officials representing economic regulatory agencies characterized agency use of administrative measures as either high to moderate; whereas only 81 percent of the respondents in the social regulatory agencies did so.

In addition, major differences existed in the degree to which different agencies were pursuing regulatory reform through statutory efforts. While 50 percent of officials in the independents were making high to moderate use of statutory reform, only 38 percent of officials in the executive agencies reported seeking regulatory changes through this means. The findings for economic and social regulators was quite similar. Here 64 percent of the respondents in agencies engaged in economic regulation rated their efforts as being either high or moderate, compared with 35 percent of the social regulators. Thus, while independent regulatory agencies had similar goal patterns to that of executive agencies, the independents apparently strongly preferred to pursue those goals through the legislative process. Several factors account for these differences. First, several independent agency representatives explained that they lacked the authority to make substantial regulatory changes without statutory changes first taking place. As a staff member of the Federal Reserve Board pointed out,

Except in certain areas of monetary policy, the Federal Reserve's flexibility is limited by the underlying statutes. For example, the complexity of truth in lending regulations could not have been substantially reduced without congressional action. Also, the deregulation of interest rates in deposits could not have been accomplished effectively without the Congress.

A second reason why independent agencies have sought statutory over administrative reform is that while many independents felt they had the necessary discretion to achieve regulatory reform by administrative means, they worried that in the absence of legislative authority, they would be excessively vulnerable to legal challenges. As an official of the Consumer Product Safety Commission commented,

The great strength of statutory reform is that it obviously legitimizes the reform. We could not make several improvements in our consumer regulations without facing litigation about our authority to do so. There was a recognition by agency staff and the Administration that basic statutory changes were needed to avoid judicial reversals at the behest of various opponents to deregulation.

As shown earlier, congressional involvement in the reform agenda of the economic regulatory agencies was relatively high. Apparently, considerable congressional support also existed for the regulatory reform goals of the independent agencies. Several representatives of independent agencies mentioned congressional interest favoring deregulation actions in their respective policy areas, thus making the statutory route a relatively more attractive one for them. Statutory strategies, however, did not appear attractive for executive agencies. Respondents from these agencies tended to view the congressional route as being impractical, anticipating almost certain congressional opposition. As an EPA official noted, "There was the awareness that the real agenda of this Administration in the environmental area would be wholly unacceptable in the Congress and probably elsewhere."

A similar pattern was observed for economic and social regulatory agencies. Economic regulatory agencies enjoyed much greater support on Capitol Hill in their efforts at regulatory reform, just as they had during the Ford and Carter administrations, while the social regulatory agencies almost universally cited the fact that congressional and interest group opposition within their policy area made the likelihood of a successful statutory reform effort slight to nonexistent. The data on usage of various types of strategies bear out these generalizations.

Reasons for Adopting Administrative Strategies

In explaining what led them to adopt an administrative strategy toward regulatory reform rather than pursuing the more traditional statutory method, very few of the surveyed officials identified the president as the

Table 3.5
Reasons for Adopting Administrative Strategies to Advance Regulatory Reforms

	Percentage of Respondents Citing Reason
Reagan Administration Factors	
Philosophy of Reagan Appointees; Presidential directives; or OMB pressure	15
Operational Factors	
Speed	21
More control	19
Accomodate complexity of issues	13
Provides flexibility	11
Structure of agency requires statutory action	8
Insufficient congressional support	6
All other factors	7

Source: Compiled by author.

major impetus (see Table 3.5). Only 15 percent directly or indirectly credited factors stemming from the Reagan administration, such as the philosophy of Reagan departmental appointees, presidential directives, and OMB involvement and pressure. Rather, both presidential appointees and careerists tended to cite various operational considerations: the ease and speed in which these reforms can be put into place, the ability to ensure that the agency maintained control of the process and content of the reforms, and the perception that through the administrative process, agency staff would be in a better position to ensure that complex policy problems and issues were addressed by policy specialists and experts.

Given the high degree of usage of administrative reform, it is not surprising that officials see these methods as having numerous strengths. Efficiency and expediency were seen as the main advantages. The ability to by-pass the legislative process through administrative actions provided an opportunity to put in place a series of regulatory reforms quickly and fairly easily. As one official within the Federal Maritime Commission commented,

The greatest strength is that reform not only can be achieved, but can be done in a more comprehensive fashion and at reduced costs—even at that it took nearly four years to achieve! Congress would spend a ton of money on hearings and then slap on a band-aid. I doubt that reform could have been achieved by any other means.

The reputed speed of the administrative approach was cited as a strength by 21 percent of the respondents. Other frequently cited strengths included: the feeling that the administrative process gave the agency more control and needed less political compromise (19%); that regulatory issues in the agency were so complex and technically oriented that it was best to keep regulatory reform in the hands of experts (13%); and that it gave the agency much desired internal flexibility in that "policy would not be cast in stone" (11%).

While respondents cited numerous strengths and were generally supportive of the administrative approach to regulatory reform, their experience with it gave them an excellent vantage point for identifying its major weaknesses. As previously discussed, a number of potential problems theoretically exist with the use of the administrative approach: (1) the possibility of great resistance to the implementation of these reforms from affected interests; (2) the likelihood of bureaucratic resistance to implementing these actions either from disagreement with the goals or methods, or from concerns that such strategies leave the agency vulnerable to external criticism or litigation; and (3) fears that such efforts may be short-lived for a new administration could turn the management strategy to quite different ends; the same technique used to deregulate could be used as well to re-regulate.

Not surprisingly, officials echoed many of these concerns in their responses. They noted that dependence on administrative strategies to advance reform had some negative consequences: a politicalization of the agency and staff which in turn severely hurt morale; a tendency for interest groups to have an enormous impact on shaping reforms from behind the scenes; an increase in the administrative burden on the staff. They also expressed concern that one needed powerful high-level political support to overcome the conflictual internal political pressures that had developed; that policy decisions were being based on a narrow collection of individual interests and ideology rather than on the technical facts or merits of the case. They also noted that action in isolation of other branches of government had frequently provoked a congressional backlash, or resulted in court challenges, leading to policy reversals.

One of the most frequently cited weaknesses was the concern that outcomes from the administrative reform process lacked certain pluralistic aspects that are built into changes effected through the legislative process. Some respondents expressed concern that the administrative reform process was a closed one, devoid of open debate, coalition building, and public participation. Such concerns were shared by several congressmen we interviewed, who saw themselves as having been effectively removed from the regulatory reform process. This feeling is reflected in comments made by Congressman Mike Synar during a 1981 hearing on the role of OMB in regulatory reform efforts:

Real regulatory reform assures all interested parties—business and labor, environmentalists and developers, manufacturers and consumers—that they are getting a fair hearing before the agencies. It is not done behind closed doors at the White House or in a private office at OMB. Real regulatory reform will come only after open hearings and full debate in Congress, where all sides have the opportunity to share their views and follow the legislative process. It is not achieved by unilateral executive order....[I]t is the Congress, as the elected representatives of the people, who have created the executive agencies, it is the Congress who have written the laws these agencies implement, and it must be the Congress who revises and reforms the laws under which these agencies operate. (Synar 1982, p. 7)

It was not just congressional forces that felt left out in the cold. Despite our earlier findings that career personnel and executive appointees played a major role in agency regulatory reform efforts, there were still many individual agency officials who felt they had been effectively removed from the process. One respondent, echoing the feelings of many, charged Reagan political appointees with favoring the "mushroom growers approach to management" which he wryly characterized as: "Keep them [the career bureaucracy] in the dark, feed them a lot of bull-shit, and cut their heads off if they stick them up."

An additional problem frequently mentioned with these administrative strategies to deregulation is how extremely time consuming they were. As an official from the Department of Transportation noted,

It is a long drawn out tedious process fraught with red tape and paperwork. It always amazes me that it is just as difficult to withdraw a regulation as it is to issue one. My experience has been to count on at least 18 months for the simple withdrawal. If controversial, you are looking at several years.

In fact, several respondents identified the failure of Reagan officials to recognize that administrative regulatory reform could take as long as working through the legislative process as a major reason why their agencies had accomplished so much less in the way of regulatory reform than had been expected. As an official in charge of regulatory analysis for the Food and Drug Administration noted,

Failure of people to recognize that the procedures to revise existing regulations are the same as those needed to issue regulations have impeded regulatory reform to the extent that reform is a longer process than might be expected.

Those offering reasons for these delays tended to fall into two camps: respondents who blamed inherent bureaucratic forces for such delays and those who placed the blame on OMB. By far the more common explanation was to blame the nature of bureaucracy itself. In the words of one respondent,

Many agencies, by their nature, are risk-adverse when it comes to regulatory reform. Moreover, there is an entrenched bureaucracy in every agency whose work and status may be jeopardized by regulatory reform. There is often at least one opposing department or division within an agency; and, without a consensus, it is difficult to adopt reforms. Delay by staff members is a common device for forestalling change.

Generally, the procedure for modifying existing rules follows the same course as for promulgating entirely new ones. There are numerous stages to this process and certain time lapses are purposely built in, for example, allowing time for public comment. Organizational inertia, the many reorganizations of agencies, the high turnover of experienced staff, the staff cuts tied to declining agency budgets—all these factors took their toll on regulatory relief efforts as well as on rule making.

Consequently, earlier notions that administrative regulatory reform could be quickly and easily put into place have not been completely borne out by events. As the case studies of individual policy areas will illustrate in a more detailed fashion, administrative reform is just as time-consuming and fraught with political obstacles as seeking reform through legislative measures.

The Use and Effectiveness of Specific Administrative Techniques

Up to this point we have discussed the administrative strategy of the Reagan administration as a whole. But to what extent were the various components of this strategy actually employed in the regulatory agencies? How useful did each specific strategy prove to be? Were different specific strategies of the administrative approach used to a greater degree in certain types of agencies than in others? To answer these questions we asked agency officials to rank the different specific strategies in terms of the frequency of use and their effectiveness. As explained previously,

Table 3.6
Extent of Use of Specific Administrative Strategies to Advance Regulatory Reform

| Specific Strategy | Percentage Characterizing Usage of Strategy As | | | | |
	Heavy	*Moderate*	*Slight*	*Did Not Use*	*Total*
Reexamination of existing rules with an emphasis on providing regulatory relief	53	28	16	3	100 (n = 162)
Mandated slowdown in the issuance of major new regulations	30	25	22	23	100 (n = 160)
Relaxation of efforts to enforce existing rules	14	15	27	44	100 (n = 162)
Significant cuts in agencies' operating budgets	38	24	24	14	100 (n = 160)
Appointment of new personnel	24	26	31	19	100 (n = 155)

Source: Compiled by author.

we identified the components of the administrative strategy as: (1) a reexamination of existing rules; (2) a mandated slowdown in the issuance of major new regulations; (3) a relaxation of efforts to enforce existing rules; (4) significant cuts in agencies' operating budgets; and (5) the appointment of new personnel.

Table 3.6 shows the extent to which respondents reported using these components. By far, the most heavily used administrative strategy has been the reexamination of existing rules with an emphasis on providing regulatory relief as mandated by Executive Order 12291. Eighty-one percent of the sample stated that their agency had engaged in either a heavy or moderate reexamination. Responses indicate that the other specific strategies are being used to a lesser degree. Of these, mention of agency budgets cuts and a mandated slowdown in the issuance of major new regulations dominated the responses.

As indicated by Table 3.7, there was little variation across the regulatory agencies in the degree of utilization of these specific strategies. As we have seen, economic and independent regulatory agencies engaged in administrative regulatory reform strategies to the highest degree. One specific strategy used to a relatively high degree within social

Table 3.7
Frequency of Use of Specific Strategies by Different Types of Regulatory Agencies

| Specific Strategy | Percentage of Respondents Rating Use as Heavy to Moderate | | | | |
| | By Agency Affiliation | | By Type of Mission | | All |
	Independent	Executive	Economic	Social	Agencies
Reexamination of existing rules with an emphasis on providing regulatory relief	90	76	95	76	80
Mandated slowdown in the issuance of major new regulations	65	50	60	53	55
Relaxation of efforts to enforce existing rules	38	24	40	25	28
Significant cuts in agencies' operating budgets	58	64	60	63	62
Appointment of new personnel	46	51	50	50	50

Source: Compiled by author.

regulatory agencies was a reexamination of existing rules together with cuts in the agencies' operating budgets. This finding probably reflects the deep domestic federal budget cuts in 1981 and the increased budgetary role that OMB plays in the social regulatory agencies. In addition, the appointment of new personnel and the relaxation of efforts to enforce existing rules were more frequently cited by interviewees in the executive branch agencies than among the independents.

To what extent have these specific administrative strategies been effective in achieving regulatory reform? This is an extraordinarily difficult question to address empirically. In our survey, we tried to measure the effectiveness of each of these strategies through the perceptions of agency personnel. But the aggregate rankings of high or moderate effectiveness reported in Table 3.8 only gives one side of the story. Through answers to other, more open-ended questions, surveyed officials often stated that such measures as agency budget cuts, the appointment of new personnel, and mandated slowdowns in the issuance of new regulations had proved to be actually counterproductive in achiev-

Table 3.8
Effectiveness of Administrative Strategies to Advance Regulatory Reform

Specific Strategy	Percentage of Respondents Rating Effectiveness as Heavy to Moderate				
	By Organizational Affiliation		By Type of Mission		All Agencies
	Independent	Executive	Economic	Social	
Reexamination of existing rules with an emphasis on providing regulatory relief	76	70	84	67	71
Mandated slowdown in the issuance of major new regulations	49	43	45	45	45
Relaxation of efforts to enforce existing rules	40	20	40	21	26
Significant cuts in agencies' operating budgets	36	40	43	37	39
Appointment of new personnel	57	50	60	50	53

Source: Compiled by author.

ing regulatory reform. These discrepancies apparently reflect the real differences of opinion that surround the controversial measures adopted by the Reagan administration—both within the agencies and in the larger society.

A large majority of the surveyed agency officials (71%) viewed reexamination of existing rules with an emphasis on providing regulatory relief—as mandated through Executive Order 12291—as having been of high or moderate effectiveness. Fairly high marks for effectiveness were given to the appointment of new personnel (53% assigned such actions as having at least moderate effectiveness). Less than half of respondents, 45 percent, thought mandated slowdowns in the issuance of major new regulations had been of even moderate effectiveness. Many fewer respondents, 39 percent, considered agency budget cuts as even moderately effective, while only 26 percent gave even a moderately effective ranking to relaxation of efforts to enforce existing rules.

Little variation in effectiveness rankings was observed among respondents from different types of agencies. Respondents from independent and economic regulatory agencies, which, as we have seen, engaged more heavily in these types of strategies, also tended to give them higher marks for effectiveness. This pattern was especially striking for the strategy of relaxing efforts to enforce existing rules.

As stated earlier, however, some agency officials apparently held strong negative judgments concerning the actual effectiveness of many of these strategies. Contradicting the high marks generally given to the reviews mandated by Executive Order 12291, one Department of Commerce official stated:

What has happened is that even though a few changes have been made, they have made the regulations more complex and have actually negated any positive change. This has led to more confusion and frustration for high tech companies and could actually hinder exports.... Although examination of the export regulations has been significant, and changes were made, the new rules and regulations have not been effective in increasing exports or in making the regulations less burdensome.

Similarly, and as might be expected, some officials were critical of the budget cuts that hit their agencies. Some administrators felt that, by reducing the number of trained and qualified personnel at their disposal, the budget cuts have impaired the adoption of some portions of the administration's reform strategy. As one Housing and Urban Development agency official we surveyed stated,

The reexamination of existing rules and its implementation requires adequate, and sufficient personnel and money. Due to the major budget reductions in our administrative budget, regulatory reform is ineffective. Although it would be quite advantageous for our Office to identify any fraud, waste or abuse, it is highly unlikely that we would have adequate personnel to ensure such a task.

The appointment of new personnel was ranked as effective by only half of the respondents. Given the reported conservative nature of many of these appointments and their commitment to less governmental regulation, one would have expected them to have a greater impact in bringing about regulatory reform in their respective agencies. Several factors were offered as explanations for this phenomenon. The most prevalent view was that these appointees brought little in the way of technical or substantive policy expertise with them to their new position. Because many dealt with issues that were highly complex, they have had to undergo a rather lengthy learning process, and thus have not been able to play much of a reform role.

A second view held that these appointees had simply been absorbed into the vastness of the bureaucracy, and while they have vigorously promoted reform efforts, they are still only one small cog in the workings of a large machine. As the following statement by a U. S. D. A. administrator indicates, "The new personnel are used to analyze the need for regulatory reform, but they do not make the decisions about whether it should occur. They are necessary before an agency can consider reforms, but they are not sufficient to bring about reform." Finally, there were those who felt that many of Reagan's political appointees simply lacked the political will to really struggle hard for the administration's position. As one respondent from the Nuclear Regulatory Commission lamented,

Our political appointees could have done much more but there has been a lack of real leadership from OMB to push appointees who may not have a strong interest to take the 'heat' to deregulate. Political appointees must go to the Hill and defend the Administration—not OMB. If our political appointees are not forced to deregulate, they have little incentive to do so.

SUMMARY AND CONCLUSIONS

Early research on bureaucratic attitudes and reactions to Reagan regulatory policy and administration were based largely on anecdotal evidence (Tolchin and Tolchin 1985; Eads and Fix 1984). The reason, no doubt, is that early findings were just that—too early for systematic analysis to be possible. Because our research was based on a survey of a representative sample of agencies that had major regulatory responsibilities, we found a more complex pattern of bureaucratic attitudes and behavior, and we were able to uncover how public managers assess the effects of the management strategy. For the most part, what we found suggests that President Reagan has been surprisingly successful turning around agency behavior in independent commissions as well as executive branch agencies. This is true even though some goals have been more widely shared than others; some types of personnel have been more reticent to accept the administration's policies than others; some elements of the management strategy were more common in some agencies than others; and some kinds of personnel were more involved in implementing the strategy in some agencies than others.

Overall, we found that while agency officials were pursuing a broad array of regulatory reform goals, economic and administrative, politically oriented goals received the greatest emphasis. The diversity found in regulatory reform goals was also seen in the mix of actors who participated in placing these goals on agencies' agendas. While OMB emerged as the most influential actor in setting executive agency regulatory policies, this did not hold true for independent agencies, whose agenda's were largely internally determined by agency staff.

Additionally, we found that to a great extent the management strategy was being aggressively pursued across all types of regulatory agencies, be they executive or independent, or economically or socially oriented. While there was some slight variation in the degree to which elements of the management strategy to regulatory reform were deemed successful by the agencies, taken together they clearly portray a picture that shows the management strategy being quite effective in bringing about the desired regulatory change.

It is also clear from our analysis, that simple generalizations about the scope of the Reagan reform effort and its effectiveness do not do justice to what has been accomplished or to what has been left undone. A major contribution of our research has been to confirm what a number of earlier researchers speculated about. After six years in operation the Reagan regulatory reform program has clearly been *institutionalized*. The goals have filtered down through the bureaucracy and, to a remarkable extent, they have been accepted across regulatory agencies. This finding in itself will surprise the many scholars who regard the federal bureaucracy as responsive to its clients and subcommittees, but impenetrable by the president. Even these skeptics will no doubt agree that getting the regulatory agencies to accept the administration's goals after decades of regulatory activism has been a giant first step toward achieving these goals. While feelings run high concerning the merits of the president's plan, and legitimate questions exist about its long-term impacts and its institutional consequences, we cannot discount the significant changes that have occurred. The past six years may not have led scholars to rewrite the book on the limits of presidential power, but Reagan has shown that presidents can make a difference in the regulatory policy area.

4 REGULATORY REFORM IN INTERGOVERNMENTAL RELATIONS

In our federal system of government, where federal, state, county, city, and town governments exist to some extent independent of each other, the relationship of the federal government to various subnational governments is complex and problematic. By the late 1970s, intergovernmental regulation—the rules laid down by the federal government for state and local governments to follow or to implement—had become a major area of intergovernmental relations.

In this chapter we first trace the growth of intergovernmental regulation since the 1960s and describe the different forms it takes. We draw a distinction between conditions attached to grants-in-aid and recent intergovernmental regulatory programs for achieving national goals such as clean air and water, safe work places, toxic waste management, and civil rights. We then discuss the rising tide of discontent in the 1970s over the growth and intrusiveness of federal regulation of states and localities. With this review as a background, we then examine and evaluate Reagan administration efforts to reform intergovernmental regulation.

This chapter focuses on the question of how successfully the Reagan management strategy reformed intergovernmental regulation. We will first evaluate the Reagan strategy by the criteria set forth by the administration itself, that is the extent to which administration efforts have actually lessened federal involvement in state and local affairs. We will then consider the intergovernmental legacy of the Reagan administration in terms of our definition of regulatory reform, asking the question: To what extent has the devolution that occurred produced a more rational intergovernmental regulatory system rather than a merely more decentralized one?

In areas where intergovernmental regulation enlists states and localities to implement programs that regulate the private sector, it is reasonable to question the extent to which easing state and local regulatory burdens may have affected the regulated entities. We consider this question in detail in Chapter 5, using the case study of environmental protection where regulatory programs are administered in partnership with state and local governments. The principal focus of this chapter, however, is the success of the effort in the state and local context, not the extent to which that translates into regulatory relief for the private sector.

THE GROWTH OF INTERGOVERNMENTAL REGULATION

Grants in Aid with Strings Attached: The Ties That Bind

Historically, when the federal government endeavored to achieve national objectives ranging from health and welfare to highways and mass transit in cooperation with state and local governments, it has relied on the grant-in-aid. From the first annual cash grant to states under the Hatch Act of 1887, federal aid outlays rose to more than $90 billion in 1980, while the number of grant-in-aid programs climbed to over 500. By the mid–1970s, a remarkable range of activities shared between federal, state, and local governments existed. Virtually every federal agency developed some type of involvement in the daily operations of nearly 50,000 state and local governments. At its peak in 1978, federal aid flowed for activities ranging from lead paint removal in public housing to wastewater treatment. The extent of involvement prompted one expert to comment that the layer cake model of federalism, long since replaced by the marble cake, was now "hypermarbleized": it had become simply impossible to sort out the responsibilities among the partners in the system (Walker 1981). From the point of view of the participating state and local governments, all the federal grant-in-aid programs came with strings attached. That is, with the carrot of federal cash came the stick of federal regulation. Overall, it can be said that the rapid expansion of grants and grant requirements in the 1960s led to a system burdened with paperwork and red tape. In response to the rising tide of complaints about burdensome grant requirements from state and local officials, every president since Johnson tried to streamline the system, reaching a high point with Nixon's New Federalism (ACIR 1977).

Such presidential efforts notwithstanding, many complained that the proliferation of new programs and requirements had outstripped efforts to reform the existing system. Thus, by the last years of the 1970s, grant conditions were increasingly perceived as a substantial regulatory burden on state and local governments. In the minds of a growing number, the federal aid system was beyond coordinating; it needed decongesting.

Strengthened Ties: The New Intergovernmental Regulation

The rapid growth of new forms of intergovernmental regulation in the 1970s further fueled state and local government dissatisfaction with the federal system. By 1980, congressional reliance on state and local governments to implement social regulatory policies had produced some 35 major intergovernmental regulatory statutes covering a wide range of issues including highway beautification, environmental protection, equal employment, and occupational safety (see Table 4.1).

As each program was added, the partnership followed a familiar pattern reflecting federal policy leadership and grants to induce state and local participation. With the passage of time, however, congressional impatience over state and local governments' failure to meet regulatory performance standards and timetables led to stiffer penalties that were harder to avoid. Whereas conditions attached to grant programs were something like a mutually agreed upon contract between different levels of government, much of the new intergovernmental regulation could not be avoided even by refusing to accept federal funds. Thus, much like the private sector, state and local governments found themselves conscripted into the battle to achieve national environmental, health and safety, civil rights, and educational goals.

The case of bilingual education is a good example. The path to a nationally mandated bilingual education program began with a modestly framed HEW memorandum to implement Title VI of the Civil Rights Act of 1964. While the department's regulations advised state and local governments to take affirmative actions to meet the special needs of children with limited English-speaking ability, few specific actions were stipulated. Also in keeping with the norms of a cooperative federalism, in 1968 Congress passed the Bilingual Education Act which provided grants to state and local governments to develop innovative bilingual education programs.

Federal involvement in bilingual education practices took a more purely regulatory turn in 1974, in response to a supreme court decision, Lau v. Nichols. Although the plaintiffs primarily sought only to assure that their Chinese-speaking children would have adequate instruction in English, and although the court had specified no particular remedy, Congress took the decision as a green light to greatly enhance the federal role. In 1974, it amended the Bilingual Education Act, mandating bilingual instruction as the only acceptable means of meeting the goals of

Table 4.1
Major Federal Statutes Regulating State and Local Governments

Title	Objective	Public Law	Type[1]
Davis-Bacon Act (1931)[2]	Assure that locally prevailing wages are paid to construction workers employed under federal contracts and financial assistance programs.	74–403	CC
Hatch Act (1940)	Prohibit public employees from engaging in certain political activities.	76–753	CC
Civil Rights Act of 1964 (Title VI)	Prevent discrimination on the basis of race, color or national origin in federally assisted programs.	88–352	CC
Water Quality Act (1965)	Establish federal water quality standards for interstate waters.	88–668	PP
Highway Beautification Act of 1965	Control and remove outdoor advertising signs along major highways.	89–285	CO
National Historic Preservation Act of 1966	Protect properties of historical, architectural, archeological and cultural significance.	89–665	CC
Wholesome Meat Act (1967)	Establish systems for the inspection of meat sold in intrastate commerce.	90–201	PP
Architectural Barriers Act of 1968	Make federally occupied and funded buildings, facilities, and public conveyances accessible to the physically handicapped.	90–480	CC
Civil Rights Act of 1968 (Title VIII)	Prevent discrimination on the basis of race, color, religion, sex or national origin in the sale or rental of federally assisted housing.	90–284	CC

Table 4.1 (continued)

Title	Objective	Public Law	Type[1]
Wholesome Poultry Products Act of 1968	Establish systems for the inspection of poultry sold in intrastate commerce.	90–492	PP
National Environmental Policy Act of 1969	Assure consideration of the environmental impact of major federal actions.	91–190	CC
Clean Air Act Amendment Act of 1970	Establish national air quality and emissions standards.	91–604	CC, CO, PP
Occupational Safety and Health Act (1970)	Eliminate unsafe and unhealthful working conditions.	91–596	PP
Uniform Relocation Assistance and Real Properties Acquisition Policies Act of 1970	Set federal policies and reimbursement procedures for property acquisition under federally assisted programs.	91–646	CC
Coastal Zone Management Act of 1972	Assure that federally assisted activities are consistent with federally approved state coastal zone management programs.	94–370	CC
Education Amendment of 1972 (Title IX)	Prevent discrimination on the basis of sex in federally assisted education programs.	92–318	CC
Equal Employment Opportunity Act of 1972	Prevent discrimination on the basis of race, color, religion, sex, or national origin in state and local government employment.	92–261	DO
Federal Water Pollution Control Act of 1972	Establish federal effluent limitations to control the discharge of pollutants.	92–500	CC, PP
Endangered Species Act of 1973	Protect and conserve endangered and threatened animal species.	93–205	CC, PP
Flood Disaster Protection Act of 1973	Expand coverage of the national flood insurance program.	93–234	CC, CO

Table 4.1 (continued)

Title	Objective	Public Law	Type[1]
Rehabilitation Act of 1973(Section 504)	Prevent discrimination against otherwise qualified individuals on the basis of physical or mental handicap in federally assisted programs.	93–112	CC
Age Discrimination in Employment Act (1974)[3]	Prevent discrimination on the basis of age in state and local government employment.	93–259; 90–202	DO
Emergency Highway Energy Conservation Act (1974)[4]	Established a national maximum speed limit of 55 mph.	93–239	CO
Fair Labor Standards	Extend federal minimum wage and overtime pay protection to state and local government employees.	93–259	DO
Family Educational Rights and Privacy Act of 1974	Provide student and parental access to educational records while restricting access by others.	93–380	CC
National Health Planning and Resources Development Act of 1974	Establish state and local health planning agencies and procedures.	93–64	CO
Safe Drinking Water Act of 1974	Assure drinking water purity.	93–523	CC, PP, DO
Age Discrimination Act of 1975	Prevent discrimination on the basis of age in federally assisted programs.	94–135	CC
Education for All Handicapped Children Act (1975)	Provide a free appropriate public education to all handicapped children.	94–142	CO[5]
Federal Insecticide Fungicide, and Rodenticide Act (1975)	Control the use of pesticides that may be harmful to the environment	92–516	PP
Resource Conservation and Recovery Act of 1976	Establish standards for the control of hazardous wastes.	94–580	PP

Table 4.1 (continued)

Title	Objective	Public Law	Type[1]
Marine Protection Research and Sanctuaries Act Amendments of 1977	Prohibit ocean dumping of municipal sludge.	95–153	DO
Surface Mining Control and Reclamation Act of 1977	Establish federal standards for the control of surface mining.	95–87	PP
National Energy Conservation Policy Act (1978)	Establish residential energy conservation plans.	95–619	PP
Natural Gas Policy Act of 1978	Implement federal pricing policies for the interstate sales of natural gas in producing states.	95–621	PP
Public Utilities Regulatory Policies Act of 1978	Require consideration of federal standards for the pricing of electricity and natural gas.	95–617	DO

Notes: 1.   Key: crosscutting requirement (CC), crossover sanction (CO), direct order (DO), partial preemption (PP).

2.   Although the *Davis-Bacon Act* applied initially only to direct federal construction, it has since been extended to some 77 federal assistance programs.

3.   Coverage of the act, originally adopted in 1967, was extended to state and local government employees in 1974.

4.   A permanent national 55 mph speed limit was established by the *Federal-Aid Highway Amendment of 1974*, (PL 93–643), signed into law January 4, 1975.

5.   Although participation is voluntary, the failure of a participating state to comply with federal requirements can result in the withholding of funds from several federal handicapped education programs. The requirements for PL 94–142 are nearly identical to those established by the Department of Education under Section 504 of the *Rehabilitation Act*, a crosscutting requirement.

Source: United States Advisory Commission on Intergovernmental Relations, 1984. *Regulatory Federalism*. A-95. Washington D.C.: Government Printing Office, pp. 19–21.

the 1968 Act. HEW, in turn, published a report detailing how the bilingual mandate was to be achieved (ACIR 1984, p. 120). According to Stewart Baker, a former deputy general counsel in the Department of Education, the guidelines were:

a breathtaking example of federal intrusion into local affairs. They demand that school districts hire bilingual experts to follow students around, jotting down the language they speak at lunch, in the classroom, in hallways and at home. They also insist that bilingual and bicultural instruction be provided whenever 20 eligible students with a common language can be found anywhere in a school district; that means a city like Chicago has to provide instruction not merely in Spanish, the nation's most widely used language after English, but in 17 tongues ranging from Assyrian and Gujarti to Indic and Serbo-Croatian. (Baker 1981, p. C–2)

The burgeoning of federal involvement in bilingual education mirrors a general pattern that developed over the 1960s and 1970s, a period of great social regulatory growth. For most of the nation's history, social regulation—especially with respect to public health, safety, and the environment—had been state regulation. Thus, it is not surprising that when those who perceived problems with the way such issues were being handled at the local level developed sufficient political clout to approach federal policymakers, the federal government was hesitant to preempt the states, trying grant-related incentives first. But, once these policy domains were breached, the impatience of national policymakers to achieve the desired results eventually led to stronger measures. This more stringent federal approach came to be the dominant one, leading intergovernmental relations into a new period, one often described as regulatory federalism (Beam 1981; Wrightson 1986).

A RISING TIDE OF COMPLAINTS

Complaints about federal intrusion into state and local affairs are not new. Debates as to the optimum balance of powers between the nation, the states, and local governments have never been entirely settled, although the twentieth century has seen a strong trend for power to consolidate at the federal level. Over the years many have argued for strong states and against particular federal encroachments on state's authority and local prerogatives. On the other hand, particular groups of people—for example, minorities experiencing discrimination or parents of handicapped children seeking special education programs—have sought relief from the federal government when frustrated by a lack of response at the state or local level. Similarly, advocates of particular issues ranging from the anti-trust movement to the anti-pollution movement have often pressed their case at the federal level.

One of the nation's most eloquent supporters of vigorous subnational government was Thomas Jefferson, yet Jefferson, himself, strengthened the federal government at the expense of the states. Overall—over the nation's history—political rhetoric advocating federal restraint has proved no match for practical politics, so that almost from the beginning federal and state affairs were intertwined. And, while state and local officials sometimes grumbled over the patronizing attitude of Washington regulatory agencies, for the most part the accent has been on co-operation even until the 1970s.

The tradition of a more or less cooperative federalism that persisted until the mid–1970s, in turn, helps to explain the strong, negative re-action to regulatory federalism. The elements of compulsion and pre-scription that marked federal regulation of state and local governments by the mid–1970s were a marked departure from earlier relations. Thus, the new intergovernmental regulation soon became the object of sub-stantial criticism among state and local officials, those that worked in state and local bureaucracies, and growing numbers of scholars.

While not all scholars agree that the current pattern of intergovern-mental relations is more regulatory than cooperative, most find the pre-scription and compulsion typical in the new regulatory programs objectionable. Criticism centers on the extent to which intergovernmen-tal regulation departs from traditional federalism norms. Critics do not dispute that the pattern of federal-state-local domestic responsibilities continues to be one of shared roles, but they do recognize a strong difference between a system in which domestic policy is a mix of national and state considerations and one in which policy is nationally determined and state administered. In the extreme, some have pictured powerful nationalizing forces as the seeds of destruction of our federal system that will eventually reduce states to mere administrative arms of Wash-ington (Glendenning and Reeves 1984). After an exhaustive review of these developments, the Advisory Commission on Intergovernmental Relations (ACIR 1984, p. 258) concluded that, "This new pattern of intergovernmental regulation represents a primary source of inter-level conflict and tension which, if unchecked, may erode the American con-cept of cooperative federalism."

The complaints of state and local officials tend to be more immediate and pragmatic. A frequent criticism is that federal requirements are not well-crafted and often have unexpected, negative side effects. For ex-ample, in testifying before Congress, many local officials charged that because those in Washington who write the regulations and set the stand-ards do not have to implement them, they pay too little attention to local differences (Senate, Subcommittee on Intergovernmental Relations 1986). Other criticism centers on a basic flaw in the financing arrange-ments. Because state and local governments underwrite a substantial portion of the costs of implementation, there is little to constrain Con-gress and the federal bureaucracy from overregulating so that costs outweigh benefits. If all funding were federal, the argument runs, Con-gress might not be so quick to enact statutes which say in effect: no price is too high, no standard too strict, and no time frame too short.

Thus, by the late 1970s and early 1980s, sentiment that intergovernmental regulation needed a thoroughgoing overhaul was strong and far reaching. And, since these regulations affected a much broader constituency as well as state and local governments, the circle of critics widened, including many of the economists, lawyers, historians, and business leaders, as explained in Chapter 2.

While rapid regulatory growth in the 1960s and 1970s left advocates for a stronger state and local role in temporary disarray, by the late 1970s these same voices constituted a relatively unified chorus of complaint. In part because federal aid growth peaked in 1978, and in part because incipient economic decline was reducing revenues available to state and local governments, obtaining a reduction in federal regulatory burdens gained in priority for them. Nearly all of the policy platforms of the major public interest groups, including the National Governors' Association (NGA), the National League of Cities (NLC) and the National Association of County Officials (NACO), contained specific calls for reform, and the generally moderate Advisory Commission on Intergovernmental Relations adopted a policy of full federal mandate reimbursement in 1982.

Dissatisfaction with regulatory federalism notwithstanding, one important caveat to the criticism must be mentioned. While it could be said that state and local governments hoped for modifications in the intergovernmental regulatory programs as well as more federal financial support, it cannot be said that they necessarily wished to undo ten years of social regulatory buildup. In the words of one top NLC lobbyist we interviewed, "Nobody wants clean air and water any more than we do, the question is who can better afford to pay for it?" As succeeding sections of this chapter will show, the perceptual differences between the intergovernmental community and the Reagan administration about what regulatory reform was supposed to accomplish proved to be a major stumbling block as the federalism reform strategy unfolded.

Voices in the Wilderness

Before Reagan took office, state and local complaints drew little national attention. There were few champions of intergovernmental regulatory reform in the White House, and fewer still on Capitol Hill. Despite his strong interest in improving management at the federal level, Carter did not take particular note of the problems of intergovernmental regulation until late in his term. Moreover, with the exception of an OMB initiative to streamline crosscutting regulations that fell victim to Carter's failed reelection bid, the efforts of the Carter administration lacked leadership and focus. As one agency staff member who had worked in both administrations summed it up, "Carter recognized certain intergovernmental areas of concern, but he lacked the initiative, philosophy, and ability to implement any changes."

For its part, Congress, which has been credited with most of the growth in intergovernmental regulation, has never been of a mind to undo its own handiwork. Over the past decade, intergovernmental regulatory reform legislation has died as often from apathy as opposition. Some legislative initiatives—such as the Uniform Relocation Amendments (which would streamline the crosscutting regulations governing the rights of those dislocated by federally aided construction projects)—were too narrowly defined to gain sufficient interest and political support for passage. Thus it failed to pass the Ninety-eighth and Ninety-ninth Congresses, despite the fact that the Congressional Budget Office (CBO) estimated no added federal costs. More controversial reform initiatives— such as those which would reimburse state and local governments for the additional direct costs of federal mandates—have been routinely introduced beginning in 1983 and just as routinely die in subcommittee.

Congressional attitudes are not hard to explain. First, the forces pushing for federal regulation are strong and well represented both inside Congress and out. Further, it is so politically difficult to oppose pro-regulation constituencies that one congressional staff member described them as "akin to apple pie and motherhood." Edward Koch, who as mayor of New York characterized intergovernmental regulation as "the mandate millstone," pondered the dilemma he faced earlier while serving in the House as follows:

I do not for a moment claim immunity for the mandate fever of the 1970s. As a member of Congress, I voted for many [of them]. . . . The bills I voted for in Washington came to the House floor in a form that compelled approval. After all, who can vote against clean air and water, or better access and education for the handicapped? (Koch 1980, p. 44)

A third factor may be that, as fewer opportunities to enact new spending programs appear, regulation seems an increasingly appealing route for congressional action. As a senator who has authored much of the recent intergovernmental reform legislation put it, "The plain fact is that as rising federal deficits make it harder for us to accomplish our objectives through spending programs regulatory programs present one of the few remaining horses we can ride."

THE REAGAN THEORY OF NEW FEDERALISM

Into this arena of regulatory activism and state, local, and popular dissatisfaction stepped Ronald Reagan, the fortieth president of the

United States. Unlike most recent presidents, Reagan did not come to Washington with a plan for new intergovernmental programs, regulatory or otherwise. His intention was quite the opposite. In his first inaugural address (1981), the new president declared, "It is my intention to curb the size and influence of the federal establishment and to demand recognition of the distinction between the powers granted to the federal government and those reserved to the states or the people." Other presidents may have sought to reform the intergovernmental system at the margins; Reagan intended to fundamentally restructure it.

As translated into actions over six years, the Reagan approach has meant a concerted effort to send back domestic program responsibilities to state and local governments. Just as the president questioned the value of federal involvement in private sector activities, so, too, he disputed the need for strong federal say-so in most domestic policy issues.

The devolutionary vision was appealing in the eyes of the public, and it was fervently shared by most Reagan appointees we interviewed. When questioned about the president's view of federalism, their answers were remarkably similar: The president wants to return domestic responsibility to states and localities where it belongs; he wants to get Washington's regulatory bureaucracy off the backs of state and local officials and let their own policy processes take over. Those we interviewed expressed the opinion that this devolution would produce a renaissance of state and local government and return the federal government to doing what it does best—protecting America from her enemies abroad and supporting vigorous economic growth at home.

Indeed, a strong connection between overregulation and a dysfunctional federalism was emphasized by top administration officials from the very beginning. As the first Reagan appointee to head the Council of Economic Advisors and top White House spokesman for economic matters, Murray Weidenbaum wrote:

The Reagan Administration is dedicated to strengthening our federal system of government.... [I]n the past decade, we have seen a boom in federal social regulation with devastating consequences for the federal system. By what lawyers and political scientists call "supersession," the federal government through its many regulatory actions, has reduced the autonomy of state governments.... This loss of autonomy has weakened the states and reduced their independence, while centralization of responsibilities better handled at state and local levels has limited the effectiveness of the federal government. (1981, p. 71)

REAGAN FEDERALISM IN PRACTICE

The Reagan theory of federalism translated into the following practical policy guidelines:

1. a fundamental reduction in the role of the central government in the federal system, in size, function, authority, and influence in domestic matters;

2. a greater reliance on state or local governments and on the private sector to carry out responsibilities that had recently come into the federal sphere; and

3. a reduction in federal aid and federal regulation, along with reduced preemption of state and local regulatory responsibilities. The administration also developed a stronger role for OMB in implementing a uniform executive branch approach to intergovernmental regulation.

Initially, the administration's intergovernmental policy was to be achieved through a combination of legislative and administrative actions. On the legislative side, proposed strategies included several statutory reforms to simplify the system overall and to achieve a new sorting out of federal from state and local programmatic responsibilities. On the administrative side, it followed the administration's general strategy for centralizing regulatory policy-making in the executive branch: the placement of political appointees sympathetic to the president's views of limited federal government; budget cuts in grant and regulatory programs in order to shrink the federal role; the relaxation of rules affecting state and local governments as well as a mandated slowdown in new intergovernmental regulation; and reductions in federal regulatory enforcement by accelerating state takeover of program responsibilities wherever possible under statute.

Early administration rhetoric suggested that all elements of the plan would be coordinated: that budget cuts would be linked to cuts in regulation. For example, Weidenbaum (1981, p. 71), reported that the administration was committed to block "budgetary actions which decreased grants to state and local governments unless there were corresponding decreases in the regulatory manacles which bind the hands of local officials and raise their costs." Moreover, he asserted:

[W]e expect that any demand by the federal government on its partners in the federal system be backed up with the revenue to meet that demand. This will require any proposed legislation that might force costs on the states to be supported by analysis of just how much it would cost them if approved. Similarly, we have task forces studying the desirability of shifting expenditure responsibilities and tax powers to the states, where that would be a more appropriate division of labor. (1981, p. 76)

Many observers have suggested that the Reagan administration has enjoyed remarkable success in accomplishing the realignment that it intended to achieve. It is apparent that denationalization of domestic policy leadership is occurring. As Doyle and Hartle (1986, p. 21) observed, "Over the past five years, a fundamental shift in government powers has occurred. New Federalism—in all but name—has arrived. Domestic policy initiatives are no longer originating in Washington; today they are the responsibility of the states."

But the Reagan successes in this area may not be as dramatic as they appear, and the effects may not be long lasting. By exclusively focusing on declining federal aid and state renaissance, researchers miss an important part of the federalism story. To a great extent, preoccupation with the budget deficit has tied the hands of national policymakers. As a consequence of the resulting fiscal adversity—but also because of a much earlier independent trend of maturing state government—some states have taken the initiative across a range of policy areas. However, more state and local responsibility does not necessarily add up to less federal involvement. Real devolution of domestic policy leadership of the kind envisioned by the administration needs more than budget cuts. It can only be achieved by linking spending cuts to the other elements of the administrative strategy such as relaxing rules, reducing regulatory requirements, cutting back on federal regulatory enforcement, and slowing down the issuance of new rules. Without major shifts of this sort, intergovernmental regulation might become more decentralized, but it would not necessarily become less federally dominated.

But such changes have not occurred—at least not on the scale hoped for by the Reagan administration. As explained later in this chapter, on the statutory side reform efforts soon lost steam in Congress. On the management side, cutting funding was emphasized to a greater degree than deregulatory efforts. As we shall see, while the management strategy was well suited to the task of intergovernmental regulatory relief in some cases, in others it was not. The strategy was especially poorly suited to the situation where state and local governments opposed the administration's relief proposals. Finally, running parallel to the efforts to deregulate were administration efforts to re-regulate, for, as explained later in this chapter, the administration itself has been responsible for a surprising amount of new intergovernmental regulation undertaken in order to advance its conservative social agenda.

As a result, when it comes to regulation of state and local governments, heavy reliance on administrative techniques has not proved itself a fast track to a less intrusive federal government. In retrospect, it has added up to less federal aid, especially in some programs, but only a little less federal interference. Further, the administration's single spectacular success—the deregulation of a range of community development, health and welfare programs—resulted from the passage of the Omnibus Budget Reconciliation Act of 1981 (OBRA), which was the product of a more traditional legislative strategy rather than a product of the administrative strategy that is the focus of this analysis.

Overall, we can say that Ronald Reagan was not the first president to express concern over intergovernmental regulation, but he was the first to give prominent attention to it by including national rules affecting state and local governments in his proposals for regulatory reform. From the White House's view, federal regulations should not preempt state laws or regulations, except to "guarantee rights of national citizenship" or to "avoid significant burdens on interstate commerce." The official position of the Task Force on Regulatory Relief was that local regulations are more responsive to local circumstances, promote greater diversity and experimentation in program implementation, and afford citizens a greater choice among divergent public policies (Presidential Task Force 1983). However, to some extent the administration's objective of maximizing local control was bound to conflict with other administration objectives such as: the desire to reduce domestic spending; the hope of reducing the amount of regulation in certain policy areas where states and localities might want to maintain regulatory levels; and the inclination to maintain or even increase federal regulatory control in specific areas of interest to business and industry or to New Right political supporters of the Reagan administration. Further, attempts to thoughtfully redesign specific regulatory programs tended to get lost in the overriding push for centralized control and reduction of regulatory proposals.

Deemphasizing Traditional Intergovernmental Administration

Because of the administration's determination to reduce the federal role in the federal system, it counted heavily on outright grant and regulatory program elimination. David Stockman became the point man for this campaign and OMB became the nerve center of the intergovernmental devolutionary strategy (Senate, Committee on Governmental Affairs 1986, p. 352). Armed with what he believed was a mandate to undo the welfare state and an armload of notebooks outlining how to get the job done, Stockman made it clear from the beginning that OMB's new responsibilities left little time for "narrow questions of grant-in-aid reform" (Senate Committee on Governmental Affairs 1986, p. 354).

One of Stockman's first actions was to cut the staff of the Intergovernmental Affairs Division at OMB. In 1981, this office had 21 full-time staff members. By 1983, it had six. By 1984, it no longer existed. According to OMB official statements, its responsibilities were transferred to other management divisions. According to congressional staff we interviewed, its responsibilities "went out the window." Lower level OMB staff we interviewed tended to concur with these congressional staff. According to one OMB staffer who survived the transition as well as several others who did not, it has been difficult or impossible to undertake traditional intergovernmental management reform since 1981. Said one such staffer of high level OMB managers: "For the most part, they're not interested in regulatory reform. For example, the review of rules that's going on over at OIRA is just a lot of paper going back and forth. They don't know what intergovernmental regulation is."

Not only was there little enthusiasm for beginning new intergovernmental management initiatives at the White House, there was also considerable intolerance of existing ones. The administration moved quickly to stop work on a proposed OMB circular the Carter administration had been working on which was intended to simplify administration of grant crosscutting requirements. OMB Circular A–85, which provided for intergovernmental advance notice and comment on agencies' proposed regulations, was rescinded. OMB abolished the Federal Regional Councils (FRC), and it sent back to the states the A–95 program of regional review and comment on intergovernmental grant and regulatory programs. According to Joseph Wright, deputy director of OMB, the A–95 devolution was "fundamental to the President's federalism concept" (Rothenberg 1984, p. 5). According to academic experts, this action sent a clear message that OMB was no longer interested in carrying out its former management activities under the Intergovernmental Cooperation Act of 1968 (McDowell 1982; Rothenberg and Gordon 1984).

The intergovernmental affairs offices in many executive branch agencies were also severely cut. A number had no director, and most had suffered disproportionate, large staffing cuts. As one staffer put it, "They give you the good news and the bad news. The good news is that you are being promoted. The bad news is that you now have to do the work of the five people they just fired." Few such staff professed any substantive knowledge of particular regulatory reform efforts and fewer still said that they monitored their agencies for opportunities to promote the intergovernmental aspects of the president's agenda. The overall impression conveyed was that while agency intergovernmental affairs staff strongly supported the president on federalism, for the most part they played the role of cheerleaders. As one state lobbyist put it, "The intergovernmental staffs in the agencies and at the White House are really just a hand-holding operation, there to promote good public relations."

This weakening of the intergovernmental perspective at the agency level strengthened the hand of OMB personnel as they negotiated with agency program staff over the content and direction of agency intergovernmental regulatory programs. As described more fully later in this chapter, with few exceptions, the centralization of power at OMB resulted in a heavy emphasis on fewer regulations and a bare bones approach to intergovernmental rules promulgated.

In the few agencies where we did find active intergovernmental affairs offices, there seemed to be evidence that the OMB staff- and budget-cut approach to intergovernmental regulation remained on the surface. In the Justice Department, for example, the accent was on "respecting the role of the states" without necessarily dismantling the federal role. Those interviewed gave a clear impression that they were applying the president's philosophy of strong states tempered by the reality that some sharing of responsibilities was unavoidable.

Overall, however, across the executive branch the overriding pressure was for fewer federal relationships with state and local governments, not better coordinated ones. Indeed, some congressional staff we interviewed regarded the few traditional reform initiatives that did appear as ironic. "[It's like] rearranging the deck chairs on the Titanic; the little guys are trying to improve the system at the same time the big guys are dismantling it." As the following sections show, the devolution was principally budget driven, but it was also an effort to substitute state for federal responsibility for implementation wherever possible, to relax federal enforcement of intergovernmental regulation in remaining areas, and to slow down the promulgation of new agency rules.

Reducing the Federal Role through Legislation

From staff reductions to rescissions of long-standing executive orders, the administration worked to cut the strings and sever the ties between the levels of government. And, with the single exception of OBRA in 1981, nearly all of its efforts have followed the administrative strategy described in Chapter 2. Interviewees concerned with the intergovernmental regulation area identified OMB as the single most important actor in the process. Also identified as significant were the ideologically oriented Reagan political appointees. OMB review of agency rules and reductions in federal enforcement of regulatory statutes—both elements of an administrative strategy—were also important in the intergovernmental relations area.

Before turning to these executive branch efforts, however, it is worthwhile to review how the administration achieved its block grant victory, and why the perception that it was a disguised first step to federal withdrawal from domestic affairs dampened prospects for additional statutory reform.

The Omnibus Budget Reconciliation Act Of 1981. In his February 18, 1981 economic policy address to Congress, the president called for the conversion of 88 categorical grant programs into seven major block grants. Reagan presented these actions as reforms that would cut administrative overhead; reduce program duplication, and allow states and localities greater control in targeting programs to local needs. The proposal promised to save the federal government nearly $30 billion dollars; as a result, it had critics as well as supporters. A coalition of 100 advocacy and special interest groups that had benefited from the categorical programs labeled the block grants "a step toward abandonment of federal responsibility" (Congressional Quarterly Almanac 1981, p. 463). In addition, some members of Congress feared that their favored programs would be lost in competition for funding at the state level. Others opposed the domestic funding cuts. Eugene Eidenberg, former state and local liaison for President Carter (1982, p. 112), summed these sentiments up this way, "The driving force behind the Administration's decisions about federalism is primarily a concern with the federal deficit . . . [a] belief that the best way to cut spending is to eliminate the substantial support that the federal government currently provides for a variety of programs administered by state and local governments."

The administration countered with the argument that the funding cuts could be made up through deregulation—by reducing administrative and program requirements written into the current set of categorical grants. Since the block grants would produce "significant savings in administration and result in more efficient management, the reductions in funding need not cause a comparable reduction in services to the public" (Congressional Quarterly Almanac 1981, p. 464).

Today, administration spokespersons adhere to the same logic. But this line of argument has long since lost its appeal among state and local officials. Looking back on the critical first year, one observer concluded that by the end of 1981, state and local governments were not quite sure into what position they had been maneuvered by the Reagan administration (Kettl 1981, p. 19). Our interviews and research, however, indicate that these officials had experienced net losses through OBRA, and they were quite sure that they would not willingly travel that route again.

Sorting Out. Even as the White House domestic policy staff were percolating the "New Federalism" proposal of 1982 inside the executive office of the president and OMB, the "Trojan horse" analogy had already found its way into the anti-New Federalism rhetoric of some Democrats in Congress, liberal Washington insiders and journalists, as well as local public interest groups and state and local lobbies. New Federalism, they argued, was budget cuts in disguise.

Undaunted, on January 26, 1982, Reagan made federalism reform the centerpiece of his state of the union address. The New Federalism proposal was to be the engine that would fire America into a "new day" for federalism. It would serve as a framework to make government accountable; the realignment it would bring about would end cumbersome administration and spiralling federal costs (Davis and Howard 1982, p. 9).

The administration proposed to federalize the Medicaid program in exchange for turning back responsibility for food stamps, AFDC, and about 40 other intergovernmental aid programs. The turnback package would have established a temporary trust fund to cushion the blow for states disadvantaged by this arrangement and it repealed some $11 billion in federal excise taxes, opening opportunities for states to further avail themselves of these revenue sources.

Had the package become law, it would have resulted in a vast reduction in grant rules affecting state and local governments. But, as in the block grants in OBRA the year before, OMB closely tied these structural changes to its plans to reduce the federal domestic budget, in effect by shifting costs to the states. As Richard Williamson, the president's assistant for intergovernmental affairs and chief architect of the plan (Conlan 1985, p. 272) later admitted, "[W]e allowed ourselves as an Administration to be trapped into an obsession over short-term budget considerations. The budget was allowed to dominate internal administration machinery and crowded out the Federalism initiative."

While the administration argued that the plan would be "revenue neutral," evidence mounted that it might not turn out that way. For one thing, revenue neutrality was predicated on anticipated budget cuts in grant programs to be turned back. This, in turn, gave the appearance of equal federal and state costs by "reducing" the up-front paper costs to the states. For another, although the White House argued that the federal share of costs would grow because of rapidly escalating Medicaid expenditures, some governors worried that if the legislation were passed, within a few years OMB would force a reduction in the minimum Medicaid payment to a level so low that states would feel compelled to supplement it (Conlan 1985). Finally, there was the problem of whose programs were being turned back. Because the costs of the Medicaid program were much higher than the costs of AFDC, responsibility for many popular joint federal and city/county programs would have to be turned back to achieve revenue neutrality. Many of the nation's local elected officials thus opposed the New Federalism, at least as it was being considered by the governors and the administration, perceiving themselves the likely losers in such a swap.

Because of such growing resistance, the OBRA 1981 legislative victory was the first and last significant legislative accomplishment in federalism reform. Since then, the administration has put forward dozens of additional legislative grant reform proposals. But, with one exception— the replacement of CETA with the Job Training Partnership Act of 1982 (JTPA)—none has been enacted.

Striking Out in Social Regulatory Reform

Insofar as intergovernmental regulatory programs were concerned, the administration found little support for even partial federal withdrawal—especially in the social regulatory programs administered jointly by the federal and state governments. The administration had expected opposition to its social regulatory policies from congressional and special interest groups. But, criticism from the intergovernmental community caught the administration by surprise. As one OMB staffer stated, "I can't understand why the mayors and governors didn't see it our way. These programs really needed fundamental statutory reform. But, I guess what they really wanted was the money."

There is truth in this conclusion. Beyond the antiregulatory rhetoric of intergovernmental advocacy groups, state and local officials were far more worried about dollars than rules. A 1980 National League of Cities survey of city officials reported that, while 63 percent of those surveyed indicated that federal agency rules and regulations made local compliance more difficult, 85 percent found the basic goals and objectives of the federal regulations to be desirable. What's more, federal regulation can be politically useful: Federal mandates have often helped state and local officials achieve their own perhaps controversial social objectives by laying the blame for strong actions on some distant federal rule maker.

In short, while the Reagan administration wanted a fundamental restructuring of the federal role in intergovernmental regulatory programs, state and local officials seemed to hold a business-as-usual attitude, looking for traditional management reforms coupled with adequate, if not generous, federal aid to get the job done. Achieving clean air and water, managing toxic waste and advancing minority and handicapped rights all required financial resources; in many cases, state and local governments had a long way to go to meet the goals of social regulatory programs and they weren't anxious to go it alone.

ADMINISTRATIVE REFORM TAKES CENTER STAGE

The administration thus faced an uphill battle on the legislative reform side, and it soon began to emphasize its executive branch administrative strategy in the intergovernmental relations area. In the remaining sections of this chapter we review each element of the strategy including budget cuts; the rescission and relaxation of existing regulation; the mandated slowdown in the promulgation of agency rules; and reduced federal enforcement.

Budget Cutting

As administration officials were quick to point out, by cutting federal aid to state and local governments—the federal carrot—the president would tend to deprive Congress and the bureaucracy of their access to regulation—the federal stick. In the absence of other measures, program funds would have to be completely "zeroed out" for this deregulatory strategy to succeed, and in a few cases even that would not bring about the intended deregulation. This strategy would further be most effective if cuts were focused in programs heavily loaded with federal requirements, preferably those which state and local governments were free to refuse. This pattern did not occur however.

While each successive presidential budget proposed domestic grant-in-aid programs for elimination, OMB was unable to convince Congress to eliminate these programs. After OBRA in 1981, OMB was forced to settle for successive, incremental cuts in intergovernmental grant programs. While some intergovernmental welfare programs have seen budget increases during this six-year period, in most cases intergovernmental grant programs have been cut substantially, in some cases dramatically. Grants for state and local expenditure programs (excluding aid to individuals) declined by an inflation-adjusted 23.5 percent between 1980 and 1985, as Table 4.2 shows. But, the only major program the administration was able to eliminate was General Revenue Sharing, an accomplishment of little regulatory consequence because this grant program involved few federal requirements.

Most of the major intergovernmental regulatory programs were significantly cut also, as Table 4.3 shows. With the exception of increased funding for two new regulatory programs, Resource Conservation and Recovery (RCRA 1976) and Surface Mining Conservation and Restoration (SMCR 1977), reductions ranged from an inflation-adjusted high of 38 percent in the clean air program to 1 percent in occupational safety and health. (OSHA programs are partial preemption programs, but administration remains largely federal because few states have sought primacy in implementation.) The heavy cuts in many of these programs are especially problematic with respect to regulatory reform. For while states and localities are at least in theory free to reject grant programs if they determine that federal dollars no longer justify federal rules, very often they are still bound by the federal requirements written into such intergovernmental regulatory programs. In a sense, the cuts in these programs have simply transferred the burden of inefficiency in existing regulations from the federal to the state and local level.

Overall, budget cutting has reduced federal support for the attainment of many former national domestic policy goals, and it has signaled state and local governments not to count on Washington for as much help financing them in the future. By and large, however, budget cuts have not been used effectively to reduce federal regulation of state and local governments. As one interviewee noted, while the White House strategy

Table 4.2
Grants to State and Local Governments by Function and Selected Programs, Including Grants That Are Also Payments to Individuals, in Constant Dollars (1980 = 100), Fiscal Years 1980–85

	1980	1985	Percent Change 1980–85
Total all functions	59,524	45,513	− 23.5
Transportation	13,087	13,027	− 0.5
Highways	8,676	9,548	+ 10.0
Urban mass transit	3,129	2,547	− 18.6
Airport and other transport	1,282	932	− 27.2
Community and regional development	6,486	3,905	− 39.8
Economic development assistance	452	275	− 39.2
Local public works and regional development	860	6	—
Community development	3,902	2,896	− 25.8
Urban development action grants	225	377	+ 68.2
Urban renewal and related grants	7,047	351	− 66.6
Education, training, employment and social services	21,783	14,503	− 33.4
Compensatory education for the disadvantaged	3,370	3,192	− 5.4
Social service block grants	2,763	2,081	− 24.7
Human development services	1,548	1,449	− 6.4
Community services program	547	285	− 47.8
Temporary employment assistance	1,797	—	—
Training and employment services	6,924	3,729	− 68.8
Other[1]	4,834	3,767	− 22.1
General purpose fiscal assistance	8.478	4,658	− 45.1
General revenue sharing	6,829	3,478	− 49.1
Shared revenues	673	516	− 23.3
Other[2]	976	664	− 31.8
All other functions[3]	9,690	9,420	− 2.8

Notes: 1. The most significant increase in constant dollars is in the family social service block grant established in 1981 and amounting to $560 million in fiscal 1985. For six programs with higher nominal amounts in 1985 the increases in real sums were as follows (in millions of dollars): impact aid + 19, special programs (education) + 2, education for the handicapped + 19, older Americans employment + 11, National Endowment for the Arts + 5, and Institute of Museum Services + 4. Decreases occurred for ten programs (in millions of dollars): bilingual education − 46, rehabilitation and handicapped research − 172, vocational and adult education − 157, higher education − 15, libraries − 30, work incentives − 83, public broadcasting − 1, Indian education − 11, and the Department of Commerce grants for telecommunication information and job opportunities programs − 5.

Table 4.2 (continued)

2. Includes payments to the District of Columbia, Puerto Rico, the trust territories of the Pacific, and other outlays in the administration of U.S. territories. Detail is not available for fiscal year 1985.

3. The U.S. Department of Agriculture grant programs related to price support and economic stabilization policies increased by $2.175 billion from fiscal 1980 to 1985. Grants for administration of the income security programs rose by $610 million, and for the health programs $397 million. Other increases were (in millions of dollars): energy +263, general government +37, and national defense (i.e., construction of National Guard armories and disaster relief) +18. The largest decrease amounting to $1.1 billion occurred in the natural resources and environment function as a result of the reduction in funds for construction grants administered by the Environmental Protection Agency. The elimination of law enforcement grants and grants for health manpower training programs resulted in cuts of $34 million and $25 million, respectively.

Source: United States Budget as reported in Congressional Research Service Report No. 86–2 E, January 2, 1986. Constant dollar totals were computed using the gross national product deflators based on the calendar 1972 prices as developed by the U.S. Department of Commerce, Bureau of Economic Analysis.

was clearly one of capping the federal role, cutting the grants, and then killing the programs, "So far they've done a lot of cutting, but the programs are still hobbling along, rules and all."

Increasing Flexibility through Block Grants

In this section we review efforts to increase flexibility in the Community Development Block Grant (CDBG) modified by OBRA (1981) and the promulgation of rules attached to the nine block grants created by OBRA, and we examine efforts to reduce federal oversight of state implementation in intergovernmental regulatory programs. Because many of the programs affected by reduced oversight are environmental programs we present only a brief overview here, reserving fuller discussion of these programs for Chapter 5.

The Community Development Block Grant (CDBG). Soon after taking over as secretary of Housing and Urban Development (HUD), Samuel Pierce announced his conviction that the CDBG program was overregulated. In order to reverse this situation, HUD unveiled new program rules: unless presented with evidence of abuse, the department would assume information local governments submitted was accurate. It would grant more waivers with respect to "nonstatutory" regulations, and it would revoke the explicit percentage standards for benefits to the poor (Notice CPD 81–5 May 15, 1981). HUD also took steps to preclude federal regional and field offices from imposing their own conditions. Taken

Table 4.3
Budgets for Selected Major Intergovernmental Regulatory Programs
Including Direct Intergovernmental Aid, in Constant Dollars (1980 = 100),
Fiscal Years 1980–85

	1980	1985	Percent change 1980–85
Bilingual Education	166.9	105.8	− 36.6
Clean Air	290.1	183.5	− 36.7
Clean Water (total)	2,864.9	2,018.0	− 29.5
Direct Assistance	2,591.9	1,874.4	− 27.6
Handicapped Education	874.5	862.7	− 1.3
Occupational Safety & Health	166.0	167.2	+ 1.0
Resource Recovery and Conservation	109.8	127.1	+ 15.8
State administrative grants[1]	18.1	43.3	+ 39.2
Safe Drinking Water	79.3	77.7	− 2.0
State administrative grants[1]	39.4	35.0	− 11.0
Surface Mining	180.0	250.8	+ 39.3
State administrative grants[1]	28.0	267.0	+787.0

Note: 1. For any given year totals may vary due to change in the number of states administering programs.

Source: United States Budget. Constant dollar totals were computed using gross national product deflators based on calendar year 1972 prices as developed by the U.S. Department of Commerce, Bureau of Economic Analysis.

together, the newly proposed rules transferred unprecedented discretion to local officials. In so doing, they followed the new, bare-bones rulemaking strategy advocated by OMB for intergovernmental regulation.

But advocates of the program inside and outside Congress worried that too much discretion might result in funds being siphoned off from intended beneficiaries. Thus, relaxing CDBG program rules met with stiff opposition. Soon after HUD published its new rules, Congress began to push back. In a House oversight hearing, Congressman Gonzalez (D-TX) castigated HUD officials for overstepping the bounds of congressional intent: "The 1981 Omnibus Reconciliation Act made some changes in the statute, but did not change at all the purpose of the Act ... and did not invite HUD to demolish all clear standards of accountability" (House, Committee on Banking, Finance and Urban Affairs 1982, p. 5).

Program beneficiaries and their advocates filled countless pages in the *Federal Register* with negative comments, and 23 groups representing minority, low income housing, tenant and neighborhood groups testified in Congress against the rules. Moreover, 45 other groups submitted written testimony protesting the changes (House, Committee on Banking, Finance and Urban Affairs 1982, p. 14).

HUD had expected a battle from client groups, but was not prepared for the negative reaction of local officials. When the department promulgated its notice of proposed rule making in October, 1981, virtually every local organization of local elected officials commented in the strongest, negative terms. Moreover, representatives of the National Association of County Officials (NACO), the U. S. Conference of Mayors (USCM), and the National League of Cities (NLC) all appeared before Congress to urge HUD to provide clearer guidelines for the program and to specify a more targeted approach to program spending. Their testimony reflected fundamental differences in the way the administration and the intergovernmental community viewed regulatory reform. While the administration was advancing wholesale devolution, state and local officials preferred to pick and choose among those rules that made their work more difficult and those that did not. Congressman Barney Frank (D-MA) (House, Committee on Banking, Finance and Urban Affairs 1982, p. 15) was quick to point out the irony:

In effect, HUD is trying to rescue the damsel in distress ... but she doesn't want to go. I think you ought to wonder why the intended beneficiaries to this rescue effort are beating you off with a stick. The answer is I think a very simple one. These are not efforts just to make this more flexible. They are efforts to undermine a Federal commitment to poorer people and moderate-income people in the cities.

City officials concurred. As one put it:

I agree with the comments ... made about making [CDBG] for low and moderate-income people.... And, I think that should be made clear in these regulations, because if it is not made clear ... believe me ... on the local level the pressures are enormous. The more we can be specific about what these funds should be used for, the better off we are on the local level. (House, Committee on Banking, Finance and Urban Affairs 1982, p. 137)

This same official was also quick to point out what happens to programs that have so few regulations that they lose their constituency:

[W]e are concerned about the same thing that you are concerned about, Mr. Chairman, and that is that the CDBG program does not turn into some kind of pork barrel, slush fund, revenue-sharing program that ultimately will be looked at by the Congress as unfocused [sic], like they have with the EDA programs and some others, and then see it disappear. (House, Committee on Banking, Finance and Urban Affairs 1982, p. 136)

In the end, HUD and its less visible allies at OMB achieved some significant changes in CDBG program rules. But, this success was limited in a number of important respects. Overall, the CDBG story strongly suggests that attempts to promulgate new, less stringent rules may not be shortcuts to devolution. Proposed changes in regulation, like changes in legislation, can be opposed. The coalition building necessary to enact regulatory reform legislation seems to be a necessary component of making changes through administrative action, as well.

Equally important, the dilution of regulatory requirements at the federal level seems not necessarily to produce a diminution in the redistributive character of programs targeted for elimination by the Reagan administration. In the CDBG program, "The programmatic changes did not appear to have affected significantly the distribution of direct benefits among income groups" (Dommel et al. 1983, p. xi). In some cases, as Dommel reported, local determination to keep to the spirit of the former rules was explicit. For example, the Albuquerque city council passed an ordinance that 75 percent of that city's CDBG monies would continue to be used to benefit poor people. Generally speaking, the CDBG efforts suggest that relying on administrative reforms that set local or state governments free to move away from statutory purposes is no guarantee that they will. Also, where local or state officials are committed to these objectives, devolution makes it possible to set a course not anticipated by the administration, one which may be inconsistent with its policies.

OBRA Block Grant Deregulation. The promulgation of vastly simplified regulations governing the nine new block grants created by OBRA (1981) suggests that even when political opposition doesn't materialize, success in achieving regulatory relief can still be problematic.

Soon after the passage of OBRA, the White House assigned OMB responsibility for coordinating the development of implementing regulations. OMB staff followed a few simple rules in pursuit of devolution: block grant regulations were to minimize paperwork; they were not to contain references to federal crosscutting requirements; they were to provide minimum guidance by using the actual statutory language; they were to assign the burden of proof of abuse to the federal government; they were to minimize record keeping and make states responsible for auditing; and they were not to be supplemented with additional agency guidance. Overall, the block grants allowed states to certify that they would administer the programs in accordance with all applicable federal laws and submit reports outlining the planned uses of the funds. There was no advance federal approval of the plans nor did many of OMB's grants management circulars apply. Finally, the audit process was principally limited to fiscal and legal compliance issues (McDowell 1982, p. 23). The philosophy was well summed up in the preamble to block grant rules promulgated by the Department of Health and Human Services (HHS):

To the extent possible, [the department] will not burden the states' administration of the programs with definitions of permissable and prohibited activities, procedural rules, paperwork and record-keeping requirements, or other regulatory provisions. The states will, for the most part, be subject only to the statutory requirements, and the department will carry out its functions with due regard for the limited nature of the role that Congress has assigned us. (*Federal Register* 42 1981, p. 48582)

As a result, in the seven block grants administered by HHS, over 600 pages of program regulations were rendered obsolete, replaced by only seven pages of block grant requirements. Other agencies had similar results. According to OMB staff we interviewed, "What the President wanted, he got. We worked through the General Counsels of the agencies to get the least regulation possible under the law."

The block grants incorporated into OBRA mark the high point of relaxing federal rules. Yet, Lovell (1983) found that while federal agencies reduced program requirements in some areas, giving states more policy flexibility, they continued to require extensive auditing and financial reviews. Moreover, the block grants did not lift the burdens of the crosscutting requirements such as historic preservation, civil rights and environmental protection. Overall, without federal guidelines, states were forced to create their own regulatory enforcement mechanisms since most of the block grant funds were passed through to local governments and nonprofit organizations. As a result the General Accounting Office (1985) found that states worried about increased liability. As one official interviewed put it, "How do you avoid getting slammed with an audit?" One likely way to avoid it seemed to be to continue to follow the old federal categorical grant regulations. According to the same GAO study,

Although considerable efforts were directed at administrative simplification at the state level, states generally did not pass on such simplification to the local level. Most of the 13 states [studied] imposed requirements on service providers in addition to the federal requirements, such as matching state funds and obtaining state approval for certain actions like hiring and procurement. Also, in some instances, program managers as well as state legislatures added administrative requirements specifically to improve program accountability. Such actions tended to emphasize increased data collection and reporting by service providers. (General Accounting Office 1985, p. 19)

After four years of state regulation many local officials surveyed registered negative views about the extent to which the block grants had produced regulatory relief at the local level. As one official put it: "Relief

...what relief? I don't think anything is different now. We just exchanged one set of regulators for another."

Reducing Federal Regulatory Enforcement

One regulatory relief strategy that seemed promising to the Reagan administration was to reduce enforcement activities of federal agencies. The administration also instructed political appointees in the regulatory agencies to reduce federal oversight by cutting enforcement personnel and mounting a concerted effort to speed up state takeover of regulatory responsibilities under a number of partial preemption statutes. These programs were especially well suited to a management strategy because most governing statutes provide for the assumption of virtually all enforcement responsibilities by states at the discretion of federal agencies. Many of the intergovernmental regulatory programs affected by these initiatives were environmental programs including clean air and water, toxic substances, and surface mining. The record of management actions in these areas is large and complex, and will be explored in fuller detail in Chapter 5, which is entirely devoted to the environmental protection area. Here, we will simply summarize our finding that devolution in environmental programs did not proceed smoothly when state and local governments opposed administration actions such as in the case of pollution discharge permits, but that it was often quite successful when the administration followed the consensus such as in the case of emissions trading. Finally, results were mixed within program areas such as surface mining where some states used the new freedoms to deregulate and others did not.

The approach to enforcement was similar to other aspects of intergovernmental regulation. Generally speaking, political appointees urged restraint in second guessing the states, preferring to leave enforcement questions to the states wherever possible. Under Reagan, said one interviewee, "There is an explicit policy to trust the states more."

The Vice President's Task Force on Regulatory Relief and OMB Review of Agency Rules

Not only did the administration make every effort to encourage agencies to implement the president's intergovernmental regulatory objectives, it also set up a presidential task force to oversee their efforts. The President's Task Force on Regulatory Relief, chaired by Vice President Bush, was charged with responsibility for reviewing existing rules—identifying those that were duplicative, inconsistent, or overlapping, or that did not measure up to the regulatory standards set forth in Executive Order 12291. Intergovernmental rules were to be given attention along with those affecting the private sector. In the end, having reviewed less than 200 rules out of thousands, the White House announced that the task force's work was complete and disbanded it in 1983.

As a starting point for regulatory relief efforts on intergovernmental rules, the task force sought the advice of state and local governments. The request brought in over 2500 submissions of rules regarded as particularly burdensome, inefficient, or inequitable. Regulations most often identified included rules governing the following program areas: clean air, clean water, safe drinking water, handicapped rights, age discrimination, wastewater construction grants, Medicaid, health planning, housing assistance planning, federally assisted single family and multi-family housing, wages in federally assisted construction projects, urban mass transit, and highway and highway safety rules.

Based on these submissions, the task force designated 27 rules for review (see Table 4.4). In August, 1982 a report was issued, recounting task force regulatory relief accomplishments. Examples of prominent regulatory relief actions cited by the administration included: withdrawal of rules governing bilingual education; revision of Transportation Department handicapped access to mass transit rules; modifications in the Education Department's rules requiring schools and colleges receiving federal grants to spend as much on women's athletic programs as men's; and changes in the Labor Department's administration of minimum wage requirements on federally assisted construction projects. Overall, of 27 rules targeted for action, 13 were reported as having been reformed, for an estimated $4-$6 billion in one-time savings and an additional $2 billion in annually recurring costs. The task force also estimated that its actions would reduce paperwork costs by nearly 12 million work hours each year.

An examination of several of these regulatory relief actions, however, suggests that the picture of success is more mixed than the report indicates. Consider action on bilingual education rules. Despite considerable publicity to the contrary, the administration did not end federal bilingual education requirements. Rather, it withdrew rules proposed by the Carter administration to codify and expand the standards long enforced by the Department of Education and the court rulings. A substantial network of other policy memos, guidelines, and court decisions requiring bilingual education efforts was left untouched. Education experts and state and local officials describe the net result as "business as usual."

Career staff and political appointees we interviewed at the Department of Education strongly believed the administration had done everything possible to set up "a decent bilingual program, one the locals could live with." The bare-bones approach of this initiative provided a philosophical statement of minimum federal oversight and involvement in the

Table 4.4
Programs Affecting State and Local Governments Designated by the President's Task Force on Regulatory Relief for Substantive Reform

Army Corps of Engineers
    Dredge and Fill Permit Program—Section 404 of the *Clean Water Act*
    Water Conservation Clause Planning Requirements (Presidential Memo July 12, 1978)

Office of Management and Budget
    A-95 Project Notification and Review
    Urban Impact Analysis

Federal Emergency Management Administration
    National Flood Insurance Program (*Flood Disaster Protection Act*)

Education Department
    Title IX—Sexual equality in athletic programs
    Section 504 of the *Handicapped Rehabilitation Act* requiring nondiscrimination on the basis of handicap
    Education for Handicapped Children Act requirements

Environmental Protection Agency
    Consolidated Pollution Control Permits
    Industrial Wastewater Pretreatment Requirements

Department of Housing and Urban Development
    CDBG regulations including: citizen participation; expected to reside requirement in housing assistance plan; small cities requirements; and, neighborhood strategy areas targeting requirements
    Environmental Impact Statements (NEPA)
    Utility allowance requirements in Public Housing Authority projects
    Lease grievance procedures in Public Housing Authority projects
    Minimum property standards in federally assisted housing units

Department of Health and Human Services
    Medicaid requirements for the states
    Health care institutions certification and surveys

Department of the Interior
    Surface Mining Regulations

Office of Personnel Management
    Federal standards for merit system of personnel administration

Department of Agriculture
    National School Lunch Program Reporting requirements

Department of Energy
    Residential Conservation Service Program

Table 4.4 (continued)

Department of Justice
  Section 504 of the *Rehabilitation Act*

Department of Transportation
  Section 504 Requirements—Transportation
  Highway statistics reporting requirements
  Design standards for highways and geometric design standards for
  resurfacing, restoring and rehabilitating highways

Department of Labor
  Davis-Bacon requirements
  Labor standards provisions of construction contracts

Source: Presidential Task Force on Regulatory Relief, *Reagan Administration Achievements in Regulatory Relief for State and Local Government: A Progress Report*, Washington, DC, August 1982 (processed).

preamble to the regulations, followed by rules that closely tracked legislative language. To the extent that this language left room for interpretation, school districts were to enjoy more freedom to interpret their responsibilities under the Act. But, interviewees also noted that the initiative was limited in a number of important respects. Said one Education Department staffer, "You just couldn't get around the law. Congress wanted it. They just don't see regulation as a problem."

The results regarding changes in section 504 handicapped discrimination rules are also rather mixed. Section 504 of the Rehabilitation Act of 1973 is a crosscutting regulation applying to all intergovernmental grant-in-aid programs. It requires equal access to and public services for those who, absent their handicap, would normally have access to or be eligible for such services. This provision is remarkably broad, affecting programs in all departments of the executive branch—administered by the Department of Justice acting as "lead agency."

Heated opposition from handicapped groups forced the Department of Justice to abandon its efforts to rewrite government-wide handicapped discrimination standards. Also, Congress proved to be a strong advocate of vigorous regulation and enforcement.

The administration did succeed in rescinding the Carter regulations concerning Section 504—requiring local transit systems to provide full access for patrons in wheelchairs and other disabled riders. But, the regulations proposed to replace the Carter rules were attacked as too weak by advocates for the handicapped, and in 1983 the administration recanted in part by proposing new transportation guidelines that were considerably more stringent.

These examples suggest that in many enforcement areas administration success was mixed. In several environmental areas, administrative enforcement enjoyed strong support from the states and succeeded. As will be explained in Chapter 5, it seems apparent that part—although by no means all—of this success lies in the fact that the administration was doing an excellent job of riding the intergovernmental reform horse in the direction it was already going.

Stemming the Growth of New Regulations

Some chroniclers of deregulation have pointed to aggregate statistics to support the argument that Reagan's management strategy—notably the OIRA review process—has substantially reduced the growth of federal regulation, and therefore has been a success. Interpreting trends in the number of rules published or from the size of the *Federal Register* is not without its methodological difficulties, particularly when applied to intergovernmental regulatory relief.

Far more telling is evidence from interviews with agency personnel responsible for the promulgation of rules, staff at OIRA who review the rules, and state and local officials who implement them. In every case, those we interviewed believed that OMB had significantly reduced the number of new federal intergovernmental regulatory initiatives. Few, however, claimed that the system effectively weeded out poor proposed regulations from better ones.

At the Transportation Department, one staff member we interviewed stated, "OMB can essentially hold regulations if they don't like them." At OSHA, where regulatory activities depend to a great extent on field-based record keeping, a staff member we interviewed cited OIRA's review powers established by the Paperwork Reduction Act:

There is more stringent enforcement of the Paperwork Act now and much more attention to the costs of regulation. Under the Reagan Administration, the record keeping process has been scrutinized and OMB/OIRA approval is necessary in order to change anything in record keeping.... We are spending more and more time justifying costs and paperwork and this slows down the process a lot. Reform works because there is less regulation primarily because it just takes longer to get things through the system.

The responses of other agency staff were much the same; when asked to gauge the effectiveness of OIRA review of agency proposed rules, the accent was generally on preventing rules from being promulgated, not tinkering with their defects.

The fact that the administration's management approach to deregulation worked primarily to slow the flow of rules raises an important question about its long-term effects. How were rules that were eventually promulgated different from having been subjected to a centralized review process? The answer, from nearly all of the agency staff we interviewed was that, "The rules are watered down." State and local government advocacy groups were quick to add that another result of OMB review is that the rules are now less clear than before the bare-bones strategy. As one interviewee stated, "Some of the rules are easier to live with, but a lot of them look just the same as when they went in [to OMB], and a lot of them are so vague its hard to tell what to do."

While watered-down rules and unclear guidelines were consistent with the administration's devolutionary philosophy, the consequences were generally less than satisfactory to state and local officials. Because subnational governments were still liable for meeting statutory goals, different states and communities often felt forced to invent their own enforcement strategies. In the case of A–95 review, this resulted in regulatory balkanization: 50 review processes instead of one. In other cases, vague rules led states to continue to follow the older, more stringent guidelines in order to play it safe.

One reason state and local governments have not benefited more from regulatory review is that OIRA evaluations emphasize the compliance, rather than administrative, costs of regulation. Since state and local costs are for administration as well as compliance, they are less apt to be fully measured. State and local officials reported that cost measurement procedures let them down in other ways as well. Both agency staff and state and local representatives we interviewed believed that OMB reviews placed primary emphasis on the monetary costs of regulations, not on assessing how intergovernmental rules might be more effective. For example, when asked what reviewing rules for their costs meant to the effort to reform intergovernmental regulation, an OSHA official stated, "Other than forcing us to justify everything and slowing the process down, the regulations have not changed. The type has not changed, the justification has just increased." When asked why nothing had changed, this official turned to the statute as the key explanatory factor. "The states' role is stated specifically in the legislation. Nothing has changed in relation to state and local governments. Yes, they are receiving less money because of blanket budget reduction, but the responsibilities are the same."

OIRA's broad brush treatment of intergovernmental impacts is also likely due to the failure of governmental associations to lobby effectively. While advocates of business and industry routinely availed themselves of OMB's help, state and local governments have had very little contact with the office. A number of those we interviewed stated that they had lost faith in regulatory reform after the lengths they had gone to in responding to the requests of the Task Force on Regulatory Relief in the early days of the administration. From their viewpoint, these efforts had tied up organizational resources without producing much in the way of real regulatory relief. As one city lobbyist we interviewed said, "Given how much we have to do on the budget side and now in tax reform, I can't justify sending the people I have out on a mission to kill a few rules. The fact is there are a whole lot more rules than I've got people."

Many state and local officials and their representatives are also suspicious of OMB staff, including those at OIRA. OMB staff are perceived as the principle architects and advocates of federal aid cuts; further that interactions with OIRA staff have not always proved helpful to these individuals. One official responsible for state and interstate pollution programs commented, "We generally limit our contacts to EPA and Hill Staff. When you give information to the people at OMB, more often than not, they use it against you later." Generally, there is a widespread feeling that regulatory relief for business and industry has a higher priority in the Reagan administration than regulatory relief for state and local government. As one interviewee summed it up, "When our problems are business's problem, then we get action. By the same token when we are business' problem, we feel the heat." The problematic aspect of intergovernmental regulatory reform—as practiced by the Reagan administration—was especially apparent when federalism values came into conflict with other administration values.

REGULATION TO ADVANCE THE CONSERVATIVE AGENDA

At the same time that the Reagan administration was engaged in these intergovernmental regulatory relief efforts, a countertrend was occurring: The administration was also making efforts to use the tool of regulation in a proactive way to advance its own political agenda. Indeed, while some of the new federal regulation that has occurred over the past five years has resulted from congressional or court action, a number of potentially burdensome regulations for state and local governments have resulted from administration initiatives. A recent study on federalism found that the Reagan administration tended to push for new regulations in cases where federal dollars could be recovered by tightening grant requirements, where business interest preferred tighter federal controls, or where certain New Right social issues were involved (Conlan 1985).

Using Regulation to Reduce Domestic Spending and Help Business and Industry

In many cases, the administration has shown a willingness to establish new federal regulation in order to reduce or cap spending on social programs. The administration promulgated tighter new regulations to limit the benefits of social programs—such as Medicaid and AFDC—to a strict, federally defined limited group of the "truly needy." Federal CDBG regulations were tightened in order to limit funds that can be spent for social services. The administration also imposed tougher fiscal sanctions on states with unacceptably high welfare program error rates.

To a surprising extent, given the administration goals of returning regulatory authority to the states, the administration has come down in favor of federal preemption of state regulatory power in specific cases where business interests were involved. The reason seems to lie in the tendency of business to be leery of substituting state regulation for national regulation in many areas. Such substitution was overwhelmingly opposed by business advocates (Gottlieb 1982). According to one chemical manufacturing lobbyist, "State regulations now, and probably during the rest of the 1980s, may pose an even greater threat to industry than do federal regulations" (McGraw-Hill 1981). The administration has been largely responsive to these business concerns, apparently giving them more priority than devolution concerns. In the last five years, of 12 proposed federal preemptions of state regulatory powers, the administration has supported nine, including the most recent efforts to nationalize product liability laws (Morrison 1982). Other examples of administration nationalizing of regulatory policy include overriding state laws regulating double-trailer trucks and Federal Trade Commission suits against individual states to override state professional licensing regulations in areas ranging from cosmetology to optometry.

Using Regulation to Advance the New Right Agenda

The Reagan administration has also showed a willingness to use federal regulation aggressively to advance certain social policies of concern to the New Right, even at the expense of devolution objectives. For example, since taking office, the president has been a consistent supporter of parental rights to influence school curricula, especially with respect to sex education. And, the administration attempts to promulgate the so-called "squeal" rule would have required local family-planning centers receiving federal health funds to report minors seeking birth control. Other examples include administration initiatives to establish a minimum national drinking age, regulate medical care for children born with severe birth defects, and require that states establish workfare programs. On these issues, the administration attempted to weaken, not widen, the regulatory discretion of state and local governments.

In the area of civil rights policy, the administration attempted to use federal regulatory authority to override the existing affirmative action plans that had been worked out and adopted by many local governments over the past few decades, often to settle long-standing and complex lawsuits. Although forcing abandonment of such local arrangements has an element of regulatory relief, such administration efforts were distinctly prescriptive, federal-dominated, and regulatory in nature. In response, several cities sued the federal government, and in 1986, the Supreme Court handed down three separate decisions affirming the right of municipalities to participate in such affirmative action plans.

Overall, then, the administration's record on the intergovernmental regulation issues includes a number of examples of nationalizing regulatory policy. These instances are troubling from the perspective of the goal of devolution of regulatory authority. These instances show that the administration's apparently strong commitment to deregulating intergovernmental relations could be—and often was—overridden by other political concerns. To the extent that these other political concerns dominated the decision-making process, the integrity of the administration's campaign to achieve true regulatory reform in the intergovernmental relations area tended to suffer.

SUMMARY AND CONCLUSIONS

In principle, President Reagan's new federalism envisioned a dramatic realignment of domestic policy responsibilities, to be achieved through a combination of legislative initiatives and administrative actions. Less than two years into the first term, however, it was apparent that beyond the achievements of OBRA 1981, legislation to reform the federal aid system was destined to fail, in large part because the White House and OMB refused to uncouple efforts to cut domestic spending from those to realign the federal system. Moreover, the Reagan transition team regarded the statutory route to social regulatory reform as exceptionally treacherous from the beginning, and did not make strong attempts to work with Congress to reshape regulatory policies. As a result, almost from the beginning the emphasis in intergovernmental regulatory reform was on the administrative management strategy.

Findings from this case study on intergovernmental relations, however, suggest that the Reagan administration administrative management strategy was only somewhat more able to sidestep the frustrations of pluralistic politics than statutory reform. Administration success was limited partially because intergovernmental regulation cuts across the executive branch and involves a wide array of outside interests at every level of government that the administration was unable to wholly shut out. Where management changes reflected a consensus of opinion or were relatively noncontroversial, the administration tended to be successful in bringing about some degree of regulatory relief. When consensus was lacking, political reactions ran the full range of opposition: interest group pressure; court suits; negative public comments on proposed rules; congressional hearings; journalistic exposés; political in-fighting; and, most of all, a desire of states and localities to go their own way.

In a number of cases the administration was clearly banking on the proposition that devolution of regulatory authority to state and local governments would result in less regulation in the aggregate. This hope often proved false. Indeed, since administrative reforms were not based in statutory changes, it became easier for states and localities to suit themselves in regard to levels of regulation. Whether from institutional habit, fear of litigation or subsequent federal audit, commitment to sta-tutory goals, or local political pressures, states and localities did not always choose to deregulate just because the administration provided them the opportunity.

Additionally, measured against its own objectives, the administration's management strategy placed too heavy an emphasis on cutting inter-governmental aid, both for grant and regulatory programs. These cuts conformed to other administration priorities: reducing domestic spend-ing; building-up defense capacity, and cutting taxes. But, intergovern-mental regulatory reform objectives have suffered.

In the future, for those programs where federal grants are actually "zeroed out," state and local governments may look forward to devel-oping their own programs free of federal conditions of aid, for, by taking away the carrot of federal aid, Washington will lose the stick of federal regulation as a condition of aid. However, if the last five years are a guide, the incremental phase-out of federal aid will not come in the programs which are the most heavily regulated. Moreover, as long as state and local governments participate in large grant programs such as Medicaid, they will continue to be covered by various crosscutting reg-ulatory requirements, and they will be vulnerable to crossover regulatory penalties as well.

President Reagan promised a dramatic realignment of responsibilities between the nation and the states. But he also promised—for better or worse—a dramatic reduction in federal involvement in state and local affairs. This chapter has shown some evidence of devolution, but the pattern has certainly not been dramatic or overwhelming. The admin-istration favored full federal withdrawal, while states and localities were much more selective about the intergovernmental regulatory and grant program changes they favored. The difference was a major stumbling block to administration efforts, one that is likely to continue to be a source of tension throughout the second term. Overall, the administra-tive deregulatory strategy, like the legislative reform strategy it was to replace, was not without difficulties when it came to implementation. These difficulties were in many ways similar to those that accompany legislative change in a pluralistic, democratic system of government.

Because much of the change that has occurred in this area has been unilateral, piecemeal, and partial, considerable question remains as to whether or not the intergovernmental system is actually more rational and workable than before the Reagan era.

5   REGULATORY REFORM IN THE ENVIRONMENTAL PROTECTION AREA

Since Earth Day in 1970, environmental protection has become a main-stay of U.S. politics. Yet, only two decades ago Americans were largely unaware of environmental problems like acid rain and toxic waste. To-day, in contrast, stories of environmental problems fill the nation's news-papers and nightly news broadcasts, and the public maintains steadfast support for an ever-increasing governmental role in the regulatory policy area.

The responsibility for environmental protection is diffused among many actors. The federal government plays the major role. No less than 82 congressional committees and subcommittees have a hand in shaping environmental laws and thousands of federal agency staff administer the statutes that protect our air and water, and conserve our natural resources. Federal and state courts also play a role in interpreting and enforcing statutes. Since many environmental statutes are administered in cooperation with state and local governments, these governments also have a share of environmental protection responsibilities as governors, state legislators, mayors, and county officials endeavor to come to terms with the everyday problems pollution poses to their communities.

Altogether, between 1965 and 1980, some 13 major federal environ-mental protection statutes were enacted. With this legislative growth has come an unprecedented number of new federally mandated environ-mental protective regulations. As might be expected in the wake of this kind of rapid growth, frequent and vociferous debates have occurred in the intervening years over whether these regulations have achieved their goals and at what cost to business, consumers, and state and local governments (Ripley and Franklin, 1984). Concerns that environmental statutes have not served their intended purposes and that they might be hindering economic growth gained much credence among members of Reagan's administration. President Reagan placed a high priority on changing existing environmental protection policy and carrying out regulatory reform in this area. In spite of evident concern and even presidential promises, Reagan has failed to change national environmental policy significantly.

This chapter examines the reasons for this policy failure. Specifically, we will explore how the Reagan administration attempted to change the rule-making process drastically and sharply curtail the growth of regulation through the use of an aggressive management approach. We will explain how it happened that —despite a combination of extensive budgetary cutbacks, personnel reductions, changes in enforcement procedure, and a redefinition of federal/state environmental responsibilities— the regulatory landscape that Reagan inherited changed very little.

ENVIRONMENTAL PROBLEMS AND PUBLIC POLICY RESPONSES

Often one can look back at particular times and events in the nation's history and clearly identify them as watershed periods in the formulation of public policy. The Roosevelt New Deal programs, Truman's Fair Deal, Kennedy's New Frontier, Johnson's War on Poverty, and Nixon's New Federalism are a few modern examples. The spurt of environmental protection legislation that occurred in the 1970s–1980s, while not identified with any one president, represents a watershed period in environmental policy. This period began with the signing of the National Environmental Policy Act (NEPA) in 1969 by President Richard Nixon. Although a relative latecomer to the environmental protection movement, Nixon made strong pleas for more forceful public policy in this area: "[T]he 1970's absolutely must be the years when America pays its debt to the past by reclaiming the purity of its air, its waters and our living environment. It is literally now or never" (Harris 1972, p. 1).

Indeed, by the 1970s many environmental problems were in the public eye, including air, water, solid waste, marine, and noise pollution. Yet only a few states, notably California, had passed strong environmental regulatory statutes. Communities were also often unwilling or unable to tackle environmental problems. Some were victims of water- or airborne pollution originating in other jurisdictions. Other communities—under pressure from powerful industries that threatened to pick up and relocate if need be—lacked the political will to regulate. A regulatory vacuum existed at the state and local levels and federal involvement grew to fill the gap. The extensiveness of environmental problems were hard for many to believe. For instance: air pollution was a major problem in all large urban areas as well as many small towns, with an estimated 200 million tons of man-made waste being released into the air on an annual basis; water pollution had reached dangerously high levels in the nation's rivers, lakes, and estuaries; more than 1,300 communities were discharging untreated sewage directly into waterways with an additional 240,000 industrial plants generating large volumes of wastewater filled with a variety of untreated toxic pollutants; the number of solid waste disposal sites for the 4.3 billion tons of solid wastes that were being annually produced were diminishing; additionally, less than 6 percent of 12,000 land disposal sites were meeting the minimum federal standards for sanitary landfills; and marine pollution was causing at least one-fifth of the nation's commercial shellfish beds and recreation beaches and bays to close, and was dramatically altering the nation's marine ecosystem (General Accounting Office 1982, pp. 12).

An Era of Vigorous Federal Antipollution Policies

NEPA was the first comprehensive national policy response to pollution. The Act called for efforts which would "prevent or eliminate damage to the environment and biosphere and stimulate the health and welfare of man" and efforts that would "enrich the understanding of the ecological systems and natural resources important to the Nation" (NEPA, 42 U.S.C. 4321, 83 Stat. 852, Pub. L. 91–190). Previous environmental legislation had attacked only isolated components of the pollution problem. In addition, much previous legislation—relying on the states for enforcement and providing little federal guidance or technical assistance—had proved nearly impossible to implement effectively (Davies III 1970, pp. 37–58).

The Council on Environmental Quality, established by NEPA to advise the president on important environmental issues, articulated this new policy direction:

1970 marks the beginning of a new emphasis on the environment, a turning point, a year when the quality of life has become more than a phrase; environment and pollution have become everyday words; and ecology has become almost a religion to some of the young. (Council on Environmental Quality 1970, p. 2)

NEPA was the response to a remarkable groundswell of public support for environmental regulation. A 1969 National Wildlife Federation poll showed that more than eight in ten Americans were at least "somewhat concerned" about environmental deterioration (Trop and Roos 1971, p 60). In addition, polls showed that the public favored government taking a forceful role in environmental protection and opposed leaving private industry alone to police themselves. One survey asked respondents to place themselves on a scale that ranged from "government should force private industry to stop polluting" to "industries should handle pollution in their own way." In 1970, 74 percent of the respondents took a strong pro-environment position. In 1972, that percentage had increased to 80. In both years, less than 15 percent of those sampled felt that industry should be left alone to handle the problem. Events such as Earth Day (1970), Clean Air Week (first sponsored by the Izaak Walton League in 1960), and the publication of books such as Rachel Carson's *Silent Spring* which documented the dangers of unregulated use of pesticides, consolidated public opinion and sent a clear message to politicians. The public wanted immediate action on long-term policies to protect the environment and curb the dangers posed by pollution.

Where was Congress amid this public clamor? One timeworn Washington maxim explains that Congress behaves like an elephant. It is large and cumbersome, difficult to excite, and moves slowly and awkwardly. When startled, however, it can move with amazing speed. The spurt in pro-environment public sentiment and the new revelations about environmental dangers to human health and ecology startled Congress: the elephant awoke and began to move. In the decade between 1970 and 1980, Congress passed in rapid succession the Clean Air Act (1970) and its amendments (1977); the Marine Protection, Research, and Sanctuaries Act (1972); the Clean Water Act (1972) and its amendments (1977); the Federal Insecticide, Fungicide, and Rodenticide Act (1972) and its amendments (1975 and 1978); the Safe Drinking Water Act (1974) and its amendments (1977); the Resource Conservation and Recovery Act (1976) and its amendments (1980); the Toxic Substances Control Act (1976) and the Superfund legislation (1980).

To gauge the degree to which Congress had involved itself in environmental issues during these years fully we should also cite legislation that had an indirect connection with preserving the quality of the environment such as: the Coastal Zone Management Act (1972); the Fishery Conservation and Management Act (1975); the Endangered Species Act (1977); the Surface Mining Control and Reclamation Act (1977); and the Occupational Safety and Health Act (1978). Indeed, this flurry of legislation prompted the Council on Environmental Quality to conclude that, by 1980, "the United States had become the first nation in history to pass comprehensive national legislation intended to protect virtually every aspect of environmental quality" (Council on Environmental Quality 1983, p. 3).

The effectiveness and utility of this legislation, however, has been a matter of some controversy. It is difficult to measure the degree to which various pollutants exist in the environment or the extent to which pollution levels vary due to government regulatory efforts. Apparently, however, some progress had been made in reducing the levels of the six pollutants for which National Ambient Air Quality Standards (NAAQS) were established under the Clean Air Act: sulfur dioxide, total suspended particulate, carbon monoxide, nitrogen oxides, ozone, and lead. The Council on Environmental Quality reported that between 1970 and 1982 total national sulfur dioxide emissions declined by almost 25 percent, particulate emissions by 58 percent, carbon monoxide emissions by 27 percent, and volatile organic compounds (a primary contributor to ozone) by 28 percent. Total nitrogen oxide emissions increased by 12 percent, however (Council on Environmental Quality 1983, p. 3).

Governmental efforts under the Clean Water Act have also apparently been responsible for reducing much pollution. Between 1972 and 1982, suspended solids were reduced by 80 percent, oil and grease by 71 percent, dissolved solids by 52 percent, phosphates by 74 percent, and heavy metals by 78 percent. More general ecological indicators pointed in the same direction: the overall quality of the Great Lakes had improved; sport fishing had returned to the Connecticut and Penobscot rivers, and some estuaries (channels and creeks) were returning to their former levels of biological activity (Council on Environmental Quality 1983, p. 4).

While few challenge the claim that governmental programs have greatly improved the quality of the nation's environment, many question whether this cleanup could have been achieved in a more cost-efficient manner. Critics have charged that environmental programs have proven to be difficult to enforce; have imposed undue financial burdens on manufacturers; and have imposed greater-than-necessary costs to achieve their desired end. Concern over the nation's trade deficit in the late 1970s afforded U.S. manufacturers a new hearing for their complaints that burdensome environmental laws adversely affected their ability to compete with foreign goods. Even dispassionate critics scorned existing environmental programs for their complex and cumbersome administration, their arbitrary and sometimes unattainable mandate deadlines; and their inflexibility in approaching widely differing regional conditions.

REAGAN ADMINISTRATION APPROACH TO ENVIRONMENTAL POLICY

In the 1980 presidential election the Republican party and Ronald Reagan signalled a new trend by calling for environmental regulatory reform. Reagan argued that governmental regulation of the environment had been excessive and was severely hindering the U.S. economy and therefore costing Americans their jobs.

[There] was a tendency on the part of the E.P.A. to insist on unreasonable and many times untried standards imposed on industry, even at the expense of productivity, when a little more common sense and reason could achieve the same end without hurting or harming productivity in our industry and business the way we have.... Just possibly, some of those who are most active, associated with the agency in Washington and all, have gone beyond the point of just being concerned about the responsibility for seeing that the environment is protected in a responsible manner. But in reality, what they believe in is no growth. What they believe in is a return to a society in which there wouldn't be the need for the industrial concerns or more power plants and so forth. (Smith 1980, p. D14)

During the presidential campaign, Reagan was often vague about his environmental values. In many instances, he was plainly wrong in his facts and statistics. Reagan often claimed that air pollution in the United States had been "substantially controlled." This statement made in a October 9 1980 speech in Youngstown Ohio, was met with disbelief by the citizens of Los Angeles who had just entered their tenth consecutive day of very heavy smog. Reagan also often insisted that, in certain instances nature contributed more in the way of air pollution than did industry. For example, in a campaign speech in Steubenville Ohio, Reagan said:

I have flown over Mount St. Helens out on our West Coast. I'm not a scientist and I don't know the figures, but I just have a suspicion that that one little mountain out there has probably released more sulfur dioxide into the atmosphere of the world than has been released in the last 10 years of automobile driving or things of that kind that people are so concerned about. (Smith 1980, p. D14)

Reagan went on to state that "Growing and decaying vegetation in this land are responsible for 93 percent of the oxides of nitrogen. If we are totally successful and can eliminate all the manmade oxides of nitrogen, we'll still have 93 percent as much as we have in the air today" (Smith 1980, p. D14). The EPA later contradicted Reagan's statements, reporting that: first, all U.S. man-made emissions of sulfur dioxide amounted to 81,000 tons a day, while the emissions from Mount St. Helens were estimated to range from 500 to 2,000 tons a day; and second, that Reagan had confused nitrous oxide (which is harmless and is the natural product of plant respiration), with nitric oxide (which is dangerous and man-made).

Reagan's was a controversial stance. As a candidate, he was constantly challenged to defend his commitment to protecting the environment. Reagan proclaimed: "I am an environmentalist," and even pointed to his record as governor of California as proof of this claim. Yet, his environmental record somewhat contradicted the claim. As governor, Reagan had called for an ambitious environmental program to combat California's smog problems, creating a centralized Air Resources board to address the problem. Yet, he later vetoed many of the Board's policy recommendations. These included such policies as mandatory auto inspections and compliance with stricter federal emissions standards. Reagan's air pollution record led the League of Conservation Voters to conclude that "Reagan was responsible for undermining what could have been the most far-reaching air pollution program in the nation" (Mosher 1980, p. 1850).

After the election, Reagan's position on the environment was strongly supported by many of his top policy advisors, notably the newly appointed director of OMB, David Stockman. While a congressman, Stockman had been a frequent and vociferous critic of EPA policy and practice. For example, in a September 1980 "Dear Colleague" letter, Congressman Stockman criticized a chemical superfund bill that would have greatly increased the federal role in cleaning up toxic waste dumps. In a section entitled "LET'S GET OFF THE SUPER BUREAUCRACY KICK," Stockman lectured other members that:

for ten years we've been in an environmental time-warp. EPA and its minions in the press and the professional environmental lobbies have assumed an absolute monopoly right to flood the American economy with regulations, litigation and compliance costs that are out of proportion to any environmental problem real and imagined that has reached the congressional calender.

Its [sic] time to get off this super bureaucracy kick unless you really believe that the present drastic deterioration of our economy, productivity, international competitiveness, and living standards will soon miraculously fade away.

It won't happen so long as we keep writing blank checks that authorize hotshot junior lawyers and zealots enscounced in the EPA to bleed American industry of scarce funds needed for investment, modernization, and job creation. (Burford and Greenya 1986, p. 29)

An advisory memorandum written by Stockman with the help of Congressman Jack Kemp entitled "Avoiding a GOP Economic Dunkirk" and distributed to the president-elect and his top advisors provides another example of Stockman's strong advocacy of environmental regulatory relief. Here, the president-elect is warned of an impending "regulatory time bomb" with environmental regulations characterized as "multibillion dollar overkill" (Greider 1982, pp. 137–159).

Certain politically conservative analysts and industry groups that had been highly critical of EPA for many years, also had the ear of the incoming president. Over the years, these groups had developed a tailor-made deregulation policy waiting for a sympathetic administration. The most vocal critic of the EPA was The Heritage Foundation, which, in a report entitled *Mandate For Leadership* (Heatherly 1981), outlined 19 administrative options and 15 legislative options to correct the "principal deficiencies" of existing policies (Cordia 1981, pp. 970–971).

Beyond favoring fewer environmental regulations and an improvement in EPA management, Reagan officials advocated replacing traditional standards and enforcement methods of regulation—so-called "command and control" methods—with a regulatory system utilizing economic/market incentives to encourage environmentally appropriate corporate behavior. The shortcomings of the command and control approach to environmental regulation had been extensively documented in the academic literature as—in the words of one set of researchers— "cumbersome, corruptible, and arbitrary and capricious in its impact" (Kneese and Schultze 1975; see also Tietenberg 1985). The fact that industrial plants may contain several pollutant discharge points, each having its own emission standard, greatly complicates the regulator's task of predicting the costs and benefits of various measures. For example, as Kneese and Schultz point out, "There are up to 55,000 major sources of industrial water pollution alone. A regulatory agency cannot know the costs, the technological opportunities, the alternative raw materials, and the kinds of products available" (Kneese and Schultze 1975, p. 88). Economists have argued that use of market-like regulatory approaches such as effluent taxes and pollution permits would produce more cost-efficient results than command and control approaches.

There had been some earlier movement toward the adoption of this market approach to regulation. Under the Ford administration, the notion of "offsets" was introduced to allow new plants locating in nonattainment areas to begin operation if they secured more emissions reductions from existing sources than they would add. Similarly, the Carter administration encouraged "emissions trading," sometimes referred to as the "bubble" concept, which allows polluters to treat their emissions as if they were enclosed in a dome. Thus, polluters can trade reduced control on some sources for extra compensating reductions on other sources. For example, DuPont's Chambers Work facility in New Jersey faced state mandates requiring 85 percent reductions in emissions from each of 119 smokestacks, vents and valves. By utilizing the bubble policy, Dupont substituted 99 percent control on seven major plant smokestacks. As a result, not only was there faster compliance, but an estimated 2,300 tons less pollution, $12 million in capital savings, and a $2 million annual savings on operation and maintenance costs (Domenici 1982, p. 20). Other incentive-based reforms have included: "netting," which exempts plants that want to modernize or expand from burdensome new source reviews, as long as other reductions ensure that "net" plant-wide emissions do not increase; and "emission banking," which gives firms credit if they reduce emissions more than is legally required. These emission credits can be stored for future use or sold to other firms who are in need of an offset.

There has been a longstanding debate between environmentalists and industry over the effectiveness of such incentive-based reforms. On the political level in 1981, however, was a growing bipartisan support for such incentives, as politicians sought to find a balance between the demands of environmentalists and the apparent distress of industries (NCAQ 1981). Because of this growing political support, market-based incentives seemed to hold great promise as a means through which the Reagan administration might further its regulatory relief goals.

REGULATORY RELIEF THROUGH LEGISLATIVE STRATEGIES

At the outset of Reagan's presidency, it was clear that the environmental reforms favored by the Administration were of such a sweeping nature that congressional action would be needed to accomplish them. As the president noted, "Existing regulatory statutes too often prevent effective regulatory decisions. Many of the statutes are conflicting, overlapping, or inconsistent. Some force agencies to issue regulations while giving them little discretion to take into account changing conditions or new information" (Presidential Task Force on Regulatory Relief 1982, p. iv).

Reagan's call for statutory environmental changes were echoed by industry representatives. Industry wanted regulatory changes, but also needed a relatively stable policy environment. Many industries had to make large capital investments in pollution control equipment, even to design and construct plants with environmental policy in mind. Thus, having regulations fixed in statute seemed highly preferable to being subject to the changeable interpretations of EPA administrators. We have more thoroughly discussed such reasoning on the part of industry in the chapters on the history of regulation and intergovernmental relations.

There were many other reasons for the president to be optimistic that he would receive the congressional support he needed to pass his new environmental legislation. The times seemed precipitous. Many important pieces of environmental legislation initially passed in the 1970s would come up for renewal during the early years of his presidency, such as the Clean Air Act (funding expired in 1981), the Clean Water Act (1982), the Ocean Dumping Act (1982) and the Safe Drinking Water Act (1982). This impending legislation promised to supply a likely vehicle through which the president might put his personal stamp on environmental policy for years to come.

Several recent institutional changes within Congress seemingly brightened prospects for regulatory reform. The Democratically controlled Senate—which had done much to spark the avalanche of environmental protection legislation and had carefully overseen its subsequent administration—was now in Republican hands. In the House of Representatives 22 incumbent Democrats lost their seats, (many of whom had been fiercely pro-environment northern and eastern liberals) and many of the legislators responsible for formulating the landmark environmental legislation of the 1970s had recently retired. In addition, congressmen sympathetic to environmental regulatory reform had begun to move into leadership positions. For instance, in 1981, Congressman John Dingel (D-MI), an outspoken critic of current environmental policy, became chairman of the house Energy and Commerce Committee which oversaw Clean Air, Safe Drinking Water, Solid Waste Disposal, Superfund, and Toxic Substance Control matters. In particular, Dingell favored reducing emission standards for new automobiles as a means of making Detroit more competitive with foreign manufacturers. In addition, in 1981, Senator Jesse Helms (R-NC), became chairman of the Agriculture, Nutrition and Forestry Committee, which was responsible for pesticide legislation oversight. Helms favored a weakening of the Federal Insecticide, Fungicide and Rodenticide Act (FIFRA), over which his committee had jurisdiction.

In spite of these pro-reform factors, however, Congress proved resistant to sweeping regulatory reform in the environmental area. Environmentalists used the highly fragmented and decentralized committee system to bottle-up reform legislation throughout Reagan's presidency. The House effectively countered the administration on numerous key environmental issues, such as the size of EPA's budget cuts, EPA's failure to meet statutory deadlines, and evidence of undue industry and OMB influence in EPA's rule-making activities. As one astute observer of the congressional scene noted, "In general, Congress wants to give EPA more money than the Reagan Administration wants to spend to accomplish things that the Administration considers unnecessary or impossible within a time schedule that EPA often believes to be unrealistic" (Stanfield 1986a, p. 393).

The administration also lacked popular support for the sweeping legislative changes they sought. For example, a September 1981 CBS News/New York *Times* poll sought to measure public support for either relaxing environmental laws so that economic growth could be achieved or for maintaining present environmental laws "in order to preserve the environment for future generations." By an overwhelming margin (73 percent to 23 percent), respondents favored maintaining present environmental laws (CBS News/New York *Times* 1981, p. 207). In fact, support for tough environmental laws actually increased during the first few years of the Reagan presidency. A majority of people (52 percent) in a 1981 national survey agreed with the following statement: "Protecting the environment is so important that requirements and standards cannot be too high, and continuing environmental improvements must be made REGARDLESS of cost" (original emphasis). By 1983, the proportion of those agreeing had substantially increased to 63 percent (CBS News/New York *Times* 1981, p. 205; CBS News/New York *Times* 1983, p. 71).

At the same time, the public remained highly skeptical of the administration's capacity to manage environmental policy. This skepticism is reflected in the fact that few individuals had much faith in EPA's ability to clean up the environment. When asked whether they had confidence in the EPA under the Reagan administration to handle problems of toxic and hazardous waste only 8 percent had a "great deal" of confidence, while 42 percent had "hardly any." In addition, when the same individuals were asked whether they felt officials in the Reagan administration were biased in favor of industries that pollute, 67 percent replied in the affirmative (CBS News/New York *Times* 1983: 72). Public confidence in the capacity of the Reagan administration to produce real regulatory reform in the environmental area was further weakened by the erupting of the scandals surrounding EPA. Charges of agency mismanagement and violations of the law developed after congressional investigations into EPA's management of the $1.6 billion toxic waste cleanup program, commonly referred to as "Superfund," accused EPA officials of political manipulation of the program, "sweetheart" deals, conflicts of interest, perjury, and the destruction of agency documents. As a direct result of these investigations, EPA Administrator Anne Burford and 20 other top EPA aides either were forced to resign or were fired. This rapid turnover of top officials at EPA was further damaging to the administration's credibility.

A final problem that statutory environmental regulatory reform faced was that—rhetoric aside—it was not a high priority item on the president's agenda. For example although in a letter to Majority Leader Howard Baker, Reagan claimed amending the Clean Air Act would be "essential" to the success of his overall economic recovery program, the White House did not aggressively push for these amendments. Efforts to scale back auto emission standards supply a good example of this contradictory dynamic.

Reagan officials made a strong start in this area, having developed a regulatory relief plan for the automotive industry that was far more comprehensive than anything previously attempted. In their "Avoiding an Economic Dunkirk" memo, Stockman and Kemp outlined five separate emission standard changes, such as simplifying auto emissions certification and testing and granting carbon monoxide waivers for the 1982 model year, that all-totaled would save industry over $600 million (Greider 1982, p. 157). The Heritage Foundation called for radical revisions in EPA's structure and function to provide regulatory relief to the auto industry. In addition, both the Bush Regulatory Reform Task Force and a cabinet-level automotive task force chaired by Transportation Secretary Drew Lewis identified various regulatory actions that could provide substantial cost savings to the automobile industry (Eads and Fix 1984b). Eventually, the Bush Task Force helped to develop an auto relief package that aimed at revising 34 environmental and safety rules. Estimated savings to the industry was placed at an annual $1.4 billion. While auto manufacturers were quite pleased with the changes taking place at EPA, as a result of the administrative strategies (discussed in the following section) they were apprehensive about the permanency of these changes. The industry continued to push for the long-term regulatory relief they felt could come only from statutory changes in the Clean Air Act. Given that the Clean Air Act was due for reauthorization in 1981, the timing couldn't have been better. Automobile manufacturers had compiled a comprehensive wish list of statutory reforms, including: emissions averaging for automobiles; abolishment of the federal vehicle certification program (to be replaced by statistical sampling of vehicles); and a rollback of emission standards.

But such proposals found generally weak support both in Congress and among the general public. In the House of Representatives, the debate over the Clean Air Act often pitted congressmen whose districts were highly dependent on the auto industry, against congressmen who had become closely allied with environmental groups. The House Energy and Commerce Committee was deeply divided over whether the Clean Air Act should be amended, and in what direction. Congressman Dingell, who chaired the full committee, strongly favored easing federal auto emission standards. His chief opponent was fellow Democrat, Congressman Henry Waxman (D-CA) chairman of the Subcommittee on Health and the Environment, who favored extending current provisions, arguing that rewriting the Act would severely weaken it. A compromise could not be reached; it proved impossible to reconcile the positions taken by industry, environmentalists, and various regional interests.

On the Senate side, the Public Works Committee led by Senator Robert Stafford (R-VT) experienced similar difficulties in fashioning a compromise Clean Air bill. Stafford—a long-time champion of the environment—wanted to "fine-tune" the Clean Air Act. He believed that the way to address many of the complaints about the Clean Air Act was by modifying regulations, not changing the legislation (Environment Reporter 1982a, p. 49). While the Committee eventually reported a reform bill in 1984 by a healthy 16–2 margin, the bill ran into trouble on the Senate floor, where it was greeted with hostility and protests—both from members who thought the bill went too far in relaxing Clean Air requirements and from members who felt the bill did not go far enough.

Throughout these protracted congressional attempts to reform the Clean Air Act, the administration stood by doing little to help. Indeed, some interventions were more harmful than helpful. For example, in 1983 EPA attempted to push legislators into changing the provisions in the Clean Air Act by making veiled threats to states that had failed to meet current deadlines on carbon monoxide and ozone standards. If current standards were not relaxed, warned EPA, the agency might be forced to ban new source construction or to cut off federal grants for highways and clean air programs. But, rather than allowing itself to be pressured into amending the Clean Air Act, Congress simply prevented the imposition of sanctions by imposing a one-year moratorium on such actions via an amendment to a fiscal 1984 appropriations bill.

Why didn't the administration take aggressive action to pass a revised Clean Air Act, if, as the president had said, it was "essential" to his economic recovery program? As explained earlier, the answer is apparently that the administration simply had bigger fish to fry. While administration leaders believed that wholesale environmental reform would benefit the economy, they also felt that its impact would be small compared with the potential impacts of Reagan's proposed tax and budgetary reforms. Indeed, Reagan's advisors had taken a warning from the legislative failures of the Carter administration: a broad-based legislative agenda that contained sweeping economic and social policy changes could fragment presidential power and make it all the more difficult to mobilize majority coalitions. Reagan advisors were convinced that, with fewer initiatives on the legislative agenda, the president would be able to concentrate his energies and successfully build the necessary congressional majorities for the highest priority concerns of the administration. As Max Friedersdorf, who headed the Reagan White House liaison office put it, "The President was determined not to clutter up the landscape with extraneous legislation" (Wayne 1982, p. 56). Even when the administration lobbied hard for statutory changes on environmental regulation, it never pulled out all the stops.

For all these reasons, the Reagan administration was never able to master the fragmented congressional process involved with environmental statutory reform. Success would have required strong executive leadership, popular support, and key allies among environmental committee chairmen. Instead, what we find is weak executive leadership, virtually no popular support, and few congressmen who are willing to fight for environmental reform. As a result, after six years in office the president cannot point to a single congressional environmental victory. Indeed, several reauthorized environmental statutes—far from offering regulatory relief to concerned industries—actually contained more stringent provisions than the old legislation. The Resource Conservation and Recovery Act, reauthorized in 1984, *tightened* federal controls over how industries handled hazardous chemical wastes, extending the coverage of the legislation to include tens of thousands of small businesses, from gasoline stations to dry cleaners. The Safe Drinking Water Act (SDWA), reauthorized in 1986, increased the number of contaminants that EPA had to regulate from about two dozen to 83. In fact, embodied in the safe water legislation we see evidence of congressional efforts to override executive control and strictly limit administrative discretion in environmental affairs. For example, the Act mandates that EPA meets a structured implementation schedule. As a high-ranking staff member from the Senate Environment and Public Works committee we interviewed commented,

We used to write simple bills that gave a great deal of regulatory discretion to the agency. Now we write 300 page bills. That's the response to Reagan management efforts. It wasn't an accident that the side-by-side of superfund was 700 pages long. We don't trust the agencies to write the regulations because all the agency does these days is just publish the statute in the *Federal Register*. So what we are doing is prescribing mandatory duties for agency heads. For example, in the SDWA we listed 83 contaminants by name and the date that EPA had to issue standards.

REGULATORY RELIEF THROUGH THE MANAGEMENT STRATEGY

The focus of this study is what we have termed the management strategy adopted by the Reagan administration to achieve regulatory reform. The congressional frustrations that the Reagan administration experienced in the environmental policy area make it clear why in contrast the management strategy appeared to offer great potential for regulatory relief. The next sections discuss how the administration applied the various components of the management strategy in the environmental regulatory area.

Administrative strategies seemed to offer the prospect of immediate regulatory relief from environmental laws that had proven to be particularly burdensome on industry. The advice the Heritage Foundation gave on this point was direct and succinct: "Proper administrative direction [in Environmental Protection] and not legislative remedy is an immediate need" (Cordia 1981, p. 970). Environmental policy seemed particularly suited to this approach, since the underlying statutes put tremendous amounts of discretion in the hands of agency officials. Many of the provisions of environmental statutes were set out in broad terms, requiring interpretation. Also, administrators were given wide latitude in setting technical standards, compliance deadlines, and defining enforcement procedures (Rosenbaum 1977, pp. 137–39).

Further, administrative reform could be put in place very swiftly and with little expenditure of political capital. Progress on regulatory relief through administrative means would please Reagan's conservative constituency, and might have some immediate impact on economic productivity. The savings from cutting agency regulatory efforts might offset the anticipated loss in federal revenue resulting from the large tax cuts underway. Finally, it was hoped that progress through administrative means would ultimately advance the cause of legislative change by establishing a "record of success" (Demuth 1982, p. 18). As outlined by one of the administration's chief architects of this strategy,

The history of deregulation is that major administrative reform is a necessary prerequisite to statutory reform. Before Congress itself will act, external changes are required to dislodge accumulated interests in the status quo and to assure the doubtful of the economy's ability to continue functioning in the absence of federal controls.... If we are to achieve major statutory reform in the last two years of President's Reagan's first term, we must first build a solid foundation of administrative deregulation in 1982. (Demuth 1982, p. 18)

Acting upon this rationale, the administration designed an environmental regulatory relief program that consisted of four components: (1) deep budget and personnel reductions in selected program areas and activities; (2) a redefinition of federal/state environmental roles and responsibilities; (3) the introduction of a market-based system of regulation; and (4) the institution of a regulatory review process designed to slow the growth in new federal regulations.

Budget Reductions and Their Impacts

Reagan's first EPA administrator Anne Burford took office with the conviction that the agency's budget could be used as an effective weapon in changing the agency's regulatory mission: "Based on my legislative experience I came to the EPA believing that the budget was the tool of management, and through it one controlled policy direction" (Burford and Greenya 1986, p. 122). The administration's strategy here was quite simple and direct. If deep enough cuts could be made in selected areas of EPA's budget, the regulatory apparatus would have to slow down. An agency staff reduced in size would be relatively limited in its ability to churn out regulations and could conduct fewer investigations and prosecutions. Strategic cuts in critical regulatory activities such as enforcement and research, would de facto result in reduced government oversight of industry. A smaller research staff would make the agency a less vigorous watchdog concerning the identification of new putative environmental dangers.

Given this management philosophy—combined with the vigorously expressed anti-environment attitudes of top White House and OMB

Table 5.1
Environmental Protection Agency Actual Budget Allocations for Selected Programs (in millions)

Program Area	1980	1981	1982	1983	1984	1985	Real Change (in percent) 80–85*
Air	248	245	218	215	223	235	− 21
Water quality	334	334	235	206	218	252	− 37
Drinking water	75	83	82	76	77	86	− 4
Hazardous waste	96	150	107	120	129	192	+ 68
Pesticides	70	69	54	54	57	67	− 20
Radiation	17	13	11	10	11	13	− 36
Noise	13	13	2	0	0	0	− 100
Toxic substances	88	103	75	68	119	85	− 19
Hazardous substance trust fund	—	75	190	210	460	620	N/A
Total EPA budget authority	4,669	3,033	3,676	3,689	4,067	4,368	− 21

*Based on a deflator of .837.
Source: Congressional Budget Office, 1986.

staff—it is not surprising that the initial budget cuts at EPA were so extreme. EPA's overall fiscal year 1983 operating budget was down 26 percent from the fiscal year 1980 level. The cuts, moreover, were quite selective in their impact. The program areas with the steepest cuts were water quality (down 37 percent between 1980 and 1986 in inflation adjusted terms), radiation (down 36 percent) and clean air (down 21 percent). (See Table 5.1.) Only the toxic waste program saw budget gains—not surprising since the program was only created by the passage of RCRA in 1977. Most of the dramatic cuts at EPA occurred under the stewardship of Anne Burford. Between 1981 and 1983, program areas such as water quality received a 42 percent budget reduction, hazardous waste 25 percent, and toxic substances 38 percent (based on a deflator of .94 for 1983). This was regulatory ventilation with a vengeance. Since Burford's departure, however, due to the adverse publicity that attended many of these cuts, as well as promises made to persuade William Ruckelshaus to return as EPA chief, many of these drastic cuts have been at least partially restored. Even so, EPA's current budget remains far below its pre-Reagan level.

The process of how these deep budget cuts came about, in itself is revealing of how executive authority was directed. Despite an overall unanimity among Reagan officials that EPA's budget had to be cut, there was little consensus on just how severe these cuts should be. In particular, several well publicized conflicts emerged between Burford and Stockman over EPA's budget. Consistently, OMB argued for deeper cuts in the agency's budget and staff. Burford strongly resisted OMB's proposed cuts. She argued that the proposed OMB budget

puts in disarray a number of major redirections I have proposed for this Agency. Those changes were based on rational decisions.... They were manageable. They were environmentally defensible. In many places where the OMB passback goes further it smacks of a bottom line in search of a reason. (House, Committee on Government Operations 1981, p. 55)

Indeed, after leaving office, Burford argued that OMB's budgetary decisions went far beyond their authority, and were blatant attempts to impose policy on the agency. As she relates,

We sent our reconstructed budget back to OMB, and it came back in *pieces*. It wasn't cut, it was shredded. And we had been using David Stockman's own revised 'bottom line' figure!
They hadn't just lowered the figures, they had made programmatic decisions! They had eliminated offices here, added others there, cut six and a half people in one obscure office, but added ten someplace else, and axed dollar amounts all over the lot. Their alterations represented management and policy decisions, not budgetary decisions. (Burford and Greenya 1986, p. 77)

Indeed, there seemed to be little analytical rationale behind some of these budget cuts. Few arguments or supporting evidence were advanced justifying such sharp reductions. Not only was this poor budget making, it proved to be disastrous politics. Shocked pro-environment congressmen resisted vigorously. Soon after information about the fiscal year 1983 budget began to leak out, four congressional hearings were called to air concerns arising out of EPA budget and enforcement policy.

The political rhetoric became quite heated. One Democratic congressmen, Toby Moffett, chairman of the House Subcommittee on Environment, Energy, and Natural Resources, charged that Burford had "ripped the heart out of the agency in her short term there." He charged that these budgetary actions were part of the administration's "concerted effort to return to the dark ages of environmental protection where the Earth, the sky, and the water were viewed as the dumping grounds for toxic wastes and poisons" (House, Committee on Government Operations 1981, p. 55, 1).

Nor were negative reactions to the EPA budget cuts confined to the Democratic side of the aisle and their allies among the environmental groups. Many Republicans and even some industry representatives felt that these cuts had gone too far. Industry representatives feared that a greatly reduced budget would prevent EPA from issuing permits efficiently. They also doubted the environmental expertise and management experience of recent EPA appointees and their ability to make selective budget cuts wisely, in other words, to cut fat and not muscle (Environment Reporter 1982b, p. 1273). Indeed, in the disputes between Burford and OMB over the extent of the proposed EPA budget cuts, industry sided with EPA, and lobbied the White House to get some cuts reinstated (Environment Reporter 1982b, p. 1274).

Personnel reductions parallel the budget cuts at EPA. The EPA work force fell 18 percent from 12,838 in FY 1981 to 10,475 in FY 1983. Indeed, in just the first three months of FY 1982, nearly 600 employees left the agency (Environment Reporter 1982b, p. 1272). Uncertainty over the eventual extent of layoffs through possible reductions in force (RIFs) caused agency morale to plummet during Burford's stewardship. At one point, the situation at EPA had deteriorated to the point where even the regulated interests were calling for management improvement. Under a headline that read "We Need a Credible EPA" the chemical industry noted that

Normally, the sight of a regulatory agency in turmoil is not calculated to bring tears to industry's eyes. But an ineffective EPA is not what the chemical industry needs.... The existence of turmoil, by itself, is no sure guide; upset, even prolonged upset, is inevitable when a new team tries to set a radically new direction for a mammoth organization. But Gorsuch's style, unless she can temper it may defeat her. Firm management at the top is good. A management attitude that turns off hundreds of competent and dedicated professionals and EPA has them is not good. (Chemical Week 1981, p. 3)

In addition to the problem of low morale, several other personnel problems hampered EPA's performance. There were long delays in getting qualified individuals to fill key agency positions. For instance, although Burford had taken office in May 1981, it took nearly nine months before positions such as the assistant administrators for water, for solid waste and emergency response, for research and development, and for policy and resource management were filled. Further, many Reagan appointees brought with them to EPA the attitude that the career bureaucracy could not be trusted. As one EPA employee lamented,

There's a lack of appreciation for what career staff can do. I think they would find people are more willing to help them accomplish what they want. There is an assumption that these people are environmentalists and are not to be trusted, which is not necessarily true. (Environment Reporter 1982b, p. 1272)

This type of mistrust was epitomized by the 1983 admission of a former EPA official that he had prepared "pro and con lists," identifying and

classifying EPA employees as being either "unacceptable to this Administration" or "supportive of the new Administration if the new Administration is for nuclear power, business and conservative interests." These
lists, which totaled 125 pages in length, assessed current staff members,
EPA consultants, and prospective new hires. This activity was defended
by EPA spokespersons as "the kind of work that's essential to any new
Administration" and that it was simply one aspect of the Reagan transition teams "educational effort" (Taylor 1983, p. B–14). Despite such
rationalizations, there were many who felt that EPA had used these lists
as a basis for decisions to hire, dismiss, or move personnel within the
agency on primarily ideological grounds. A number of appointments
and dismissals in EPA's research and development seemed particularly
driven by considerations of ideology rather than competency (Marshall
1983, p. 1303). As one senior EPA scientist commented,

We need an EPA that is impartial. But the Reaganites are not trying to improve
the agency's science. Instead of trying to solve the problems they inherited, they
are taking the easy way out by abolishing many of our programs. How can you
regulate properly without doing the monitoring for health effects? Our workload
is increasing, not decreasing, and we need more competent people, not somebody
else's rejects. It just breaks your heart to see what's happening. (Mosher 1982,
p. 637)

Reducing Federal Enforcement Efforts

Agency enforcement activities are what give the regulatory process
teeth. Agency enforcement staff monitor compliance with federal regulations and can apply legal action if necessary. One of the main functions of an enforcement program, however, is to encourage voluntary
compliance on the part of the regulated industry. Without voluntary
compliance the level of resources needed to ensure that all industries
were actually obeying the law would be prohibitive. Generally, industry
voluntary compliance is heightened when: the rules and standards for
compliance are clear; there is a high probability that failure to comply
will be detected; and significant penalties exist for noncompliance. Voluntary compliance with the law suffers when polluters perceive that
environmental standards are not being detected or that instances of
noncompliance that are detected are not vigorously prosecuted.

Enforcement activities have traditionally been hindered by a lack of
resources on the federal, state, and local levels. But the regulatory relief
priorities of the Reagan administration overrode such considerations
and dictated the reduction of the federal enforcement role through a
combination of budget cuts, agency reorganization, and a change in
enforcement philosophy. Thus, budget reductions in the enforcement

Table 5.2
**Major Activity Funding Levels for Selected Environmental Protection
Agency Programs, 1980–85**

| Function | Budget Levels (in millions of 1983 dollars) | | | | | | Change (in percent) |
	1980	1981	1982	1983	1984	1985	1980–85
Research and development	223	191	193	152	137	140	−37
Enforcement	85	87	73	52	58	63	−26
Abatement and control	727	621	456	411	414	406	−44
Total	1035	900	721	615	608	609	−41

Notes: Data through 1983 reflect actual obligations; 1984 and 1985 data reflect budget
    authority. Details may not add to totals due to rounding.
Source: Congressional Budget Office, April 1984.

division at EPA were particularly steep. As Table 5.2 indicates, between
1980 and 1983, Burford reduced the enforcement budget by 39 percent.
Since her departure, some of these cuts have been restored, but by 1985,
the enforcement budget was still 26 percent below its 1980 funding level.
A 35 percent reduction in enforcement personnel between 1981 and
1984 accompanied these budget declines.

Administrative reorganizations also apparently played some strategic
role in redirecting the operations of EPA. Burford carried out several
reorganizations of the enforcement division. The first reorganization,
in July 1981, abolished the assistant administrator-level Office of Enforcement and combined it with the General Counsel's Office to create
the Office of Enforcement and Legal Counsel. This change was severely
criticized by environmental interest groups, who viewed it as a deliberate
ploy to downgrade enforcement activities. As Burford later explained,
this move had devastating consequences on the morale of enforcement
personnel:

First of all, a number of Enforcement division lawyers were unhappy with the
switch because they were used to a degree of autonomy (and, yes, power) under
the old arrangement, and did not take kindly to being bossed by the top legal
officer—and they carried that attitude into their new offices. A few of them were
actually disruptive. Second, I had a number of EPA employees, lawyers and
nonlawyer alike, who simply believe what they read in the newspapers and
thought they no longer had to be very concerned about enforcement....Clearly
there was the normal disruption that goes along with any big change in an
organization, and there were malcontents who fought the change, and finally

there were those on the inside who thought they'd been given a signal by the new Administration to go slow on enforcement, if not to disregard it entirely. (Burford and Greenya 1986, p. 91)

Not surprisingly the number of cases the enforcement division referred to the Justice Department for prosecution dropped dramatically, from 283 in 1980 to 81 in 1981, a 71 percent reduction (Environment Report 1982, p. 1273). EPA also began to drop proceedings on cases that had already been filed. According to one Democratic congressman, EPA dropped 43 such cases in the first six months of Burford's tenure (House, Committee on Government Operations 1981, p. 45).

Fundamental changes were also made in their environmental enforcement philosophy. The hazardous waste and Superfund programs were given priority over air and water pollution programs. The official rationale was that air and water programs were older and therefore many of the significant violators were already under consent decrees (Environment Reporter 1982, p. 1273). This turns out to be a dubious claim, however. For example, one report prepared by the General Accounting Office examined the degree to which effluent guidelines established under the Clean Water Act were being met. After randomly auditing 242 municipal waste treatment plants, GAO found that 211 (87 percent) had violated the terms of the effluent discharge permits for at least one of the 12 months for which the plants were monitored (GAO 1980). Additional enforcement activity in this and other areas were clearly still needed.

A deeper change in enforcement philosophy involved the handling of those industries found violating the law. EPA took a jawboning approach, trying informal negotiations with violators rather than threatening them immediately with stiff fines and prosecution. Environmentalists charged that this approach to enforcement would amount to nothing more than a "letter writing campaign" doomed to prove ineffective. They argued that if industry perceived that EPA had lost the will to litigate, voluntary compliance would suffer. Clearly, the approach taken by EPA represented a major change from traditional enforcement philosophy—as enunciated by Nixon's Secretary of the Interior, Walter J. Hickel, who claimed that the only way to deal with pollution violators was: "You've got to hit them with a two-by-four to make them believe you" (Rosenbaum 1977, p. 129).

This approach also opened EPA to the charge that back room deals were being struck with industry. For example, eyebrows were raised over the treatment of the Thriftway Company, a small New Mexico oil refinery. Under the lead phasedown program, small refineries were allowed an average lead content of 2.65 grams per gallon in the gasoline they manufacture. In November 1981, Thriftway applied to EPA for a waiver or suspension of the lead limit, only to be told by EPA's Mobile Source Enforcement staff that no such easing of enforcement would be possible. Just one month later, however, Thriftway representatives privately met with Burford and other top EPA officials. At this meeting Burford expressed her commitment to regulatory relief, and noted that lead phasedown regulation review was one EPA's high priority items, that she hoped that the regulations would be abolished in 1982, and that EPA would not be committing resources to enforce regulations that it intended to abolish. In essence then, Burford informed Thriftway officials that EPA would not enforce the lead phasedown regulations against them (House, Committee on Government Operations 1982, pp. 71–49).

In summary, administrative enforcement actions clearly played an important part in EPA's regulatory relief effort. Through a combination of budget and personnel reductions, reorganizations that negatively affected staff morale, and a clear liberalization in enforcement philosophy, EPA administrators left the agency in a weakened position to enforce the law.

Cuts Made in the Pursuit of "Good Science"

Scientific inquiry is inextricably linked with environmental policy-making. Policy decisions concerning which pollutants to regulate, how to regulate them, and the timetables of imposing regulatory standards depend on information supplied by the scientific community concerning the risks attending various pollution levels and the costs and benefits of various policy options. From its earliest days, however, EPA's scientific research has been routinely criticized by Congress, environmentalists, industry, and the National Academy of Sciences. Charges have been made that EPA manipulates data, fails to adhere to standards of quality control, employs improper validation methods, and carries out inadequate cross-checking of data (Office of Technology Assessment 1976; National Academy of Sciences 1977; EPA 1979; GAO 1979; GAO 1980). In particular, industry and conservative groups had argued that improper analysis at EPA had led to the adoption of unreasonable and noncost-effective regulatory standards.

Immediately upon taking office, Reagan officials announced that one of their primary objectives would be to "improve the quality of the scientific basis underlying the regulatory decision-making process" (Congressional Quarterly 1982, p. 1829) In practice, however, the Reagan administration sharply cut funds for research and development at EPA. While the budget for research and development activities grew by 80 percent in real terms during the Carter administration, it has declined by 37 percent under the Reagan administration (1980–1985). (See Table 5–2.) These research cuts were selective, however. Almost all of these cuts, 98 percent, were made in long-term basic research conducted outside of the agency, primarily by universities and private sector institutions, focusing on long-term issues such as the basic nature of pollution, its sources, effects, and possible controls. The budget for internal EPA scientific research, in contrast, has risen by 60 percent since 1980. These internal research efforts tend to be geared towards translating present scientific information into upcoming standards.

It seems highly questionable that these research cuts were really intended to improve the scientific base of decision making at EPA. For one thing, the outside research conducted for EPA has generally produced far more credible products than EPA's own internal research. Further, in 1981 the National Council on Air Quality (NCAQ) specifically recommended that EPA should strengthen long-term, anticipatory, and basic environmental research—the very type of research that is generally conducted by outside groups (NCAQ: 56). Far from following these NCAQ recommendations, EPA officials took policy actions that practically eliminated such outside research activities. Agency officials steadfastly argued that increased in-house research was needed to develop the environmental standards mandated by law properly. As an EPA research staff member explained,

There is a narrowing of focus to conduct research for identified needs in support of regulations. The shift is being motivated by good management that is opposed to the pursuit of something for its own sake. Our job is to determine what the environmental standards should be and then enforce them. (Mosher 1982, p. 638)

An alternative explanation for these policy actions is that by reducing outside research funds, new environmental dangers are less likely to be discovered and scientifically documented, thus reducing the number of new regulations coming out of EPA in the future. Greater reliance on internal research tends to narrowly focus agency concerns on existing standards. It favors an orientation toward the status quo of regulating known pollutants rather than toward emerging environmental dangers.

Another environmental research program that has been adversely effected by Reagan administration budget cuts is that of the Council on Environmental Quality. Established in 1970 under NEPA, and located within the Executive Office of the president, the Council was empowered not only to advise the president of environmental matters but also to "conduct investigations, studies, surveys, research, and analyses relating to ecological systems and environmental quality" (NEPA 1969). In 1981, Reagan reduced Council staff by 69 percent (from 49 to 15 people) and cut the budget in half. Environmental groups responded with outrage. These cuts in the Council on Environmental Quality coupled with the changes taking place in EPA's research division, seemed to be clear evidence that the Reagan administration was wiping out the nation's environmental research capacity as a shortcut to regulatory relief. As the Conservation Foundation argued,

Because of the budget cuts the information base for environmental policy, always weak, is likely to be even weaker in the future. We will be less able to sort out important problems from unimportant ones, less able to tell which environmental programs are working effectively and which are not. Perhaps most important the perennial dilemma of whether available information is sufficient to justify action will become more pervasive and difficult. (Mosher 1982, p. 1306)

Thus, while the Reagan rhetoric has championed the notion of "good science," in practice, the White House has done little to promote it. Instead, the administration has apparently used research budget cuts as a means of reducing the number of items on the nation's policy agenda. In so doing, it has moved EPA from its once progressive research stance to one that is decidedly more oriented towards the status quo.

Slowing the Regulatory Process: The Impact of Executive Order 12291

Executive Order 12291, which as we have seen was the centerpiece for the Reagan regulatory relief program, was applied particularly forcefully in environmental programs. Critics claim that in the environmental area, the regulatory review process established by EO 12291 slowed down the regulatory process, thereby establishing a de facto system of regulatory relief; and that it gave policy generalists (OMB's attorneys, economists, and policy analysts) authority over substantive issues in which they had no technical training or expertise.

Regulatory Delay: OMB's "Black Hole." The stringent review process and other administrative actions of the Reagan administration have resulted in a general slowdown in the number of new regulations that have been promulgated at EPA. During 1981, EPA carried out only 18 regulatory actions. Of these, eight involved proposals for waivers, relaxations, or extensions of environmental standards and deadlines; three sought to weaken environmental controls; five reviewed new source performance standards, and two involved financial reimbursement and reporting requirements (Environment Reporter 1982, p. 1274).

New review powers established under EO 12291 and EO 12498, have given OMB the role of EPA's gatekeeper. All proposed and final rules must first pass through OMB and receive its stamp of approval. OMB officials have vigorously contended that the slowdowns due to the new review process have not been excessive, and that, in any case, it is unfair to expect quick review of complicated rules at OMB, some of which took the agency years to formulate. As one OMB official asked, "How do they expect us to analyze a complex regulation that took them four years to develop in just a matter of days? What agencies are really complaining about is not 'delay,' but that they are required to come here in the first place."

OMB had indeed delayed the enactment of environmental regulations. Internal EPA records show that from 1981 to 1985, OMB held up 86 of 169 proposed EPA regulations an average of 91 days (Stanfield 1986a, p. 392). In addition, an internal memo written by Charles Elkins, the acting chief of EPA's air division, charged that OMB "grossly" delayed Clean Air Act regulations. Elkins noted that OMB missed its official review deadlines for 11 out of 12 air quality regulations, and that some had been awaiting OMB clearance for well over a year (Peterson 1985, p. A21).

Despite such claims by OMB officials, their record in handling environmental regulations remains highly suspect. Many of the individuals interviewed at EPA were convinced that OMB had used the review process both to block rules they disliked and to intimidate EPA staff. One EPA staffer pointed out that

OMB has mostly used its power to stall or completely kill the regulatory efforts of the agency, rather than to repeal existing regulations. They do this by sitting on packages which are sent over to E.O. 12291 review. The more difficult it is to get packages through OMB, the greater is the chilling effect on future rule development.

Such delay and intimidation tactics may be clearly seen in a revealing retrospective account by Burford concerning one experience with OMB and EO 12291 review:

About halfway through my time at EPA we found ourselves in a real crunch. We were under a court order to release some pollutant guidelines for pharmaceutical manufacturers. We had done our work, and then submitted the guidelines to OMB for review as required. The manufacturers had put on a lot of pressure for certain changes, which we had resisted, but the court deadline was swiftly approaching, and there was still no word from OMB. Finally, they told us that they weren't approved, though OMB would not put it in writing, as required by the Executive Order, which might have allowed us to buy some time from the judge. This despite the fact that an Executive Order said that if OMB held anything past a certain length of time, they had to put their objections in writing.

All Tozzi [James Tozzi, OMB deputy administrator for OIRA] would tell us was 'They're not approved.' That continued to be OMB's response right up to the last minute. It was the night before the deadline, my last day to obey the

court order and sign and release the regs. It got so dark in my office that we
could see the moon outside. Finally, John Daniel [EPA chief of staff] said, 'Anne,
I recommend you sign the regs without OMB approval.'

We called OMB to tell them what we were going to do. I called Stockman,
who had surprisingly little to say, and John called Tozzi. Tozzi didn't say anything
for a few moments after he'd heard the news. Then he said in a quiet voice,
'Daniel, I hope you people know that there's a price to pay for this, and you've
only begun to pay.' (Burford and Greenya 1986, pp. 82–83)

One not unexpected result of these delays attending the new regulatory review process has been litigation. The Environmental Defense
Fund sued EPA for failing to issue regulations that had been mandated
by the Resources Conservation and Recovery Act (RCRA) 1984 amendments. In this case, failure to issue regulations had been a direct result
of delays in OMB's review process. In a victory for environmental groups,
the District Court ruled in 1986 that OMB may not delay the issuance
of a regulation beyond the statutory deadline. Judge Thomas W. Flan-
nery of the U.S. District Court for the District of Columbia found that
"OMB's propensity to extend review" beyond statutory deadlines was
"incompatible with the will of Congress and cannot be sustained as a
valid exercise." (Environmental Defense Fund v. Thomas, Civil Action
No. 85–1747, D.D.C. January 23, 1986).

Delay in regulatory review as practiced by OMB has had two effects.
First, it has slowed the regulatory process, thereby creating de facto
regulatory relief. Second, it has created a climate that discourages EPA
officials from attempting to issue new rules. The administrative changes
made in the regulatory process under the Reagan administration have
thus put OMB in a remarkably powerful role to control EPA's regulatory
agenda. As a senior attorney with the Natural Resources Defense Council
Inc. summarized the situation, "Right now, EPA is really in thrall to the
overlordship of OMB" (Stanfield 1986a, p. 392).

Estimating Costs and Benefits. One of the most controversial aspects of
EO 12291 is that it seeks to quantify the costs and benefits of regulation
in policy areas where such quantification is highly problematic. The
technical issues involved are highly complex. As one economist notes,
developing a primary standard for any given pollutant, such as a particulate standard, requires consideration of at least six issues: (1) the
pollutant indicator; (2) the form of the standard; (3) the averaging time
for the standard; (4) the exceedance level that determines a violation;
(5) the method for determining exceedance; and (6) the actual concen-
tration level specifying the standard. Many of these factors cannot be
definitively measured. Further, only the first two of these issues are
generally taken into consideration in the cost-benefit analyses conducted
for air quality standards. (Smith 1984, p. 25).

Another difficulty with applying cost-benefit analysis to the environmental area is that empirically it is easier to quantify the associated costs of a new regulation on society (and particularly on affected industries) than it is to measure the social benefits gained. How do you quantify improvements in health, aesthetics, the preservation of different species of wildlife, and so on? Roy N. Gamse, deputy associate EPA administrator for policy and resource management, provides the following example of the complexity of these issues:

Take one of our water pollution effluent guidelines. It will be set at, say, 10 micrograms per gram of water. So you have an immediate measurement possible—the number of tons of pollution you will avoid putting in the water and a percentage reduction from the previous level.

But that's not very meaningful, in terms of measuring benefits. So you try to convert that into the standard's effect on water quality. Using models of a stream's rate of flow, you can tell when you have done enough to make the ambient water quality good, but of course, the quality will vary from the Mississippi to some small river. It costs a bundle to develop models, and often we just don't have data on individual streams.

But if you can reach the judgment that a stream's water quality now will be improved enough to sustain fish life and to permit industrial use of the water without further treatment so that a brewery might be possibly located there, you have now characterized the uses of the water and you have started to characterize the actual benefits.

If you want to quantify benefits, you must assign a dollar value to swimming or fishing. You must estimate the number of recreational visits there will be and how much they are worth. You must calculate the number of adverse health effects avoided and assign a dollar value to them.

Each step is very uncertain. The water quality models are uncertain. The projections of how many fishing trips and illnesses there will be are uncertain. The range of error is larger and larger. Is it really worth the expense entailed going to the end of the chain? Why compound error by building sand castles. (Clark 1981, p. 1385)

In addition, the question arises as to whether or not OMB personnel have the necessary scientific and technical capability to carry out such reviews competently. One political scientist, Chester Newland, believes that the Reagan administration, by placing undue emphasis on the ideological outlook of OMB personnel, has further undermined OMB's already weak capacity to undertake just such analysis.

The politicalization of OMB since the 1960s is not a matter of partisan use of reliable expert information; it is a deterioration of capacity to produce believable information due to displacement of professional expertise by political partisans at levels below the director. Reagan, with his inexperienced partisan appointees, has given a far greater unprofessional cast to OMB than Carter. (Newland 1983, p. 12)

As previously explained, the critical actor within OMB that oversees E.O. 12291 review is OIRA. Yet, few OIRA staff have formal training in policy analysis and even fewer are scientific specialists in any area, let alone the environmental area. Such staff composition raises the question of whether OIRA is qualified to assess the cost and benefit impacts of highly technical environmental regulations accurately. As George Eads, formerly a member of President Carter's Council of Economic Advisors, and chairman of the Carter Regulatory Analysis Review Group (RARG) effort points out,

Considering the stress the Reagan program lays on formal cost-benefit analysis of regulations, taken both individually and in groups, the meagerness of OIRA's analytical resources cannot help but undermine its credibility. Even more serious is the likelihood that OIRA will miss opportunities for reform. Important issues may fall between the cracks because no one knows enough about their significance to challenge them, or because none of the parties involved has the incentive to raise them or the capability of analyzing them properly. (Eads 1981, p. 22)

This weakness of analytical capacity at OIRA poses a particular problem in the environmental area, where the number of regulations is voluminous, highly technical, and scientifically complex. When queried about this problem, OMB staff openly admit that they do not have the technical competency to review environmental regulations. Rather, as one OIRA staffer we interviewed noted, their role is confined to being an "issue spotter":

We first read the regulation, and we ask does it pass the laugh test. If it does, we ask, what are you doing and why are you doing it? What are you trying to accomplish? How will this regulation do it? Do you have adequate information to do it? If they can't answer these questions we return the regulation. (Emphasis added)

The fact that many OMB staff members do not have the requisite skills and time to carry out detailed regulatory reviews, combined with the use of heavily subjective "laugh tests," in which OMB staff merely eyeball a regulation to determine if is "reasonable or absurd," suggests that what is taking place within OIRA is not adequate policy analysis. Rather it suggests the working of an ideologically directed administrative strategy aimed at a goal that might be characterized as regulatory birth control.

Given these and many other problems associated with measuring the costs and particularly the benefits of environmental standards, some scholars have questioned the adequacy of the RIAs prepared under Reagan's executive order. One review of all of the RIAs prepared in 1981 (including three prepared by EPA) found serious quality problems (Grubb et al. 1984, pp. 136–137). The level of sophistication of the studies varied widely. "[T]he best of the RIAs provide extensive information, even when they commit serious analytical errors; the worst of them are uninformative and misleading." Further, the analysis of social benefits was largely rejected. "[M]any of the RIAs prepared under EO 12291 have spent a great deal of energy estimating the reduced costs to corporations from deregulation, while virtually ignoring the reduced benefits to consumers and workers." In these reviews, costs tend to greatly overshadow benefits, putting a brake on the adoption of new regulations even when a proposed new standard might be truly cost-effective.

REFORM THROUGH ECONOMIC INCENTIVES

As discussed earlier, Reagan officials favored the use of economic/market incentives as alternatives to traditional command and control regulatory methods. Such leaning toward economic incentives fit well with the Reagan view that regulations should not seriously compromise economic growth. As the *Regulatory Program of the United States Government* states, "[When] federal regulatory activity is necessary, such activity must avoid wherever possible disrupting the efficient operation of the market. It should cause firms to internalize the costs of pollution damages, work-place hazards, transportation accidents, and other risks" (OMB 1985, p. xv).

Given this disposition, a natural area for Reagan administration regulatory reform activity would seem to have been substitution of economic devices—such as offsets, emission-trading, bubbles, and netting—for command and control methods. Such reform concepts enjoyed broad support among environmental advocates and industry officials. After six years in office, however, the administration has not been very successful at introducing these types of regulatory reforms. The main factors producing this failure seem to have been a lack of leadership on the part of EPA officials, adverse court decisions, and bureaucratic infighting among EPA staff members.

EPA head Burford was initially very skeptical of the emission-trading concept, apparently considering it a Carter administration "gimmick" (Tether 1986, p. 28). However, after hearing supportive comments from the industry, the administration was convinced and in April 1982 came out with an emission-trading policy that incorporated the use of bubbles. Unfortunately for the industry, their victory was very short-lived. By August 1982, the U.S. Court of Appeals for the District of Columbia ruled that the use of netting in areas that had failed to meet federal clean air guidelines was not permissable, and as a result the bubble concept could not be applied (Natural Resources Defense Council, Inc. v. Gorsuch: 685 F.2d 718) (1982).

While this decision was eventually unanimously overturned by the U.S. Supreme Court in June 1984 (see Chevron U.S.A. v. National Resources

Defense Council, Inc. 52 LW 4845), the bubble process essentially came to a standstill during the two-year interim (Tietenberg 1985, p. 201). Having survived a Supreme Court decision, however, the bureaucratic debate over bubbles erupted anew. EPA's bubble policy would for the first time allow polluters subject to new source performance standards to generate and trade emission reduction credits. While this policy received the support of EPA's Office of Policy Planning and Evaluation's Regulatory Reform Staff, it has been "strongly opposed" by the Office of Air Quality Planning and Standards as well as nine out of ten of EPA's regional offices. (For a good discussion of the different viewpoints in this debate, see: Levin 1985; Doniger 1986; Levin 1986; Liroff 1986; Tether 1986.) EPA's air quality staff has contended that "our experience is that emission trading has been used only as an escape from compliance" and that the new bubble policy would allow industry to earn emission credits they did not rightly deserve (Stanfield 1986b, p. 821). Indeed, some "horror" stories have surfaced to suggest that such fears were justified. For example, the EPA air office found that in 1982 Texas allowed Union Carbide Inc. to avoid controls on a storage tank in exchange for emissions reductions that resulted when the company shut down an obsolete facility four years previously. In addition, they found that four steel plants paved or watered down dirt roads to reduce dust in exchange for not placing controls on smokestacks (Stanfield 1986b, p. 821). In a study of 37 of the 40 bubbles approved as of January 1985, EPA's air office found that while 23 trades resulted in decreases in pollution, 14 did not and may have actually resulted in increased emissions.

In summary, a combination of factors have inhibited the progress the administration has been able to make in furthering the use of market incentives. A lack of administrative leadership on the part of Burford, adverse court decisions, and bureaucratic disputes over the utility of such incentives, have ironically left the Reagan administration making substantially less progress in this area than either the Ford or Carter administrations.

CHANGING THE STATE ROLE

As discussed more thoroughly in Chapter 4, the Reagan administration expressed a strong early commitment to restructuring the relationship between the federal government and state and local governments. In line with this general disposition, the administration attempted to make fundamental changes in the federal-state environmental partnership. The Reagan environmental program sought not only to ensure that federal regulations imposed as few burdens as necessary on the private sector, but also that the federal regulations be imposed only in cases where state and local governments have failed to regulate or where regulatory uniformity is necessary to promote interstate commerce.

Administration officials portrayed state and local governments as the appropriate front-line regulators of the environment. As outlined by Robert Bedell, OMB deputy administrator of OIRA:

Our view is that there should be federal regulatory intervention only in the case of a market failure and then only if the state and local governments are unable to or possibly unwilling to deal with the problem. It [federal regulation] should not be used as an authority of the first use. (Environment Reporter 1984, p. 1387)

In theory, the states have always been major actors in setting environmental policy. As explained more fully in our discussion of intergovernmental relations, environmental programs traditionally have been implemented under a federal–state partnership as partial preemption programs, with the federal government setting minimum national standards and the states ensuring through state implementation plans (SIPs) that the standards are being met. However, during much of the 1970s, there was deep skepticism on the part of federal officials concerning the willingness, technical capacity, and ability of the states to enforce these environmental regulations. As a result, federal officials tended to hold on to much of the regulatory power.

The Reagan administration took several immediate steps to return authority to the states. Burford sought to transfer administrative responsibility for running environmental programs directly to the states. She had promised at her confirmation hearings to "restore the States to their rightful place as partners with the Federal Government in policy-making as well as policy implementation" (Burford 1986, p. 56). Eventually, she was successful in increasing state environmental program responsibility from 33 to 66 percent (Stanfield 1984, p. 1034). While states welcomed this delegation of power, however, they were not pleased by the accompanying budget cuts. As one environmental lobbyist we interviewed noted,

When [Burford] came on the scene, the first thing out of her mouth was 'delegate, delegate, delegate,' which the states didn't mind because they wanted the responsibility to implement the programs. The problem was that at the same time she slashed, slashed, slashed federal financial assistance and federal technical assistance.

Sharp budget cuts in federal financial assistance for state administration of environmental regulations hit states hard, for they relied heavily on federal funding in implementing these programs. While some states received more assistance than others, federal funds in 1982 provided on average approximately 45 percent of state air program budgets, 46 percent of state water quality program budgets, and 69 percent of state hazardous waste program budgets (National Governor's Association 1982, p. 71). Table 5.2 documents these budget cuts for environmental regulation. A dramatic example is provided by steep declines in abatement and control funds, which are devoted to developing standards and providing assistance to states for the implementation of their environmental programs. Abatement and control funds dropped (in 1983 dollars) from $727 million in 1980 to $406 million in 1985, a 44 percent real decrease.

The Reagan administration's message was clear: States must assume a greater proportion of the costs as well as the responsibility of environmental regulation. Yet, because of fiscal impacts the 1982 recession had on many states, and marked differences in their fiscal capacities versus environmental regulatory needs, many states were in a poor position to assume these costs. The cuts had come so suddenly and gone so deep that many states found themselves unable to develop alternative funding plans even when the political will to do so existed (CBO 1984, pp. 7–8). The trend of the deep cuts in federal financial assistance to the states came to an end with the departure of Burford from EPA. Since Ruckelshaus took over as administrator in May 1983 grants to states have stabilized and were only reduced by 5 percent between 1983 and 1985.

In addition, Ruckelshaus sought to counteract the perception that EPA had lost its interest in enforcement. While calling the present enforcement staff "pussy cats" (because of their apparent unwillingness to go after polluters or to press the states to enforce the law), Ruckelshaus urged his staff to become "gorillas":

Unless [the states] have a gorilla in the closet, they can't do the job. And the gorilla is EPA. . . . The states can't enforce these laws by themselves. They need us. They'll complain and scream, but if they don't have us, they are dead. (Stanfield 1984, p. 1035)

One question raised by this transfer of regulatory authority from the federal government to the states is whether or not it has significantly reduced burdens on industry. Certainly, easing the burden of compliance was an important administration goal. In some cases, strip-mining is a major example, industry seems to be benefiting from significantly reduced enforcement activities by the states. But this outcome varies greatly from state to state and from industry to industry. There are some indications that industry has not benefited a great deal from the transfer. Some states have proven to be tougher on polluters than the federal government. Consider the following examples: Massachusetts cleaned up 51 hazardous waste dumps in a three-year period, while EPA on a national level managed to clean up only 16. California, Massachusetts, and New York set tougher standards on the pesticide ethylene dibromide (EDB) than did EPA. By 1984, 19 states had more extensive programs to control toxic air pollution than the federal government (Stanfield 1984, pp. 1034, 1038). In 1981, state legislators considered approximately 400 pesticide-related bills, a number expected to jump to 1000 bills by 1983 (Wines 1982, p. 1927). Another industry concern is that all this state activity promises little guarantee of national regulatory uniformity. Manufacturers of household chemicals, for example, might long for the days when they faced only one pesticide standard rather than 50. As one state administrator aptly commented, "It's a classic example of the pendulum swinging too far in the other direction" (Wines 1982, p. 1927).

SUMMARY AND CONCLUSIONS

While the Reagan administration took office seeking sweeping environmental changes and applied an aggressive management approach towards that end, after six years in office relatively little has changed. True, fewer federal dollars are currently being spent on protection of the environment, and enforcement and research activities have been sharply curtailed. But at the same time, there has not been anything approaching the "regulatory ventilation" that Reagan officials had hoped to bring about. Instead, what we see is greater activism on the part of the Congress to tighten current environmental laws and oversee their implementation, greater support for the environment by the general public (environmental groups have reported sizable increases in their membership), and increased activism on the part of some states in setting environmental standards that are stricter than those maintained by the federal government. None of this resistance bodes well for business leaders or conservative ideologues who expected the administration to get government off industry's back. Nor are the changes that have taken place permanent. The administration has yet to win a single environmental victory on Capitol Hill; the regulatory relief that has been brought about through administrative means could be quickly overturned by future administrations.

Idealists of any ideological school who envision the formulation of public policy as based on sound theory and developed in an orderly fashion have reason to be disappointed in environmental policy-making under Reagan. Indeed, the old adage, that people who like sausage and public policy should never watch how either are made, definitely fits the situation here. Environmental regulatory reform under the Reagan administration was fashioned out of a patchwork of ideas, loosely tied together, and driven by ideologues who were more concerned with crippling and/or dismantling the ability of EPA to carry out its statutory functions than with authentic regulatory reforms. Administration efforts to achieve regulatory reform in the environmental area have been marred by such questionable practices as abuses in the Superfund program (that eventually led to the resignation of Burford and her top appointees), budget reductions haphazardly made rather than in a planned fashion, evidence of undue industry and OMB pressures on EPA rule-making activity, nonenforcement of the specific environmental standards mandated by law, and the blacklistng of EPA personnel. All this adds up not to the "record of success" that Demuth had hoped would pave the way for later statutory changes but to a record of disaster that could pave the way for more and stronger federal regulation. The Reagan administration's actions in environmental policy have poisoned the atmosphere in Congress for even debating anything resembling environmental reform. While EPA Administrators Ruckelshaus and Thomas, two very skilled managers, have been successful in giving EPA greater environmental credibility and restoring EPA morale, neither one has been successful in overcoming congressional skepticism towards the administration's environmental policies, and have not been successful, nor very interested, in moving reform efforts along.

6 REGULATORY REFORM IN THE NUCLEAR POWER AREA

The policy area of nuclear-generated power offers us the opportunity to observe President Reagan's regulatory reform initiatives in an environment in which the agency with primary responsibility for regulation is an independent commission, not an executive branch agency. It is also a policy area in which an industry—buffeted by serious economic, technical, and management problems—has been calling out for regulatory relief. And, involving nuclear technology as it does, this is also a highly controversial area, in which a consensus about what course to take has been extremely difficult to achieve among all the parties involved: Congress, the regulatory agencies involved, concerned watchdog organizations, communities around nuclear power plants, and the nuclear industry itself.

In this chapter, we will first look at the state of the nuclear industry and the case for regulatory reform of the nuclear licensing process. We will examine the economic, technical, and management problems that have troubled the industry. We will describe industry's regulatory reform agenda and the reception these proposals have tended to receive in Congress. Next, we will look at the nuclear regulatory initiatives of presidents before Reagan. Then, we will examine the nuclear policy and licensing reform initiatives of the Reagan administration. We will describe both the attempts to change nuclear licensing laws and the attempts to create regulatory relief through various administrative means. Of particular concern to our analysis here will be to point out which elements of the administration's management strategy proved themselves effective in dealing with an independent regulatory commission.

Finally, we will evaluate the success of these different strategies and of administration reform efforts overall in this policy area.

THE NUCLEAR INDUSTRY AND THE CASE FOR REFORM

Today, nuclear power rarely makes the news except when accidents occur such as the partial meltdown at Three Mile Island in Pennsylvania in 1979, or the explosion at the Soviet power plant at Chernobyl in the Spring of 1986. Yet nuclear power has come to play a significant role in the U.S. energy picture, generating about 16 percent of the nation's electricity. There were 101 operating nuclear power plants in the United States in 1986, with another 26 under construction. While nuclear power plants are in operation or under construction in 35 states, states vary greatly in their dependence on this energy source (see Table 6.1). Nuclear energy supplies more than half of the electricity in Vermont, Maine, and South Carolina, supplies less than one-third of the electricity generated in Illinois, Wisconsin, and New Jersey, and supplies less than 5 percent of the electricity generated in Washington and Colorado. In addition, a total of 15 states make no use of nuclear power. In general, states in the northeast and south make the heaviest use of nuclear power, while states in the west use it least. While nuclear energy is an important energy source in this country, its role is far less than many other industrialized nations: France, for example relies on nuclear power for 65 percent of its electricity; West Germany 31 percent; and Japan, 23 percent.

The nuclear power industry in the United States suffered many setbacks in recent years. No new plants have been ordered since the March 1979 accident at Three Mile Island (TMI). In the last ten years over 100 plants that were either planned or actually under construction have been cancelled. All of the orders placed between 1974 and 1977 have been cancelled, and construction has yet to begin on the two plants ordered in 1978. In addition, 18 nuclear power plants that are in various stages of completion have been identified by the Department of Energy as being "highly vulnerable" to cancellation at abandonment costs estimated at between $4.5 billion to $8.1 billion combined (Department of Energy 1983).

The decline of the nuclear power industry can be seen as the result of three sets of factors: economic problems (such as declines in demand for electric power, and periods of extremely high double-digit interest rates), technical problems (such as lengthening construction schedules for nuclear plants, and the lack of a solution for long-term disposal of nuclear waste), and facility mismanagement problems (such as the events that caused the accident at Three Mile Island).

Table 6.1
Electricity Generated by Nuclear Power by State, 1983 (megawatt-hours in millions)

State	Nuclear	Total	Nuclear (%)
Vermont	2.9	3.9	74
Maine	5.7	9.7	59
South Carolina	25.6	46.0	56
Virginia	18.7	37.7	50
Connecticut	11.6	23.9	49
Minnesota	11.8	30.0	39
Nebraska	6.1	17.1	36
Maryland	11.7	32.6	36
Alabama	25.1	76.2	33
Illinois	28.0	99.2	28
Arkansas	7.6	30.1	25
Wisconsin	9.3	39.3	24
New Jersey	6.3	27.3	23
Michigan	16.4	70.9	23
Tennessee	14.1	69.4	20
Massachusetts	6.1	34.7	18
North Carolina	12.4	74.7	17
Florida	14.8	91.5	16
New York	16.4	105.0	16
Pennsylvania	14.7	123.6	12
Georgia	7.8	66.6	12
Iowa	2.3	22.3	10
Oregon	3.7	49.2	8
California	5.6	117.7	5
Ohio	4.9	105.9	5
Washington	3.5	95.1	4
Colorado	0.7	25.2	3
Total U.S.	293.7	2,310.3	12.7

Source: U.S. Department of Energy 1984.

Economic Problems

The economic recession of the mid–1970s and the double-digit interest rates that followed it hit the capital-intensive nuclear industry particularly hard. The impact of high interest rates was worsened by lengthening construction schedules (resulting from such factors as increased government regulations and labor problems), so that interest costs rose to a substantial portion of the total cost of plant construction (Department of Energy 1982a). As a nuclear reactor supplier noted, "Nuclear power has become an investment with tremendous financial risks to utilities, and the utility industry itself is in such poor financial health it can no longer afford to purchase nuclear generating stations" (Hamilton 1982, p. 22).

The general economic downturn of recent years has also caused a decline in demand for electric power. As a result of a number of economic factors—industrial plant closings; conservation efforts by industry, consumers, and the U.S. government; and efforts by the Organization of Petroleum Exporting Countries (OPEC) to control the price and availability of oil—use of electric power actually declined during the period between 1978 and 1982. To make matters worse, nearly all utility companies had forecast *increased* energy consumption for this period, and had planned aggressive plant construction programs. The unexpected decline in demand for electricity has caused a general slowdown in building all types of power plants: coal, hydro-electric and nuclear, but the nuclear industry was the most adversely affected.

In addition to the economic difficulties affecting the entire electricity production industry, the nuclear power industry had special problems of its own. The inflation-adjusted costs of building a nuclear plant jumped between 1960 and 1980. During the mid–1960s, utilities believed that nuclear power plants would be far less costly to run than coal-fired plants. The vision of cheap, clean energy production led utilities to commit more resources to nuclear power (Department of Energy 1982a, p. xviii). However, the commanding economic advantage nuclear power once enjoyed has long since evaporated. While the costs of both nuclear and coal-fired plants have escalated since the 1960s, nuclear plant capital costs have escalated more rapidly. As a recent Department of Energy (DOE) report stated, "(The) . . . gap between future nuclear and coal-fired costs has narrowed to the point that, for a new plant entering service in 1995, the two options are in a virtual dead heat in most regions of the country" (DOE 1982a, p. xviii). If other factors such as construction time, capacity, the expected operating life of the facility, and general operating and maintenance costs are considered as well, it is projected that electricity from a nuclear power plant ordered today would be twice as costly to purchase as the electricity from a coal plant (Hellman and Hellman 1983, p. 28).

The causes of dramatic increases in cost for nuclear power production are not entirely clear. Industry officials have charged that the major cost factor has been overregulation by NRC of the nuclear power plant construction process. Critics in the nuclear power industry claim that NRC imposes design requirements that significantly raise labor and material costs but do not increase the public safety. Industry spokespersons also blame NRC regulation for the dramatic lengthening of construction schedules for nuclear plants. Plant construction schedules expanded nearly 70 percent between 1974 and the mid–1980s (DOE 1982b, p. 3).

In particular, the time required for NRC application review, hearings, and ultimate approval of final construction plans increased substantially. NRC's imposition of new regulatory requirements in the wake of the accident at Three Mile Island has created even more delays in the development and construction of nuclear power plants (DOE 1982b, p. 3.). The nuclear industry argues that overregulation has made the nuclear option appear prohibitively costly in terms of both time and money in the eyes of utility managers.

Technical Problems

In addition to these economic problems, the nuclear power industry has also been beset by two serious technological problems: the difficulty of nuclear waste disposal and the possibility of nuclear accidents. Science has yet to discover a satisfactory solution to the problem of storing nuclear waste safely over the long term. Short-term disposal sites are hard to find and space in existing sites is running out. Uncertainty over future waste disposal is a concern to utility managers. Moreover, publicity concerning the industry's waste disposal problems has stiffened existing public opposition to the further development of nuclear power. Negative public opinion, in turn, has increased the hesitancy of utility officials to commit themselves to new plants.

Widely publicized scandals concerning employee safety have further undermined the image of nuclear power generation as a safely managed industry. The Karen Silkwood case, for example—in which a nuclear plant employee who had been accidentally exposed to high doses of radiation died in ambiguous circumstances (an automobile accident) on the way to meeting with federal officials—has been the subject of much publicity and debate.

The accident at Three Mile Island—a partial meltdown and subsequent release of low levels of radiation into the atmosphere—caused hundreds of nearby residents to flee their homes, brought lawsuits from those fearing a health hazard from the accident, and shut down the plant for several years. This accident had a powerful effect on the nuclear industry in the United States. The NRC issued no new licenses during a 17-month moratorium during which it reviewed licensing and inspection procedures and examined new safety alternative measures (Civiak 1983). This moratorium may in itself have been responsible for some of the post-TMI delays in plant construction. Also, since the accident, NRC has imposed new regulatory requirements on both new and existing nuclear plants many of which involve significant time costs. For example, a new post-TMI ruling by the NRC requires the completion and approval of state and local emergency evacuation plans prior to licensing. And, since the accident, NRC has imposed a large number of new safety

procedures, many of them likely to further lengthen construction schedules and increase plant costs.

The most important effect of the well-publicized plant failures at
Three Mile Island and later at Chernobyl is that these accidents fundamentally changed the public's view of nuclear power. Nuclear energy
had enjoyed the strong support of a substantial majority (71 percent) of
the U.S. public in the early 1970s. Now in the 1980s, a growing majority
opposes new plant construction. As a 1981 *NBC News/Associated Press* poll
reported, "A majority of the public—56 percent—do not want more
nuclear power plants built in the United States. This opinion is the
reverse of our findings four and a half years ago, when nearly two-thirds
of the public favored new nuclear power facilities" (NBC News 1981,
Poll #72). A Washington Post–ABC News poll taken in the wake of the
April 1986 accident at Chernobyl found that an unprecedented 78 percent of those questioned were now opposed to the construction of new
nuclear plants. (Sussman 1986, p. A6)

Concern over Facilities Management and Public Safety

There is much evidence that poor management has contributed its
share to construction delays and thus to increased plant costs. A report
by the Federal Power Commission found over 45 instances in which
managerial problems accounted for construction delays (Reiber and Halcrow 1974, p. 3). Indeed, as *Energy Daily* reported, two utilities that
introduced strict managerial control over plant construction were able
to beat construction averages by half—completing one facility in just
under six years, and the other facility in just over seven years (1977 to
1983). And, as one of the utility managers involved in this success story
noted, "NRC and the regulatory side has not been a problem . . . I think
it's a lame excuse that many executives use when they get into trouble.
NRC basically never held us up" (Myers 1983, p. 4).

In the nuclear industry, poor management has tremendous implica-
tions for public safety. A majority of NRC commissioners have consistently argued that—while there have been isolated problems with utility
mismanagement—overall the nuclear power system is quite safe. As NRC
Chairman Nunzio Palladino has testified, "It is the Commission's firm
belief that all operating reactors in the U.S. today are operating at a
level of safety that ensures that the health and safety of the public is
adequately protected" (Palladino 1983, p. 1). Despite such official assurances, evidence continually surfaces of serious problems with management practices. Consider the following examples:

• Disenchanted employees at the Zimmer nuclear plant in Ohio documented so
  many safety problems and examples of poor workmanship and construction

errors that the plant owner decided to abandon the plant and try and convert it to a coal burning facility—even though the plant at the time was 97 percent complete.

- Numerous electrical and construction errors kept the nearly completed Texas Comanche Peak nuclear plant from being licensed for more than four years. There were problems with valves, welding, and concrete and estimates suggest that one-third of all the pipe supports and electrical preparations need replacing.

- The Tennessee Valley Authority was forced to shut down all five of its nuclear plants due to poor management practices that seriously jeopardized plant safety.

- Licensing delays for both the Shoreham plant on Long Island in New York, and the Seabrook plant in New Hampshire occurred because of public concern that these plants are located in areas that cannot effectively be evacuated if an accident should occur. (Stanfield 1986c, p. 1649)

In summary, the nuclear power industry has recently experienced many serious problems—economic difficulties, technological stumbling blocks, and facilities management weaknesses. While some of these problems might have been avoided or lessened by industry behavior, most could not. Over-building might have been avoided to some extent by more prudent strategic planning, but not entirely. Clearly better management could have helped in many cases to mitigate costs, avoid delays, and improve the public image of individual facilities and the nuclear power industry as a whole.

The technological problem of waste disposal has remained an unavoidable stumbling block, however. The economic misfortunes that resulted from the decline in demand for electric power also clearly lay beyond the control of the nuclear power industry itself. Also, although it might be argued that avoidable management error contributed to the accident at Three Mile Island, the dramatic shift in public opinion that followed concerning nuclear power generation as a whole clearly could not have been anticipated. Similarly, the relevance of the accident at Chernobyl to the U.S. nuclear power industry is to some extent unclear; yet, the industry's public image suffered sharply from that event.

With this troubled recent history as a backdrop, let us now turn to the regulatory reform goals of the nuclear power industry and then to the way that Congress, past administrations, and the Reagan administration have responded to them.

The Regulatory Reform Agenda of the Nuclear Industry

With so many adverse events seemingly outside its control, the nuclear power industry has given much attention in recent years to one thing that might be within its power to change: government regulation. As we have seen, the nuclear industry has long perceived the tight regulatory policies of the NRC as an important contributor to its frustrations. And, as last discussed, regulations tightened considerably after the accident at Three Mile Island in 1978. In recent years, the nuclear power industry has launched an extensive lobbying effort in Congress to gain some degree of regulatory relief—particularly in the area of the licensing procedures used by NRC.

Industry Concerns over Regulatory Delays. Industry lobbyists argue that the present NRC licensing process imposes unnecessary delays and in some cases presents undue burdens on nuclear plant operators. They point out that the time frame for putting a nuclear facility into operation—from the determination of need for power until the issuance of the operating license—has lengthened dramatically in recent years. While the nuclear industry admits that other factors play a part in causing delays in the building of nuclear facilities, they strongly believe that the main culprit for these time delays is the regulatory process (Large 1982, p. 1). As the American Nuclear Energy Council, a major industry association argues,

During the last decade, the time from planning to operation of a nuclear power plant has increased significantly. A major component of this scheduled escalation, and the consequent increased costs, is the instability and unpredictability of the Nuclear Regulatory Commission's . . . regulatory requirements. Delays caused by the licensing process can add as much as one million dollars for each day of delay to the overall cost of a plant. One of the Council's highest priorities is to seek fundamental changes in the licensing and regulatory process. (American Nuclear Energy Council 1985, p. 4)

Following this line of reasoning, the cumbersome nature of the regulatory process itself is largely blamed for the recent cancellation of so many previously ordered nuclear plants. An interviewee representing the American Nuclear Energy Council stated: "A utility will never order a power plant again under the existing system. The system must be reformed. The current system has created too many impediments to building a new plant because of its instability and unpredictability."

Political Reaction to Nuclear Industry Concerns. Since the development of nuclear power, political officials have been intimately involved in issues that affect the health and well-being of the nuclear power industry. This situation is not surprising considering the enormous resources involved, the potential dangers of the technology used, and the fact that public utilities purchase much of the electric power produced. Nuclear power plants necessitate investments of billions of dollars, provide thousands of jobs in local areas and produce millions of dollars in profit for corporations involved in plant construction. The list of companies that make up the nuclear power industry include many of the largest and wealthiest corporations in the United States: General Electric Company, Westinghouse Corporation, Exxon Nuclear Company, Bechtel Power Corporation, Goodyear Aerospace Corporation, Kerr-McGee Corporation, Rockwell International Corporation, as well as numerous utility companies. Obviously such organizations have the resources to carry out extensive lobbying campaigns. In addition, some well organized and very vocal environmental groups lobby against the building of nuclear power plants. While these groups cannot match the nuclear industry in terms of economic resources available to promote their point of view or to hire legal talent to fight their case through the courts, anti-nuclear groups have quite successfully employed grass-roots political techniques (such as canvassing, protest marches, and rallys), to get their point across to elected officials.

Not surprisingly, given the strong lobbying efforts on both sides, nuclear energy receives a great deal of attention from congressmen. During the Ninety-eighth Congress (1984–1985) legislative, budget and oversight jurisdiction over nuclear energy was shared by 29 congressional committees, including 53 subcommittees, on which a total of approximately 200 members serve. Over 100 bills relating to nuclear power were submitted that session and hearings were held before 44 congressional committees or subcommittees. Topics included: nuclear waste management and disposal, emergency planning, transportation, nuclear export policy, decommissioning, licensing reform, uranium supply issues, fuel cycle issues, risk assessment, TMI cleanup, and research and development expenditures (American Nuclear Energy Council 1985).

While the nuclear industry has won some major victories on a variety of these issues (such as federal funds for cleaning up the TMI reactor and the defeat of amendments to the Nuclear Waste Policy Act of 1982 and the Export Administration Act which would have curtailed nuclear exports) it has found political support for its primary concern—regulatory reform of the nuclear licensing process—to be weak or nonexistent.

In general, congressmen have remained skeptical of industry's assertion that the current regulatory process is the principal cause of nuclear licensing and construction delays. Congressman John Dingell, chairman of the House Subcommittee on Energy and Environment, expressed such skepticism upon opening the 1978 hearings on the Carter administration nuclear licensing reform bill (The Nuclear Siting and Licensing Act of 1978):

This bill is premised upon the assumption that the length of time required to license and construct a nuclear power-plant is a consequence of certain defi-

ciencies in the existing process, especially those procedures relating to environmental issues, and that the way to shorten this process is to modify those
procedures. The extent to which this is valid has yet to be established. There is
abundant evidence that the amount of time needed to license and construct
nuclear powerplants is related to the process itself and which are not addressed
in this proposal. (House, Committee on Interior and Insular Affairs 1978, p. 2)

Indeed, studies performed by a variety of government agencies have
consistently contradicted industry views of the delaying effects of regulation. A comprehensive study conducted by the Congressional Budget
Office found that nuclear licensing and construction delays were caused
by economic, not governmental, factors, including unanticipated decline
in the demand for power, as well as the difficulty utilities faced in trying
to finance a project. CBO concluded that two-thirds of the delays were
not inherent in the regulatory process and most likely could not be
ameliorated through regulatory changes. CBO's assessment was that regulatory reform legislation could have only a "moderate effect" on expediting nuclear plant licensing and construction (House, Committee on
Interior and Insular Affairs 1978b, p. 578).

In the most detailed analysis to date, the Department of Energy examined the causes of the cancellation of nuclear power plants and the
costs associated with them. The major reasons for cancelling planned
nuclear units, in order of importance, were identified as: (1) a drop in
the projected demand for electricity; (2) financial constraints; (3) a loss
of the nuclear cost advantage over coal-fired plants; (4) regulatory
changes and uncertainty at the federal level; and (5) the denial of nuclear
certification approval by state authorities. Of these, DOE analysts considered the first three factors as having been responsible for most of the
nuclear plant cancellations (DOE 1983, pp. 3–32). Out of the 100 cancellations analyzed, only one was attributed solely to governmental regulatory changes and uncertainty. Indeed, in 68 percent of the cases, the
utilities did not even cite the regulatory environment as a reason for
plant cancellation (DOE 1983, pp. 8–14).

Environmental groups have utilized CBO and Energy Department
studies to argue that regulatory reform of nuclear licensing would be
unnecessary at best and dangerous at worst. Testifying on behalf of eight
environmental and safe energy organizations, Ellyn Weiss summed the
argument up this way:

No amount of regulatory "reform", however sweeping, will cure all [the nuclear
industry's] ills. The nuclear industry's safety, reliability, financial and public
acceptance problems will not be resolved by curtailing adjudicatory hearings or
placing restrictions on backfits so onerous as to prevent the correction of serious
safety defects. On the contrary, adoption of this legislation will produce two
negative results: it will simply hide many of the real problems from view and

make it less likely that they will be addressed until after the next accident or near-miss, and the mere fact of its passage will further reduce public confidence in the technology and its regulators. (House, Committee on Interior and Insular Affairs 1983, p. 3)

The nuclear industry, for its part, contends that such studies have been based on inadequate data and tend to mask regulatory causes for construction delays. George Gleason, vice-president of the American Nuclear Energy Council states: "(T)he true cause of delay is often masked by what is known as the 'ripple effect.' For example, a change in [NRC] regulatory criteria will necessitate a design change which will require an equipment change which in turn will result in a construction delay. More often than not, the equipment change will be labeled by [the NRC] as the cause of delay . . . " (House, Committee on Interior and Insular Affairs 1978b, p. 352).

In summary, the nuclear power industry has initiated a strong campaign for regulatory reform, blaming NRC licensing as a major cause of the lengthening schedules and escalating costs that have severely troubled the nuclear industry. However, as we have seen, many people in Congress and elsewhere have remained skeptical that the regulatory process, rather than economic, technological or management factors have caused these problems. As a result, industry proposals to reform licensing procedures have not found much support. Moreover, industry advocates have also had a difficult time making the case that licensing and inspection procedures could be streamlined without jeopardizing public safety and health. This persistent congressional skepticism has, as we will see, also dogged administration attempts to achieve statutory change in the nuclear licensing area.

NUCLEAR LICENSING REGULATION

As we have seen, NRC's licensing procedures have emerged as the focal point of nuclear regulatory reform efforts in recent years. Before we examine specific reform initiatives, therefore, let us describe in some detail the institutional history, procedures, and issues involved in nuclear licensing.

The administrative process for the licensing and regulation of nuclear power plants was established by the Atomic Energy Act of 1954. This act created the Atomic Energy Commission (AEC) as an independent regulatory commission charging it with the responsibility for ensuring that nuclear plants would be constructed and operated in a manner to ensure protection of the health and safety of the public. Like many of the regulatory statutes which created independent commissions, the Atomic Energy Act gave broad responsibilities to the AEC with little specific guidance on how to carry out these responsibilities. Specifically, the 1954 Act set forth the basic framework for the regulatory process without additional guidance concerning criteria or standards to be applied by the AEC in its regulatory decision making and enforcement. For example, while the Act called for the "adequate protection" of the public's health and safety, and "adequate assurance of no undue risk" from nuclear power, Congress chose to leave it to the AEC to define the meaning of these terms precisely.

It has proved rather problematic for the AEC to carry out this general mandate over the ensuing 30 years. In the 1950s, when nuclear technology was in its infancy, many questions about regulation were unresolved, including basic questions of reactor design and health dangers and environmental effects of radiation (Rolph 1979, p. 155). In addition to its regulatory role, the AEC was also charged with encouraging the commercial use of nuclear energy—corresponding to recommendations within President Eisenhower's "Atoms for Peace" program. In the next 20 years, between 1954 and 1974, the AEC found it difficult to play these two roles: the impartial regulator and the promoter of commercial uses of nuclear energy. This dual role led to charges that the AEC had become intimately intertwined with the nuclear industry. As Senator Abraham Ribicoff, chairman of the Senate Committee on Government Operations observed in introducing a bill that would later change this relationship,

[T]he development of the nuclear industry has been managed by the same agency responsible for regulating it. While this arrangement may have been necessary in the infancy of the atomic era after World War II, it is clearly not in the public interest to continue this special relationship now that the industry is well on its way to becoming among the largest and most hazardous in the Nation. In fact, it is difficult to determine . . . where the Commission ends and the industry begins. (Ribicoff 1974, p. 14869)

This role conflict was resolved in 1974 when the Energy Reorganization Act of 1974 split the AEC into two organizations: the Nuclear Regulatory Commission (NRC), which assumed the "regulator" role, and the Energy Research and Development Administration (ERDA), with the responsibility of promoting the development of nuclear and other forms of energy. In 1977, ERDA and several other agencies and offices were combined to create the Department of Energy (DOE), an executive branch agency that retained ERDA's promotional role as part of agency responsibilities.

The creation of the NRC did not bring about any major transformations in regulating policy however. As one study of the U.S. nuclear regulatory history found, "[The NRC] . . . has inherited the same regulatory traditions, it faces the same technical problems and uncertainties that plagued its predecessor, and its basic approach to safety through engineered safeguards has not changed" (Rolph 1979, p. 155)

The licensing process administered by NRC is a complex one, taking an average of 12 to 14 years to complete. Planning takes about four years and the construction process takes eight to ten years. The utility planning stage involves site acquisition, development of a preliminary facility design, the process of applying for a construction permit from NRC, NRC's review of the application, and public hearings. At these public hearings individuals and organizations may present their views concerning the proposed plant, introduce evidence, call their own witnesses, and cross-examine witnesses called by NRC or the utility company.

Once these preparatory hurdles are overcome, NRC will issue a preliminary construction permit on the basis of a general design pending later full specification of the exact characteristics of plant assemblies and equipment. Plant construction can now begin. But the length of the construction process may vary considerably as a result of several factors: financial cost overruns; added regulatory requirements; construction delays; or bad weather (DOE 1982b, p. 6). During the construction period, the plant design is further specified according to NRC regulation. NRC staff review the entire construction process to ensure compliance with NRC safety regulations. The application for an operating license that the utility thereafter submits to NRC is based on a design that is essentially complete. The NRC staff reviews the application for an operation license in detail, and a second public hearing may even be held at this point. Normally, the operating license is granted at the time of the opening of the facility.

Most regulatory reform proposals have centered around modifications of three aspects of the nuclear licensing process: backfitting requirements, standardization of design rules, and hearing procedures. Because these issues lie at the center of the regulatory reform debate and are highly technical in nature, we will briefly define each term and describe the issues involved.

Backfitting. Backfitting is a shorthand term for government requirements to make changes in the design or operation of nuclear facilities even though construction may be already underway or a facility may be in operation. NRC justifies its policy on the rationale that—even after 31 years of experience—nuclear power is still not well understood, that many important safety problems are as yet unresolved, and that a policy of extreme caution should be followed. Backfitting is a way of taking advantage of new safeguards immediately as soon as they are developed.

Although the nuclear power industry does not object to backfitting in principle, strong objections have been raised concerning the implementation of backfitting requirements. One set of industry concerns deals with the standards by which NRC imposes backfitting requirements. NRC's general rule appears to be this: if a design change would improve the safety of the plant by any degree, it should be made, even if the plant has been previously licensed and certified as safe to operate (DOE 1982b, p. 12). The costs of making such changes are not considered. Industry considers NRC's backfitting policy as needlessly inflexible and costly. Another set of industry criticisms concerns the lack of coordination or priority setting among the backfitting requirements coming from different divisions of NRC. Until recently, there was no central unit within NRC responsible for reviewing and coordinating new safety rules. Backfit requirements were issued by several different offices in an apparently haphazard, unsystematic manner (DOE 1982b, p. 12). Because of this unsystematic approach, say industry spokespersons, opportunities for making important changes in a timely fashion might be crowded out by unimportant changes; and several backfitting tasks that might have been accomplished in a single consolidated shutdown period instead necessitated several uncoordinated plant shutdowns (DOE 1982c).

Standardization. There has been little standardization of nuclear power plant design. Past practice—rationalized as the best way to maximize public safety and accommodate individual utilities—has been to design each nuclear power plant individually. As a result, designs of plants across the United States differ radically from one another (House, Committee on Interior and Insular Affairs, 1983). The nuclear industry is now arguing that—since originals are always more expensive to design and carry out than copies—this practice has raised costs. The industry also says this practice has hampered the transfer of technology, management practices, and safety improvements, between various plants. As William S. Lee, chairman and chief executive officer of Duke Power Company, testified before the House Subcommittee on Energy and the Environment,

The encouragement of standardized plant designs will benefit safety by concentrating the resources of designers, engineers and vendors on a few improved designs. This will stimulate improved construction practices, including improved construction quality assurance. Training of operating personnel will be facilitated. Improved standard designs will also enhance plant maintenance and operating practices and make possible more effective and efficient inspections. (House, Committee on Interior and Insular Affairs 1983, p. 5)

It also seems likely that such standardization would remove one obstacle to the smooth functioning of the two-step licensing process—the tendency of utilities to under-specify the plant design submitted to obtain the preliminary construction permit. Industry conservatism in this regard is understandable given the costs associated with developing a complete, original design measured against the likelihood that the NRC would require changes in it (DOE 1982b, pp. 15–16).

Advocates of standardization discount the concerns of those who fear standardized plant designs may entail significant health and safety risks, instead arguing that standardized plant designs could be readily tailored to specific geographical sites—both cost effectively and safely. Under proposed plant standardization regulatory reforms, NRC would approve certain "generic" manufacturers' plant designs as safe to operate on a range of geographical sites. Then, a utility wishing to construct a nuclear plant could purchase a site meeting NRC specifications and a standardized design licensed to be built on that site. By following such a procedure, industry reasons, a utility could obtain a preliminary construction permit without undergoing the detailed review currently required by NRC. These same standardized plans would later facilitate the review that precedes the issuance of the operating license (House, Committee on Interior and Insular Affairs 1983, pp. 5–10).

Public Hearings. The NRC has traditionally conducted two sets of hearings when deciding whether to license a plant: the first at the construction permit stage and the second before the operating license is issued. At each of these stages, NRC staff go before a panel of administrative law judges presenting recommendations for accepting, modifying, or rejecting license applications. The applicant utilities may respond to these presentations. In addition, other individuals or organizations—generally reflecting community and environmental interests or concerns—may air their views. These formal hearings are conducted similar to trials, involving witnesses, evidence, and cross-examination. And, as with trials, licensing hearings may be contentious events in which a great deal of technical information is presented, perhaps lasting for months.

Nuclear industry officials have criticized NRC hearing procedures as extremely expensive, overly burdensome, and ill-suited to investigating the complex scientific issues involved in nuclear plant planning and licensing. To streamline the public hearing process without sacrificing the public's right to participate in licensing decisions, some industry experts have proposed a "hybrid" system—one melding the formalities of adjudication with the informality of a legislative hearing. Under this proposal, hearings would involve two stages. The initial stage would provide an opportunity for the public, the utility, and other interested parties to testify before the licensing board. However, no testimony would be accepted by the judges as official evidence, and examination and cross-examination would not be allowed. The second stage of the hearing would involve the presentation of evidence and the examination and cross-examination of witnesses. After the first stage of the hearing, the licensing board would determine which of the issues aired in the first stage of the hearing would be addressed in the second stage. This hybrid process, say proponents, would accord adjudication only where it is clearly needed, saving time and money for all concerned (Shapar and Malsch 1974, pp. 539–555).

As we have seen, the nuclear industry has experienced many serious problems and considers regulatory reform a way out of some of its difficulties. We have discussed the major issues involved in industry proposals for regulatory reform. With this background in mind, we will briefly describe the reform activities in this area of presidents before Reagan, and then examine the regulatory reform initiatives of the Reagan administration.

PRESIDENTIAL NUCLEAR REGULATORY INITIATIVES BEFORE REAGAN

The first president to call for major reforms of the nuclear energy process was Richard Nixon. Nixon saw nuclear power as indispensible to meeting the nation's future energy needs and was concerned about the constraints imposed by the complex licensing process. Nixon saw a "need to streamline our governmental procedures for licensing and inspections [of nuclear plants], reduce overlapping jurisdictions and eliminate confusion generated by the government" (Nixon 1973, p. S7692). Jimmy Carter also saw a need for nuclear licensing reform. On April 20, 1977, in an Energy Address before a Joint Session of Congress, Carter stated that

We must . . . reform the nuclear licensing procedures. New plants should not be located near earthquake fault zones or near population centers, safety standards should be strengthened and enforced, design standardized as much as possible, and more adequate storage for spent fuel assured. However, even with the most thorough safeguards, it should not take ten years to license a plant. I propose that we establish reasonable, objective criteria for licensing, and that plants which are based on a standardized design not require extensive individual design studies for licensing. (Congressional Quarterly 1981, p. 255)

Trained as a nuclear engineer, President Carter often expressed an interest in the peaceful use of nuclear power (Ferrey 1978, pp. 294–297). However, he also stated that because of safety, waste disposal and national security concerns, nuclear power should be the energy source of "last resort with the strictest possible safety precautions," to be used only if traditional energy sources, such as coal, oil, hydropower, or alternative sources such as solar power, did not fill the country's energy needs (Ferrey 1978, pp. 294–297). Carter's doubts about the nuclear option helped him gain the support of environmental organizations in his 1976 campaign (Metz 1977, p. 592).

In spite of such reservations, the Carter administration came to embrace nuclear energy after DOE energy demand projections indicated that a substantial number of new power facilities would be needed by the year 2000 in order to meet projected consumer demand. To the Carter administration in the mid–1970s, nuclear power seemed more attractive than other alternatives—cheaper than coal, not dependent on foreign oil, and reasonably safe. Based on these assumptions, the administration through DOE mounted an effort to overcome the obstacles to full utilization of nuclear power posed by NRC's strict licensing procedures.

Carter's Energy Secretary, James Schlesinger, was a strong advocate of nuclear energy and licensing reform (Ferrey 1978, p. 294). Schlesinger kept work on the administrations' reform proposals within the province of a relatively few staff members, but still formulated with an eye to balancing the competing interests involved. Key components of the proposed regulatory reform legislation centered around two major issues that greatly resemble those we have detailed in the previous section as still of primary concern to the nuclear industry: aspects of NRC's licensing process and standardization of plant design. The DOE draft focused primarily on encouraging the use of standardization. Backfitting was not directly addressed. The draft recommended hybrid-type hearings, but only for concerns related to the *environmental* effects of plant operation, not on the more lengthy and more significant hearings concerning the *safety* of the plant.

The DOE draft legislation proved very controversial when it surfaced. Several agencies commenting on the proposal vigorously objected to its provisions. The White House Domestic Policy Council rejected the original draft bill on the grounds that it was too pro-nuclear. The President's Council on Environmental Quality objected to provisions of the bill that would reduce citizen participation in licensing hearings (Metz 1977, p. 592). After 11 months of bureaucratic infighting, Carter himself had to make the final choice on several crucial issues. In the end, the final product was strikingly similar to the version that Schlesinger had originally proposed.

One important item added to the DOE draft as a result of Carter's review was the provision to fund the efforts of so-called intervenor groups. Environmental and other public interest groups often attend NRC licensing proceedings to present their views and are granted the same rights to present evidence and cross-examine witnesses as NRC and the utility enjoy. These organizations had pointed out that a lack of sufficient funds prevented them from participating effectively. They argued that the present system was unfair because no funds were provided to them to advance the cause of public safety while the attorney fees for the industry were supported by utility rate payers (NRC, Ad Hoc Committee for Review of Nuclear Reactor Licensing Reform Proposals 1982, pp. 1–5). Following what has been characterized as a "Christmas tree" strategy, White House officials incorporated this provision to pay the expenses of intervenor groups in an apparent attempt to gain the support of environmental and consumer interest groups.

Even with the addition of the intervenor funding provision, however, environmental groups remained strongly opposed to Carter's reform package. As Anthony Roisman, a leading environmental attorney in this area, noted,

It's a badly conceived, badly drafted, and badly motivated piece of legislation. [The bill] represents the final corruption of the President's moral and political courage on the nuclear issue.... The President has chosen to pay the price of losing his environmental constituency. This is curious politics for an election year. (Congressional Quarterly 1979, p. 105)

The nuclear industry strenuously objected to the intervenor funding provisions. They regarded the final version of the proposal as having been so "emasculated" as to be "worse than nothing at all" (Metz 1977, p. 198). Industry officials laid the blame for this situation on factions within the White House staff. As Craig Hosmer, then president of the Atomic Nuclear Energy Council, stated,

There are two White Houses instead of one. There is the White House symbolized by Schlesinger and Co., where a courageous effort goes on ... and there is the White House, populated by no-growth, counter-culture activists.... There is no reason why Jimmy Carter can't torpedo a few rebellious, anti-nuclear pipsqueaks. (Congressional Quarterly 1979, p. 110)

The proposed legislation was introduced into both chambers of Congress on March 21, 1978 (S.2775; H.R. 11704), but it failed to move beyond the hearing process. The Carter nuclear licensing reform bill never came to a vote, in committee or on the floor. As already indicated, the proposal in its final form pleased none of its interested constituencies. Moreover, the late 1970s was a time of growth of anti-nuclear sentiment across the country. Public concern about safety and waste disposal increased rapidly and the actions of key congressional committee members reflected these concerns (House, Committee on Interior and Insular Affairs 1978c, p. 176). Even more important, as explained in a previous section, the nuclear industry was not able to convince many in Congress that NRC was guilty of overregulation or that licensing reform would decrease construction costs, speed up schedules, or otherwise improve the future of nuclear power. The Carter administration had failed on two fronts in its attempt to affect change in the nuclear policy area: not only did it fail to get a bill out of its bureaucracy that balanced industry needs with environmental group concerns and that had the full support of the NRC, but also Carter forces had made almost no attempt to attain the support of key congressional allies who would fight for passage of the bill.

There was some attempt to bring up the bill again in 1979, but then the accident at TMI occurred, and DOE permanently withdrew its bill from consideration. Between 1979 and 1981 neither the Carter administration nor Congress took any significant steps toward nuclear licensing reform. The accident at Three Mile Island had made nuclear power into a politically explosive issue that no one wanted to touch.

REAGAN NUCLEAR POLICY AND LICENSING REFORM INITIATIVES

With the election of Ronald Reagan to the presidency, the nuclear industry felt confident that the leadership mistakes of the past would not only be corrected, but that the new president would embrace changes even more sweeping than those advocated by Carter. As an official from the Atomic Industrial Forum stated, "The [1980] election produced mixed emotions in our industry: ecstasy, joy, pleasure, and euphoria" (Large 1980, p. 27).

During the 1980 campaign Reagan expressed strong support for developing nuclear-generated electricity. In his initial presidential policy statement on nuclear power, Reagan gave industry executives every reasons to celebrate.

I am directing the Secretary of Energy to give immediate priority attention to recommending improvements in the nuclear regulatory and licensing process. ... Consistent with public health and safety, we must remove unnecessary obstacles to deployment of the current generation of nuclear power reactors. The time involved to proceed from the planning stage to an operating license for new nuclear power plants has more than doubled since the mid–1970s and is presently some 10–14 years. This process must be streamlined, with the objective of shortening the time involved to 6–8 years, as is typical in some other countries. (Reagan 1981, p. 24-E)

Unlike previous presidents, Reagan gave a good deal of credence to the industry view that government regulation was to a great extent responsible for the sad state of affairs in the nuclear power industry:

The U.S. has developed a strong technological base in the production of electricity from nuclear energy. Unfortunately, the federal government has created a regulatory environment that is forcing many utilities to rule out nuclear power as a source of new generating capacity, even when their consumers may face unnecessarily high electric rates as a result. Nuclear power has become entangled in a morass of regulations that do not enhance safety but that do cause extensive licensing delays and economic uncertainty. (Reagan 1981, p. 24-E)

Attempts to Reform Nuclear Regulatory Statutes

Given this strong presidential support, the main thing nuclear licensing reform advocates seemingly lacked was a strategy to translate this new philosophy into policy. The set of actions we have termed the management strategy would be difficult to implement completely, given that the NRC was an independent commission not directly under executive branch control. Moreover, the nuclear industry was not very interested in administrative regulatory reform. Given the fact that it takes over a decade to complete a nuclear power plant, the nuclear industry needed assurances that any regulatory changes achieved would remain in place for many years. Such type of long-term assurance of regulatory stability could only be achieved through changing the regulatory statutes. Thus, the administration was resolved to seek nuclear regulatory reform through the legislative process.

DOE's Reform Effort: The Nuclear Industry Writes a Bill

In November of 1981, pursuant to Reagan's Nuclear Energy Policy Statement, Secretary of Energy Edwards formed a Nuclear Licensing Reform Task Force. The Task Force included some 15 representatives from three offices in DOE: the Office of Nuclear Energy; the General Counsel's Office; and the Office of Environment and Policy. This broad representation from different segments of DOE was very different from the close to the chest Carter-Schlesinger approach. As the Task Force evaluated possible reform alternatives, there was little, if any, conflict or confusion about goals—another difference with the Carter experience. Department of Energy officials we interviewed recalled that the Task Force understood that—even in the absence of explicit direction—the Reagan legislation was to reflect the concerns of the *nuclear industry* closely. Consequently, little attempt was made to build in a compromise between the conflicting interests of industry versus environmental groups.

Apart from philosophical considerations, practical circumstances reinforced the Task Force's conclusion that its principal mission was to provide relief from the burdens of the nuclear licensing process to the nuclear industry. Task Force members generally agreed that increasing public and interest group resistance to nuclear power after the TMI accident soured any chances the administration had for satisfying the opposition. These groups would fight any bill Reagan produced. Thus, from the Task Force's vantage point, the best choice was to formulate a bill which would achieve the ends desired by the president and the industry, without attempting to compromise in an effort to win over the opposition.

The Task Force worked closely with the industry, meeting officials in drafting the bill, to solicit their views and benefit from their expertise. The main issues involved were backfitting, hearings, and standardization. Originally, the DOE Task Force did not intend to include backfitting provisions in its legislative proposal, preferring instead to rely on an administrative solution to what it believed were overly stringent back-fitting requirements. But the nuclear industry argued that, to provide much-needed stability, new backfitting standards should be firmly embedded in statute, subject to change only by Congress and the president. The nuclear industry felt it needed a modified backfitting provision covering safety standards applied to *existing* as well as new plants in order to support the bill. In the end, the Task Force accommodated industry officials by including provisions designed to relax backfitting provisions applied to existing nuclear plant facilities in the administration's legislation.

On the two other important issues—hearings and standardization—DOE and industry officials agreed from the outset. Reagan's nuclear policy—as outlined in his 1981 policy statement—called for simplified hearing procedures and increased standardization in plant design. Because these were the industry's goals as well, discussions between the DOE Task Force and industry experts centered around specific technical adjustments.

NRC's Legislative Efforts

While DOE was drafting its bill, with some input from NRC, NRC was preparing a nuclear regulatory reform bill of its own. While there had been some hopes on the part of administration officials that NRC might drop its potentially competing legislative efforts, it soon became apparent that the differences between NRC and DOE could not be reconciled. While DOE favored a broader change in licensing procedures, NRC had a more conservative approach to the three main areas in which industry had lodged complaints: relaxing backfitting requirements; modifying hearing procedures; and encouraging standardization in design of plant facilities.

These different emphases between agencies notwithstanding, the NRC had wanted regulatory reforms in the nuclear licensing area for many years. After all, the nuclear licensing process had changed little since its enactment 29 years ago under the Atomic Energy Act of 1954, and many within the NRC wanted to change licensing procedures to reflect the changes that had taken place during those almost three decades. By 1983, commission members had established a rather vague mandate calling for regulatory reform in several areas: the creation of a more effective process for resolving legitimate public safety and environmental issues regarding applications under review; the development of a more effective method of utilizing NRC resources in the licensing of new plants; the avoidance of regulatory uncertainty and placement of un-justifiable economic burdens on utilities; and the accomplishment of the above without impairing the public's health or safety (Palladino 1983, pp. 1–2). This vagueness of the reform objectives reflected papered-over differences among some commissioners as to what changes the NRC needed and how far changes ought to go. While there was a general consensus favoring regulatory change, there proved to be little agree-ment on how these changes were to be instituted or how far these reforms should go.

While many within NRC wanted to seek changes in the regulatory statutes, others believed the changes could be accomplished through modifications of the agency's internal administrative procedures. There were several reasons why NRC chose to go ahead with a legislative strat-egy in spite of this disagreement. First, as Chairman Palladino (1983) argued, congressional imprimatur would protect NRC from both polit-ical criticism and legal challenges resulting from the proposed changes. Also, NRC did not want to leave rewriting nuclear licensing legislation completely in the hands of DOE. Several commissioners reported to us that, while they supported the "general thrust" of the 1978 DOE bill, they strongly objected to the proposed cutback in NRC's regulatory role, the restructuring of its adjudicatory proceedings, and what they viewed as DOE's overall intrusion into its policy domain. Rather than having a DOE reform bill once again foisted upon them, NRC decided to submit their own reform legislation, even if this meant competing with DOE.

In addition, the nuclear power industry stepped up its pressure on the NRC to sponsor and support regulatory reform legislation. The industry argued that a combination of factors—Reagan's election, the presidential "honeymoon period," and the fact that several years had passed since TMI—had created a "window of opportunity," a time dur-ing which a licensing reform bill stood a good chance of passage. Indeed, Congress itself had indicated some modest interest in such licensing reform, at least to "fine-tune" the licensing process—an example of this can later be seen in the NRC's Authorization Act of 1982 (P.L. 97–415), where the Congress inserted a few provisions which sought to reform NRC administrative procedure.

Moreover, the nuclear industry continued to press its view that a leg-islative rather than administrative solution was necessary for reform efforts to be successful. It felt that only legislation could bring the necessary stability and predictability to the licensing process. In addition, industry officials argued that the NRC had attempted on several past occasions to reform its licensing procedures through the administrative process. Each of these attempts, they felt, had met with either limited success or downright failure due to several factors: a lack of discipline within the NRC bureaucracy; a lack of ordered and systematic review of applications; and an absence of concern by NRC staff for delays and costs caused by unjustified regulations. As one industry official bluntly told us: "The NRC will not approve licenses efficiently and without unnecessary imposition of safety requirements *unless it is forced by statute to do so.*"

Clearly, there was something to be said for both sides of the administration versus legislation argument. In the end, the NRC compromised among its members and staff by adopting a "two-prong" approach to licensing problems. The idea was to develop *both* legislative and administrative packages, so that if legislation was not acted upon by Congress, the NRC would still be prepared to go forth with administrative reform. On the other hand, if legislation was enacted, the Commission would revisit its administrative package and modify it to correspond with the legislation that emerged from Congress. As the two-prong effort continued, it became clear to NRC officials that certain issues could best be handled administratively. The two most important were changes in backfitting requirements and the public hearing process. On these issues, the NRC wanted to retain its internal flexibility, producing significant differences between the legislative approaches of NRC and DOE. As a staff attorney for DOE and a member of the Nuclear Licensing Task Force explained in an interview with us:

Each of the two bills had a particular perspective that the agency that drafted them wanted to get across. We each believed strongly in the approach we took. In the end, our feeling was that we would never have a more captive audience in the Republican controlled Senate. So, we decided to go for the whole nine yards.

This decision may have to some extent involved an unwillingness of NRC to make organizational changes. The chairman of the Regulatory Reform Task Force stated the situation this way: "The fact is, NRC does not want to change. They say they want to change but they don't. Change is difficult. It is easier for DOE to objectively say what change in the regulations should be, because NRC does not want to acknowledge it."

Throughout its legislative drafting process, NRC—extremely aware of its independent agency status—shunned outside comments from both DOE and the White House. Since the NRC is an independent agency, the president could not directly order the commission to give priority attention to nuclear licensing reform. However, he did give strong hints to the NRC in his October 1981 nuclear policy statement as to the direction he would like to see the NRC take. Here, Reagan stated: "I anticipate that the Chairman of the Nuclear Regulatory Commission will take steps to facilitate the licensing of plants under construction and those awaiting licenses" (Reagan 1981, p. 24-E). Unlike the experience of many regulatory agencies—even independent agencies—during this period, OMB adopted a hands-off attitude toward NRC's drafting process. While OMB played a major role in the legislative reform efforts of other agencies, asking to review and approve all proposed legislative packages, this was not the case with the NRC. This situation partly reflected the determination of commission members to keep OMB out of agency efforts at statutory reform. As one NRC commissioner commented in reference to OMB's right to review legislative proposals, "I feel very strongly that in the role of an independent commission, that unless it is strictly a budgetary matter in which case we do go to OMB, other than that, we give them a courtesy copy simultaneous to going to the Hill. This is a point of principle" (NRC 1983, p. 11).

The NRC Regulatory Reform Task Force did seek advice and comments from other actors who had a stake in the outcome, including the nuclear power industry and environmental interest groups. It proved very difficult to walk the narrow line between these competing interests. Environmental and intervenor groups tended to oppose the entire legislative package. From the perspective of these critics the NRC's proposed changes in the backfitting and hearings areas "would generally streamline and speed up the licensing process to the benefit of the nuclear industry at the expense of interveners" (NRC 1982a, p. 3). Many of these groups questioned the need for any licensing reform. They pointed out that no new nuclear plants had been ordered since 1978. Indeed, as a representative from one such group put it, "The nuclear industry is so far gone that nothing can revive it at this point" (Large 1982, p. 8).

Industry officials generally favored the NRC's proposals, although they wanted the NRC to go even further toward regulatory relief and reform, particularly in the area of legislating changes in backfitting requirements. Because it failed in the end to address major industry complaints about backfitting and licensing procedure, the NRC bill was not warmly received by the nuclear industry. Industry representatives reiterated their view that without mandated legislative change, the NRC would have excessive discretion over licensing reform. As one industry lobbyist commented, "The type of reform changes being considered in the areas of backfitting and hybrid hearings would be so major, the NRC would not have the clout to pull it off." Given their concerns over the

NRC version, and the fact that DOE's version was tailor-made to industry specifications, it is not surprising that the nuclear industry put its full weight behind DOE's version, and that it testified before Congress against NRC's proposal, stating that it did not address the industry's licensing problems.

During the 1983 congressional debate on the proposed legislation, it was apparent that the coalitions that would be needed to move either of these legislative proposals could not be formed. On one hand, the DOE bill was perceived by key congressmen as catering to the narrow self-interest of the nuclear power industry. These congressmen aligned with environmental interest groups to successfully block the DOE proposal. On the other hand, the NRC proposal died from apathy. Because there was little to be gained by supporting it—either from the administration or from interest groups—it became an orphan: the NRC introduced it, but no member of Congress wanted to adopt and support its passage.

THE MANAGEMENT STRATEGY AND NUCLEAR REGULATORY REFORM

The cold reception given the NRC's and DOE's licensing reform legislation on Capitol Hill, made it clear that—at least for the short term—legislative regulatory reform was not to be. As one of the NRC's congressional liaisons candidly admitted to us, "Seeking these reforms through the legislative process is a waste of time. There is simply no consensus up there. It won't get done."

Support within NRC for Administrative Reform Strategies

Many at NRC had expected few results from the legislative effort and had favored an administrative approach from the beginning. While this legislative setback left the DOE at a loss because it had no alternative to legislative reform, the NRC was able to fall back on the second prong of its two-prong approach: if legislation was not the answer to licensing reform, the answer could be found in administrative action. Many NRC staffers believed that essentially every proposed reform objective that commissioners had articulated in 1983 could be accomplished administratively. They argued that by utilizing the administrative approach, the NRC could bypass the Congress, put the reforms in place sooner, and maintain a greater degree of control over final versions of rules. As one NRC staff member told us: "If you go to Congress you don't have control. You never know what will be done or when. Additionally, through administrative reform you avoid the 'not invented here' syndrome. It becomes more acceptable to the internal bureaucracy. Our philosophy comes down to this: it is always better to beg the Congress for forgiveness than to ask them for permission."

Several commissioners gave strong support to staff that advocated administrative change. Administrative reform found a home for reasons of history as well as current events. After all, independent commissions historically have enjoyed substantial discretion based on broad regulatory statutes. As Commissioner Gilinsky reminded enthusiasts of legislative reform, "Ever since I came here in 1975 I think there is no subject on which we have spent more time to less purpose than reform legislation. I regard this effort a continuing of that. I wouldn't pursue it. There are a few things here and there that you could tune up through legislation, but what we really ought to address ourselves to is how we can deal with these problems by administrative means" (NRC 1982b, p. 48). Indeed, the NRC had already paved the way for future reform initiatives by undertaking a number of significant administrative changes on its own in 1980 and 1981. These earlier changes were intended to implement some of the less controversial elements of DOE's 1978 reform proposal (see, for example: 46 Fed. Reg. 28630 [May 28, 1981]; 46 Fed. Reg. 30328 [June 9, 1981]; 46 Fed. Reg. 58280 [August 28, 1981]).

While the Commission had the discretionary power to modify its licensing procedures, the prospect of testing the limits of its statutory mandate by radically departing from the status quo in licensing regulation worried many members. It was obvious that should a major nuclear power accident occur, and if the accident were tied to commission licensing reform decisions, the blame would surely be placed at the Commission's doorstep. In addition, individual commissioners—as well as the nuclear power industry officials—were still concerned that administrative licensing reform would achieve very little, in that it would only serve to promote instability over the long term. Several of those we interviewed at NRC expressed concerns that the next administration might appoint commissioners who would reverse all of these reform changes leaving the nuclear power industry worse off than before.

Despite its reservations, given the hostility toward licensing reform on Capitol Hill, and the cross-pressure from industry lobbyists to take some action to modify the 29-year-old licensing process, the commission forged ahead with its administrative reform plans. One top official of the NRC's Regulatory Reform Task Force we interviewed explained why:

This new reform effort is the result of a swing in the pendulum of how we think about nuclear regulation. Everything done to the utilities after Three Mile Island was not completely justified—no new plants, etc. There was a pent up need for reform. Before Three Mile Island, there was too much confidence, but the accident sent a shock wave through the agency: when in doubt, lay an additional regulation. Now the commission questions the desirability of this [overreaction]. Additionally, from a broad standpoint, every agency felt it should do something for reform to bring it in line with the wishes of the [Reagan] Administration.

Thus, long-term perspectives within NRC favoring an administrative approach to regulatory change dove-tailed to some extent with the emerging regulatory strategy of the Reagan administration—what we have termed the management strategy.

Using the Power of Appointments

By 1982, three out of the five NRC commissioners were Reagan appointees, thus giving the president numerical control of the Commission. By 1985 all five were Reagan appointees. By law, no more than three commissioners can be of the same party. Therefore, three of the appointed commissioners were Republicans: Nunzio J. Palladino (Chairman); Frederick J. Bernthal; and Thomas M. Roberts. The other two members were considered to be "Independents": James K. Asselstine and Lando Zech Jr. The Reagan-appointed commissioners did not have to look very far to see that the administration favored handling of "regulatory relief" through administrative rather than statutory means, and that NRC efforts to manage change would be positively regarded by the White House.

In the early days of the administration, according to those we interviewed, when the balance of power in the commission had not substantially tipped in favor of the White House-appointed commission members, the NRC moved slowly and incrementally in the direction of licensing reform. This was the period when the NRC drafted its own reform legislation because it regarded the DOE version as too radical and too invasive of the commission's discretion. By 1982, however, given Reagan's numerical control of the commission, NRC's regulatory policy began to reflect administration views to a greater extent.

Reexamination of Existing Rules and Mandating a Regulatory Slowdown

There are clear indications that the NRC has been extensively involved in reexamination of their existing rules with an emphasis toward providing regulatory relief, as well as putting in place a mandated slowdown in the issuance of major new regulations. The vast majority of those interviewed characterized the extensiveness of the NRC reexamination effort and efforts at mandating a regulatory slowdown as moderate to heavy.

Reexamination of existing rules has primarily taken place under the jurisdiction of the Committee to Review Generic Requirements (CRGR), established in October 1981. Composed of senior career agency personnel, this committee examined the "appropriateness" of all new proposed generic requirements, that is, requirements to be imposed upon all nuclear plants. The appropriateness of a new requirement was to be defined through a highly technical cost-benefit analysis, a technique that has been highly criticized both inside and outside the Commission. As NRC Commissioner Asselstine (1986) points out in regards to applying cost-benefit analysis to backfitting rules,

[T]he list of factors to be considered under the rule in evaluating the benefits and costs of proposed backfits heavily weighs the evaluation in favor of cost considerations. Potential benefits such as the reduction in the likelihood of serious operating events and accidents, avoiding the loss of on-site property, and assuring the long-term availability of the plant's generating capacity are ignored, while every possible cost, including such questionable "costs" as the NRC resource burden, is emphasized. (49 *Federal Register* 47040)

While the NRC has argued that the CRGR has proven to be a "catalyst for better management oversight" and that it "has been accepted by the NRC staff as a reality," CRGR review has been highly criticized by concerned groups outside the Commission. Intervenor groups have charged that the real purpose of the CRGR is to create a de facto system of regulatory relief by erecting such stubborn administrative barriers that it becomes virtually impossible for any new regulations to be approved. As the Union of Concerned Scientists argued:

While the concept of improving the process to assure that new requirements are well-considered and justified is certainly supportable, NRC actions have aimed less toward this goal and more toward creating a system in which licensees can avoid or substantially delay the implementation of needed safety improvements. These actions demonstrate a dangerous retreat from the "safety first" standard of the Atomic Energy Act. (Union of Concerned Scientists 1985, p. 39)

In fact, NRC staff have reported that the CRGR review process has been the direct cause of a substantial reduction in the number of new generic requirements that have been issued by the Commission. Data available for 1982 indicates that the number of new generic requirements issued for that year dropped 53 percent—from 1900 new operating reactor licensing actions to 900 new actions (Murley 1983).

By 1983 the Commission came to the realization that CRGR review by itself would not be effective in managing backfits that occurred on an individual plant basis. Consequently, the NRC began to work administratively on a program that would ensure better management of the plant-specific backfitting process. The result of this effort was a new backfitting rule that became effective October 21, 1985. This rule sought to define not only what backfitting was, but what was required of the NRC staff when backfits are to be imposed, what exceptions to the rule would be allowable, and who within the Commission staff would be responsible for the proper application of the rule. The new backfitting rule specified that the Commission would require the backfitting of a facility only when it determined:

based upon a systematic and documented analysis, that there is a substantial increase in overall protection of public health and safety or the common defense and security to be derived from the backfit and that the direct and indirect costs of implementation for that facility are justified in view of this increased protection. (NRC 1986, p. 3)

One NRC commissioner—James Asselstine—has expressed open opposition to the new backfit rule. Despite the fact that he is a Reagan appointee, Commissioner Asselstine has rarely sided with the other commissioners, and in many cases has been the lone dissenter to the new regulatory direction the Commission has taken. His opposition to the backfit rule and the regulatory direction the Commission has embarked upon is evident in comments he submitted to the Congress:

In adopting this backfitting rule, the Commission continues its inexorable march down the path toward non-regulation of the nuclear industry.... The Commission's rule in effect says that nuclear reactor risks are so acceptable and so well understood that the burden of proof for lowering the risk to the public must be placed on the proponent of improved safety even if that proponent is the Commission itself. This optimistic view of the risks posed by nuclear power plants is unjustified. The Commission's adoption of this rule is truly an unprecedented step in the annals of regulation. I can think of no other instance in which a regulatory agency has been so eager to stymie its own ability to carry out its responsibilities. Indeed, the adoption of this rule is the most compelling evidence to date of the Commission majority's open hostility to the regulatory mission of this agency. (Asselstine 1986, pp. 1–2)

NRC administrative reform actions have also involved the question of public access to agency deliberations. Under the 1977 Sunshine Act, regulatory agencies are required to open their meetings to the public. On May 16, 1985, by a 3–2 vote the Commission, for example, changed its rules so that staff briefings and discussions could be held in secret. No official transcript of what transpired during these meetings would be kept. The NRC argued that the Sunshine Act's open meeting policy had simply become "unworkable" and had needlessly slowed down the entire regulatory apparatus.

NRC has always resisted Sunshine requirements to some extent. A study on the implementation and effect of the Sunshine Act sponsored by the Administrative Conference of the United States found that between 1977 and 1981 the NRC failed to publish seven-day advance notice of its meetings in the Federal Register approximately half the time (Welborn, Lyons, Thomas 1984, pp. 37–38). In addition, on several occasions, the NRC has been found by the courts to have violated provisions within the Sunshine Act (see: *Common Cause et al.* v. *Nuclear Regulatory Commission* 674 F. 2d 921 [D.C. Cir. Feb. 26 1982]; *Philadelphia Newspapers Inc.* v. *Nuclear Regulatory Commission*, 727 f. 2d 1195 [Feb. 10, 1984]).

In its recent attempts to relax requirements for open meetings commissioners argued that open meetings limited their ability to engage in frank discussion with their colleagues. As newly appointed NRC Chairman Lando Zech Jr. noted in congressional testimony,

Collegial decision-making and efficient management are not well suited for each other. For example, prompt decision-making is difficult because time must be afforded for each Commissioner to consider the issues and provide separate views. As a result, there is frequently delay in responding to requests from Congress, in issuing adjudicatory decisions, making rule-making decisions, and providing policy direction to the NRC staff. Debate of issues is often unduly prolonged in an attempt to develop a consensus position, and because of the diverse Commissioner views, the NRC staff and the public sometimes received confused signals.

Moreover, the Government in the Sunshine Act has greatly diminished the exchange of diverse views which is the primary benefit of a Commission structure. The Commission cannot usually meet as a body except in public meetings. This requirement that Commission deliberations be held in scheduled public meetings greatly diminishes the opportunity and quality of such exchange of views. (Zech 1986, pp. 7–8)

To avoid being charged with noncompliance with the Sunshine Act requirements, the NRC deftly redefined what constituted a "meeting," arguing that "brainstorming sessions" and "agenda-planning meeting" do not require public access or a transcript of the proceedings. Critics have argued that such changes would effectively eliminate public participation in the hearing process since transcripts of NRC meetings have been used by intervenors as the basis for lawsuits concerning licensing of nuclear plants.

NRC has also moved forward with administrative plans to make certain procedural changes in the hearing process. The new rules would make it more difficult for outside parties to raise issues, cross-examine witnesses, and generally partake in licensing hearings before the Commission. As in the past, intervenors have strongly opposed any such changes. As the general counsel for the Conservation Council of North Carolina pointedly argued in a letter to commissioners,

Since the early 1970's, [we have] intervened in both the construction permit and operating license for Shearon Harris Nuclear Power Plant (Carolina Power & Light) and we strongly urge you not to make the process even more a sham than it already is. The entire licensing process is overwhelmingly skewed to the benefit of the Applicant, with the NRC staff in most instances taking an active role supporting the Applicants in discouraging all public involvement. If you will review the history of the plants which have been cancelled, indefinitely postponed, or have had licenses denied, you will see that second to the finances involved, safety issues first proposed by Interveners are the major cause. The ability for concerned citizens to bring forward issues concerning the environment, safety, safeguards, emergency planning, and management has so far greatly enhanced the process rather than detracted from it. . . . [T]he proposed "licensing reform" rules are a pure and simple attempt to make meaningless public participation through intervention. There is not one instance of the hearing process unjustifiably delaying plant licensing, although there are documented instances when serious safety and environmental issues were raised by intervention. The rights of the public must be protected. (Runkle 1986, p. 2)

It should be noted that intervenors have not been the only groups that have complained of difficulty in participating and overseeing NRC rule making since the Commission attained a Reagan-appointed majority. Congress itself has been hampered in its ability to oversee NRC activities. While the Atomic Energy Act provides that the Commission shall keep the Congress "fully and currently informed with respect to the activities of the . . . Commission" (42 U.S.C. Section 303a), the Commission has not been highly cooperative in recent years in regards to responding to subcommittee inquiries and document requests. This lack of responsiveness in certain instances, has had impacts on the administrative rules the NRC has promulgated. For instance, a congressional request for information over NRC's proposed changes in its licensing process was delayed seven months, by which time the proposed licensing changes had already been made into a final rule. This delay effectively removed Congress from having any input into the matter. This and other similar NRC actions brought forth a sharp response from one congressman charged with overseeing NRC activities, who wrote in a letter to Chairman Palladino that

[I]n the past several months, there have been a number of instances wherein the Commission has not only failed to keep the relevant committees informed, but has withheld, for an unnecessary period of time and without authority, information which should have been submitted to Congress and which had been specifically requested by such committee[s]. The number and nature of these instances form a pattern of behavior on the part of the Commission which is inconsistent with its statutory responsibility and which constitutes a totally unacceptable level of performance on the part of the Commission, its Chairman and members. While the Commission's efforts to withhold or delay the release of information is not unique within the context of this [Reagan] Administration, the number of instances and the length of the delays set the Commission apart. (Ottinger 1982, p. 1)

In summary, the NRC had undertaken several administrative actions that have clearly flowed from the Commission's new found support for achieving regulatory relief through administrative means. Many of the administrative actions taken by the NRC have had a direct and immediate effect on the promulgation of new rules, while other administrative actions have been notably more indirect. As one commissioner confided to us, "In many instances the Commission has not directly sought to slowdown the issuance of new regulations. To do so might have important political overtones. Instead, the Commission has moved to indirectly erect barriers to new regulations. Through changes in our internal review process, and by developing a new generic process, we have created bottlenecks so that the entire process slows down."

Relaxation of Enforcement of Existing Rules and Budgetary Pressures on NRC

Perhaps the most difficult area to assess the degree to which regulatory reform has taken place is in the area of relaxation efforts to enforce existing rules. This is true for several reasons. First, it is not in the agency's best interest to admit candidly that it is not enforcing regulations that are legally called for, since this would have obvious legal and political ramifications. Second, empirical evidence of nonenforcement is extremely difficult to acquire. In many cases, one has to rely on watchdog groups that closely monitor enforcement efforts, even though the reports of these groups may represent a particular bias. Given the above problems, we sought to diversify our sources of information as best we could, and have utilized data collected from interviews, congressional testimony, and evidence collected by intervenor groups. In general, we found that the NRC had not significantly relaxed efforts to enforce existing regulations. Respondents overwhelmingly characterized NRC relaxation efforts as being slight to nonexistent. However, despite these assertions, there were several indications that the NRC would not be able to enforce its rules or develop new regulations with the same vigor it had shown in the past.

One reason for this decline in vigor is that Reagan administration officials have the power of the purse over NRC. Through its control of the budget, Reagan officials—particularly those within OMB—have apparently wielded a significant long-term impact on NRC's regulatory agenda. Budgetary changes at NRC during the Reagan years tell us something about changing agency emphases and even indicate some-

Table 6.2
**Nuclear Regulatory Commission Budget Allocations for Fiscal Years
1981–87**

Program Area	Nuclear Regulatory Budget Allocation (in millions)							*Percent Change 1981–87*	*Inflation Adjusted Change (in percent) 1981–87[3]*
	1981	*1982*	*1983*	*1984*	*1985*	*1986[1]*	*1987[2]*		
Nuclear reactor regulation	81	87	91	93	86	80	80	− 1	− 9
Inspection and enforcement	53	59	69	82	94	94	98	87	72
Nuclear regulatory research	227	220	207	191	150	129	113	− 50	− 54
Nuclear material safety and safeguards	34	37	35	38	40	39	39	17	7
Total budget authority	449	466	467	466	448	413	405	− 10	− 17

Notes: 1. Net appropriation after Gramm-Rudman-Hollings sequestration
2. Congressional Budget Office estimate
3. Based on a deflator of .837.
Source: U.S. Congressional Budget Office, 1986.

thing about the quality of enforcement. As Table 6.2 indicates, between 1981 and 1987, NRC's budget fell by 10 percent—17 percent in inflation-adjusted dollars. During this same time period, a number of new nuclear plants became operational and new safety issues have arisen, so NRC activities and these expenditures might have been expected to increase. Moreover, if we look beyond the overall reductions toward specific budget areas, we can see that there is cause for concern that NRC's capacity to carry out its regulatory function may be deteriorating.

As Table 6.2 shows, the only area that has shown any substantial growth during this period has been the inspections and enforcement area, whose budget has been increased by a seemingly healthy 72 percent (adjusted for inflation). This growth is confirmed by the figures in Table 6.3, which show the number of nuclear licensees inspected and the over-all number of inspections carried out between 1981 and 1985. In general, the number of licensees inspected and inspections carried out have either increased or remained stable during this time period across program areas. As one commissioner explained to us, "Events such as Three Mile Island have precluded cutbacks in our inspection and enforcement ef-

Table 6.3
Total Number of Licensees Inspected and Number of Inspections
Conducted by the NRC: 1981–85

Program	Number of Licensees Inspected				
	1981	1982	1983	1984	1985
Power reactor construction	93	76	62	50	40
Operating power reactors	82	70	79	85	92
Other reactors	84	36	41	42	53
Fuel facilities	50	35	153	295	42
Materials	8,769	2,107	1,624	1,685	2,048
Vendors	300	109	131	90	n/a
Shipments of spent fuel	n/a	22	55	55	96
Program	Number of Inspections Conducted				
	1981	1982	1983	1984	1985
Power reactor construction	1,669	1,471	1,383	1,386	1,210
Operating power reactors	1,931	1,995	2,043	2,272	3,136
Other reactors	85	56	70	66	86
Fuel facilities	222	279	238	464	233
Materials	2,261	2,196	1,669	1,751	2,131
Vendors	181	143	275	160	150
Shipments of spent fuel	426	292	475	475	98

Source: U.S. Nuclear Regulatory Commission, Annual Reports 1981–85.

forts. You have to enforce given the current environment." Nonetheless, several commissioners testified under questioning by the House Subcommittee on Energy Conservation and Power, that funds allocated for inspections and enforcement are still far below the levels that are actually needed to ensure an adequate inspection program, and consequently, safety inspections of nuclear facilities in terms of maintenance, equipment testing and fire protection would have to be reduced. The program areas of nuclear reactor regulation and nuclear regulatory research have both declined in inflation-adjusted terms. Cuts have been most severe in the area of nuclear regulatory research, where reduced spending fell by 54 percent in inflation-adjusted terms between 1981 and 1987. Moreover, the share of Commission resources going to research is shrinking. While in 1981, nuclear regulatory research made up 51 percent of the total NRC budget, it is estimated that this figure will shrink to 28 percent by 1987.

These cuts in research activities have been highly controversial. Critics see them as OMB's attempt to impose future regulatory ventilation. The reasoning behind this change is as follows: NRC's nuclear regulatory research program develops and tests new technologies; if the Commission is not able to conduct research on new technologies or complete experiments on what new dangers may be posed by present-day nuclear plants, the chances that new regulations will be needed and instituted (thereby forcing utilities to make costly backfits) will be dramatically reduced. These actions make it likely that there will be fewer new regulations in the future, since the decline in NRC research activities will produce even less of a scientific basis for justifying need for them. OMB officials have denied this charge, arguing instead that NRC's research budget received the lion's share of the cuts for two reasons: (1) NRC officials did a poor job of justifying the need for these monies; and (2) because research funds represented the largest pool of money in their budget, these cuts were easier to make here.

Added to these budgetary pressures that either have slowed down the pace of new regulations or will do so in the future, intervenors have charged that the NRC over the past decade has simply been lax and arbitrary when it has come to regulatory enforcement. For example, the Union of Concerned Scientists has charged that:

The NRC's treatment of its regulations and the law have suffered when the agency's *de facto* priorities—licensing reactors, keeping them on line and minimizing financial hardships on utilities—are at stake. When a problem could not be put aside by labeling it generic (because the issue has already been formally resolved in a regulation), or a hearing might have impeded speedy licensing, the NRC has sometimes simply ignored its regulations. In other cases, where plants do not meet the regulations, the NRC has hastily changed its regulations to match the plants. Other NRC actions have shown disrespect for the legal requirements of the federal Administrative Procedure Act and the Atomic Energy Act. (Union of Concerned Scientists 1985, p. 107)

As a result of the limited amount of evidence that is available over nonenforcement activities, we cannot conclusively say whether the NRC is or is not engaging in this particular regulatory reform strategy. However, it is clear that when relaxation efforts as a strategy are compared with clear evidence of use of several other elements of the management strategy at NRC, there seems to be a good deal of evidence suggesting that this has not been one of their primary strategies to date.

Indirect Administrative Intervention by Executive Officials

While it is clear that the Reagan administration has been able to influence NRC's regulatory process through the use of its appointment and budgetary power, it has not stopped there. The Reagan administration has sought to realize even more of its regulatory relief agenda than the NRC seemed likely to produce on its own. Since NRC is an independent regulatory commission, it has been relatively isolated from executive branch intervention. Even so, however, the Reagan administration has been able to use the executive branch agencies DOE and OMB to some extent to apply pressure on NRC. Such pressures have been most notable in two areas: DOE's activist stance in championing the licensing of nuclear power plants and OMB's monitoring of NRC rule making as provided under the Paperwork Reduction Act.

Department of Energy Intervention. Under the leadership of Reagan's Energy Secretary Donald Hodel, DOE increasingly sought to play an activist role in nuclear power affairs. We have already seen the aggressive role that the Reagan Energy Department has played in the formulation of nuclear regulatory reform legislation. In addition, in recent years, DOE has increasingly sought to intervene in administrative regulatory matters that have traditionally been the sole province of the NRC. This new activist stance first became evident in a speech Secretary Hodel gave before a conference of nuclear industry executives, during which he declared that in an effort to speed the licensing of nuclear plants, DOE would become more involved in proceedings before the NRC: "The NRC has been buffeted in recent times by a great deal of controversy...I think it's just time for the Department of Energy to be out there to point out how these plants affect [national energy] policy" (Russakoff 1984, p. C2). Specifically, Hodel outlined several areas where he felt DOE could become more involved: testifying in more state and federal proceedings on licensing and rate increases, and helping NRC conduct "readiness reviews" of plants under construction. These plans have troubled some NRC officials. For instance, Victor Gilensky, a past NRC commissioner, feared that DOE participation in readiness reviews would "defeat the purpose of an independent safety review. DOE is too involved with the utilities. It is not proper to conduct safety reviews on plants that you yourself are helping" (Russakoff 1984, p. C2).

One issue in which DOE intervention has been quite noticeable was in the struggle over licensing the Shoreham nuclear power plant operated by Long Island Lighting Company (LILCO). Federal law requires that each nuclear facility operator must have an effective evacuation plan. Shoreham county officials as well as New York Governor Mario Cuomo, however, maintained that the plan developed by LILCO was inadequate in that it did not provide for the safe evacuation of residents. As a result of the objections of county officials and their failure to ratify or participate in LILCO's evacuation plan, the $4.2 billion plant was blocked from going into service. When LILCO asked the federal government to intervene and overrule state and county officials, President Reagan refused, stating: "This Administration does not favor the imposition of Federal Government authority over the objections of state and local governments in matters regarding the adequacy of an emergency evacuation plan for a nuclear power plant such as Shoreham"

(Wald 1985, p. C1). Despite the president's assertion, however, investigations into the Shoreham case by the House Energy and Commerce's Subcommittee on Energy and Conservation and Power found that DOE had been working secretly behind the scenes to develop proposals through which the president could use his authority (as vested in the Civil Defense Act of 1950) to intercede and overrule state and local officials, thereby allowing the plant to operate.

OMB Control via the Paperwork Reduction Act. NRC's independent status precluded President Reagan from direct oversight of NRC regulatory reform efforts through the new executive orders 12291 and 12498. However, as the Reagan administration quickly discovered, other vehicles existed through which the president could oversee NRC regulatory activities. One likely vehicle was the Paperwork Reduction Act of 1980. Under this Act, Congress granted the chief executive broad powers to oversee and control the amount of paperwork generated by federal agencies. In particular, the Act gave OMB control over all federal reporting requirements and forms that requested information from the public or businesses. The impact that the Paperwork Reduction Act could have on the generation of new regulations—which almost always carry with them new reporting and record-keeping requirments—was quite evident. If OMB found that a proposed regulation would create additional burdensome reporting requirements, it could disapprove it for failing to comply with the criteria for approval as outlined by the Paperwork Reduction Act.

The Reagan administration lost little time in outlining to NRC commissioners its philosophy toward new regulations and how it planned to implement its reviews under the Paperwork Reduction Act. In the first months of the Reagan administration, Christopher Demuth (OIRA chief administrator) sent a letter to NRC Chairman Palladino, outlining actions NRC had to take in order to receive approval of new rules in the future:

NRC's needs and the practical utility of the data must be balanced more effectively against the burdens and costs involved.... Assuring the practical utility of the information for NRC will help minimize burden on licensees and applicants. This means NRC should be collecting only such data as it can use: seeking only that level of detail needed; having it submitted no sooner than the likely time of actual use; and precisely defining record-keeping requirements and retention periods, based on likely periods of actual inspection and use. Once the data is obtained, NRC should be actually using it, following up promptly and conclusively with the respondent, as necessary. (Demuth 1981, p. 2)

Thus, for NRC to get OMB approval to institute new regulatory requirements, new rules had to meet the Paperwork Reduction Act's dual criteria of "practical utility" and "burden reduction." Failure to do so would mean disapproval of the new rule. Since these terms had not been explicitly defined in the act, a lot of latitude was left for OMB interpretation. OMB has utilized this power to block several new regulations that the NRC had proposed.

One example of OMB's wielding its new power over NRC is the rejection by the budget agency of the many reporting and record-keeping requirements recommended by NRC to its "Insider Safeguard Rules" (amendments to 10 CFR, Parts 50 and 73, proposed August 1, 1984, 49 FR 30726–30739). One of the new rules proposed by the NRC called for psychological assessment and behavioral observation of those persons that are granted unescorted access to restricted or security areas at nuclear power plants. The NRC felt that only through such protective measures could the commission ensure the trustworthiness and suitability of these individuals.

OMB, however, rejected this proposed rule on grounds that it failed to meet the budget agency's definition of practical utility and burden reduction. As a member of OMB's regulatory analysis staff informed NRC Chairman Palladino:

Our first problem relates to the practical utility of the proposed psychological assessment. It is to be used to predict whether the licensee's employees or contractor personnel have 'a potential for committing acts that are inimical to the public health and safety or present a danger to life or property' (49 FR 30733). To be useful, the psychological assessment has to have a validated history of success at predicting the characteristics sought to be identified. The proposed rule neither specifies the psychological assessment test to be used, nor defines the psychological characteristics to be identified, nor explains how any identified characteristics are to be weighed in determining employee trustworthiness.... Our second problem relates to the burden that would be imposed by using the proposed psychological assessment for the purpose stated in the proposed rule. To the extent the data collections and record-keeping requirements are invalidated, the regulation would impose an undue burden. (Coad 1984, pp. 1–2)

Consequently, the rule was disapproved and returned to NRC. Thus, while NRC's status as an independent commission precluded the administration from fully using the types of regulatory management tools that were available when dealing with executive branch agencies, nonetheless, OMB has been able to intervene in NRC regulatory policy-making and significantly affect the regulatory direction taken by the NRC.

SUMMARY AND CONCLUSIONS

In this chapter we have examined the regulatory reform efforts of the Reagan administration in regard to nuclear licensing—a policy area in which the industry involved is financially troubled and eager for regulatory reform; a highly technical area in which the costs of mistakes are potentially catastrophic; a very controversial area in which the watch-dog organizations are strong and well organized; and an area in which the primary regulatory agency is an independent commission, thus to some extent insulated from direct executive branch control. In this policy area, the Reagan administration tried going the route of statutory reform, and then fell back on whatever elements of the management strategy that could be applied within a policy area chiefly governed by an independent regulatory agency.

The administration—partly at the behest of the nuclear power industry, which was quite convinced that regulatory changes of the necessary breadth and stability could only be achieved by changing the statutes governing licensing regulations—made a serious attempt to achieve regulatory reform through legislative means. DOE prepared draft legislation that was closely in line with what industry wanted. At the same time, also at the urging of the nuclear power industry, NRC prepared its own draft legislation that was somewhat more protective of the NRC role and somewhat less reflective of industry desires.

Both legislative attempts fizzled in Congress, however. The statutory reform effort was hurt by the general lack of cooperation between NRC and DOE in developing a reform bill, the traditional unwillingness of Congress to legislate in this highly technical area, and the inability of industry spokespersons to make a convincing case that the regulatory reforms recommended would actually address the underlying economic, technical, and management problems of the nuclear power industry.

In contrast, the administrative approach has been much more successful. Through administrative strategies, NRC and a sympathetic Reagan administration have been able to provide the nuclear power industry with at least some degree of short-term regulatory relief. Although not able to apply all of the requirements for centralized regulatory administration put in place for executive branch agencies, President Reagan has skillfully been able to work around NRC's independent status and bring about regulatory changes through a combination of appointments, budget cuts, DOE intervention, and OMB reviews under the Paperwork Reduction Act. Moreover, the budgetary changes initiated at NRC during the Reagan years have significantly diminished the commission's regulatory research activities, a change in agency emphasis that promises a slowing down of the production of new regulations in the future.

The regulatory relief that has been gained through administrative means—such as modifications in NRC's backfit rule and hearing procedures—are viewed by the Commission as an important beginning in reducing the regulatory burden on the nuclear power industry. But it seems unlikely that these changes alone will significantly reduce the costs and time it takes to construct nuclear facilities or that they will effectively revive the economically troubled nuclear industry. At most, these types of reforms will help only those utilities that are currently operating nuclear facilities.

Most important, the administrative reforms that have been made in no way address the two major concerns of the nuclear power industry in regards to regulation—the necessity for increasing the predictability and stability of the regulatory environment. These goals can only be met through major statutory changes, for example, by establishing standardization of plant design or creating some type of hybrid hearing process. Thus—in spite of Ronald Reagan's sincere belief in the need for regulatory reform and his administration's evident sympathy for the reform agenda of the nuclear power industry—the administration's regulatory reform efforts in the nuclear arena can only be considered a very partial success.

7 THE LIMITS OF THE MANAGEMENT STRATEGY

It is a truism that the U.S. political system is one of checks and balances: among the legislative, executive, and judicial branches of government; between the federal government and the states; between the appointed bureaucracy and elected officials; and among the crosscurrents of influences on public decisions from public opinion, the media, and different interest groups. This chapter focuses on these types of institutional constraints as they were brought to bear on the regulatory reform initiatives of the Reagan administration, and then moves on to make an evaluation of these efforts.

We will first look at the role of Congress, an institution that, as we have seen, traditionally bears a major portion of the responsibility for regulation. We will examine congressional responses to the regulatory initiatives of the Reagan administration. We will then look at the responses of other potentially constraining institutions: interest groups, public opinion, the courts, the media, and the federal system itself. Then we will evaluate Reagan's regulatory reform strategy in terms of its overall effectiveness and its appropriateness. We will see how Reagan's apparent dramatic regulatory successes measure up against two different standards: the standard of regulatory relief and the standard of rational regulatory reform. Finally, we speculate about the lessons our findings might hold for students of the presidency and for future presidents themselves.

INSTITUTIONAL CONSTRAINTS ON THE MANAGEMENT STRATEGY

Congress and the Management Strategy

A long line of learned commissions has urged strengthened presidential management of regulatory policy. Fisher commented that while many of these studies caution Congress to leave regulatory administration strictly to the president, Congress has followed this advice only to a limited extent, and has stuck to its strong regulatory role, for reasons that are fundamental to our system of government. "Presidents and their supporters face continued frustration because they ignore, or try to overlook, the legitimate stake and interest of Congress in administrative matters" (Fisher 1981, pp. 108–109).

The Reagan administration, as we have seen, seized the early initiative in its struggle with Congress in the regulatory administrative arena. Reagan launched his management strategy to gain control of the regulatory bureaucracy in the earliest days of his presidency. During 1981, Reagan issued Executive Order 12291, which established a centralized regulatory review process, and he vigorously exploited his powers under the new Paperwork Reduction Act, which created OIRA (the Office of Information and Regulatory Affairs) within OMB as the agency responsible for coordinating this process.

Very soon, however, Congress began to reassert itself in regulatory administration. By 1982, Congress had rebounded, more energetically conducting oversight of such aspects of regulatory administration as OMB regulatory review activities, delays in the promulgation of rules, and laxity in the enforcement of existing regulatory requirements. Congress blocked a number of administration budget rescissions and deferrals in favored grant and regulatory programs, and it consistently appropriated more funds for agencies that administered social regulatory programs than the administration requested.

Congress did not merely attempt to prevent the president from making substantive regulatory changes through the management strategy, it also took aim at the review process and the legitimacy of OIRA as an institution. Nor was it unmindful of Reagan appointees; it locked horns with several highly unpopular administrators of regulatory agencies, contributing to their forced departure. In retrospect, it is clear that the onslaught of unilateral administrative actions during the so-called honeymoon period offended congressional sensibilities and hardened some members' resolve not to compromise with the administration on statutory reforms.

The strategy of appointing political and ideological loyalists undermined support for the president's regulatory program not only because of the inflammatory styles of certain administrators, but also because White House demands on administrators violated conventional norms governing regulatory responsibilities held by agency and department heads. When making regulatory decisions, agency heads are responsible to the president, but not exclusively; they must also make quasi-legislative judgments required by statute and judicial interpretation. Because the administration centralized regulatory decision making at the White House and OMB, traditional working relationships between agency and congressional staff were often impaired as agencies became sometimes unable to deliver on agreements made with Congress. This, in turn, limited avenues for negotiated settlements on regulatory issues of substantial importance to both sides. As a result, Congress intensified its oversight of agency activities, in some cases involving emotionally charged, confrontational incidents. For example, in the case of the Civil Rights Commission—created as an independent commission in 1957— Congress was sufficiently displeased that it voted to cut drastically the agency's funds for fiscal year 1987. Civil rights advocates accused the commission majority of using ideologically compatible consultants and political appointees as a way of bypassing the career staff. A GAO report found that the chairman, Clarence Pendleton, had turned his part-time post into a full-time job, billing the commission for more than twice the number of days charged by any other commissioner. Indeed, the situation between the embattled commission and Congress and its supporters among civil rights activists had so deteriorated by 1986 that the few civil rights leaders and liberals who remained on the commission were calling for the commission to be abolished, presumably because it was harming, not helping, the cause of civil rights. In response, the Senate first voted to cut the commission's budget in half, while the House initially voted to eliminate funds altogether. Thereafter, a compromise was struck between the two bodies which allowed the agency to continue, contained in an omnibus appropriations bill passed in October, 1986—the so-called continuing resolution.

When Congress recognized that many sensitive administrative decisions, especially in agency rule making, were being heavily influenced by OMB, the budget office became a special target for oversight. Chapter 2 described how under the Executive Orders 12291 and 12498 OMB applied strict efficiency tests to agency regulatory decisions, often contrary to congressional intentions. OMB's emphasis on reducing the costs of regulation to the federal government (as in the case of intergovernmental regulation), as well as to the private sector (as in the case of nuclear licensing and environmental protection), and its disregard for equity considerations offended some key members of Congress. Unfortunately for OMB, no congressional champions emerged to counter the growing opposition.

The cost-cutting emphasis at OMB left it particularly vulnerable to congressional rhetoric. However neutral the concepts of efficiency and risk assessment seemed to be to the economists at OIRA, such terms were readily translated into pejoratives by congressional critics, pejoratives implying quick relief for industry at the expense of the general public. Consider the following exchange between Senator Albert Gore, Jr. (D-TN) and OMB Director James Miller during an oversight hearing.

Senator Gore: You said in your testimony just a moment ago that OMB concluded that the grain dust standard as submitted to OMB for review was deeply flawed because, for one thing, this risk to the three workers who were killed in Knoxville was grossly overstated?

Director Miller: That is not the appropriate use of the term, 'risk'.

Senator Gore: They faced a risk when they walked into that grain elevator.... The risk was identified before they walked in, and a distinguished panel of scientists, the agency responsible for assessing that risk, and others had said, 'We have to remove this risk.... It can cause loss of life.' After that decision was made by OSHA, they submitted their assessment of the risk and their proposed remedy to OMB. OMB decided, in your view, that the risk was grossly overstated. While OMB held [the rule] up, the risk continued. The measures to remove the risk were not allowed to be put into place because of OMB's interference. Subsequent to OMB's interference, these three men walked into the grain elevator and faced that same risk, which should have been removed, and they lost their lives as a result. My question to you is, in retrospect, do you believe that the risk faced by those three workers, when they walked into that grain elevator was grossly overstated? (Senate, Subcommittee on Intergovernmental Relations, January 28, 1986)

From the congressional viewpoint, the most damaging aspect of OIRA's application of cost-benefit analysis has perhaps been that, in practice, it has only benefited those who oppose regulations, principally business and industry. This apparent bias led Congress to attack OMB for substituting its economic judgement for agency scientific expertise. The comments of Congressman Gerry Sikorski (D-MN) at a 1986 House oversight hearing illustrate these concerns:

From our April 1985 hearing on OMB's interference in EPA's formulation of asbestos regulations [it is clear] that OMB is simply acting as a back-door conduit by which industry can lobby in secret to save its own selfish interests. OMB blocked the proposed asbestos regulations saying a life saved was only worth $20,000 and calling for more study—even though asbestos has been a known carcinogenic for 20 years, and the regulations themselves were proposed before, and the scientists and doctors and health experts said act now. So the instruments of this zippered-lip, secret decision making process are not informed professionals or doctors, scientists or environmentalists. Instead, the health and safety of 240 million Americans is left to faceless, unelected and unaccountable economists and lawyers, equipped only to say, no, go slow, what about our friends in industry? (U.S. House of Representatives, May 8, 1986)

As these comments also illustrate, Congress has objected as well to the secrecy that surrounds OMB's review of agency rules. OMB has resisted public disclosure on two grounds: first, disclosure would violate executive privilege, and second, disclosure is not required because OMB comments are advisory only. Few members of Congress have been persuaded by these arguments, however. For example, Senator Dave Durenberger (R-MN), chairman of the Subcommittee on Intergovernmental Relations, Committee on Governmental Affairs that oversees OIRA, has urged the need for disclosure on several grounds: "OMB can delay proposed rules for any length of time. It can interfere with statutory deadlines. It can serve as a secret conduit for industry opposition to rules. It can impose its own limited interpretation of cost-benefit analysis to the exclusion of other relevant considerations" (Senate, Subcommittee on Intergovernmental Relations, January, 1986, p. 61).

As these comments suggest, in many cases, it was the manner in which the administration conducted regulatory review as much as the content of the administration's regulatory agenda that produced the greatest congressional backlash. Opposition has been stronger in the House, led by Congressman John Dingell (D-MI), chairman of the subcommittee on Oversight and Investigations, Committee on Energy and Commerce. Under his leadership, House oversight activities have been almost constant, resulting in thousands of pages of hearings, transcripts, and committee reports. For example, in 1982, the Senate overwhelmingly passed S. 1080, the Regulatory Reform Act, but, largely due to Dingell's efforts, this legislation failed to pass the House. Beginning in 1985, Dingell dramatically stepped up his oversight efforts. In June, 1985, he and four other committee chairmen, William Ford (D-MI), Augustus Hawkins (D-CA), Peter Rodino (D-NJ), and Jack Brooks (D-TX), joined Public Citizen Health Research Group in suing the executive branch regulatory agency, OSHA, for failure to promulgate regulations governing the short-term exposure of hospital workers to the carcinogen, ethylene oxide (C_2H_4O) (D.C. Circuit Court of Appeals, No. 84–1252 [1986] p. 57). In June, 1986, Dingell moved to eliminate appropriations for OIRA under the rationale that the Paperwork Reduction Act, which provided legislative authorization for the office, had expired in 1983. He convinced Brooks, chairman of the Committee on Government Operations, which oversees the Paperwork Act and OIRA in the House, to join him, urging the Appropriations Committee to defund the regulatory review unit. Because of these efforts, in July, 1986, the House Appropriations Committee voted to eliminate OIRA's entire budget of $5.4 million and to bar OMB from using any other funds to support presidential regulatory review.

Growing opposition in the House during the mid–1980s alerted the Senate. As evidence of OMB heavy-handedness mounted, the Senate increased its oversight as well. Initially, most activity was centered in the Environment and Public Works Committee, which, beginning in 1985, held frequent subcommittee hearings on agency delays in environmental rule making. Oversight activities included such emotionally charged problems as toxic substances regulations, leaking underground toxic storage tanks, groundwater pollution, and drinking water quality regulations. In 1986, several members of the Governmental Affairs Committee introduced S. 2023, the Rulemaking Information Act, intended to open up the OMB regulatory review process to unprecedented levels of public scrutiny. This legislation also proposed to limit the length of time OIRA could take to review rules to 60 days. Despite requests for comment during drafting stages, OMB remained silent on the legislation for several months. Finally, when called to Capitol Hill to testify on the bill in January, 1986, OMB Director Miller objected to the proposed legislation in the strongest terms, stating that it would fundamentally interfere with the president's ability to execute his management responsibilities (Senate, Subcommittee on Intergovernmental Relations, January 1986).

Later, however, in an effort to head off House defunding action, OMB negotiated an administrative agreement with the Senate bill's authors, Senators Durenberger and Carl Levin (D-MI), trading increased disclosure for a promise that the Governmental Affairs Committee would report out a reauthorization of the Paperwork Reduction Act. Following several weeks of elaborate negotiations, OMB consented to a number of disclosure provisions including the publication of all drafts of rules sent to OMB by agencies, a monthly list of rules returned to agencies and an offer to all executive branch agencies to participate in trial procedures identical to those used by EPA described earlier in Chapter 4.

While satisfactory to key members of the Governmental Affairs Committee, OMB's disclosure provisions failed to mollify House members. Dingell (June 1986) characterized the procedures as limited in scope, which largely failed to address the constitutional problems entailed in presidential review. Asked to comment on the House reaction, Durenberger expressed disappointment, but he acknowledged that, given OMB's past behavior, he understood the House response (Haveman 1986). Shortly thereafter, the depth of Dingell's dissatisfaction became quickly apparent when the Governmental Affairs Committee reported out a governmental management reform bill, S. 2037, which, among other things, reauthorized the Paperwork Reduction Act. The chairman of the Governmental Affairs Committee, William Roth (R-DE) had planned to pass the bill quietly, by unanimous consent of the Senate. But, almost immediately, Senator Gary Hart (D-CO) placed a hold on Roth's bill, at the request of Chairman Dingell.

The hold that Hart placed on the reauthorization bill was especially important because time was running out on the Ninety-ninth Congress. According to Senate parliamentary procedures, such a procedural hold makes it impossible to pass legislation by unanimous consent. Thus, while a quick and painless passage through the Senate was foreclosed by Hart, a scheduled vote following floor debate also seemed treacherous to both key members of the Senate and to the administration. For one thing, 1986 was an election year—one in which many were predicting the Democrats would recapture control of the Senate. And, while the Republican leadership was understandably anxious to send its members home to campaign, the Senate agenda was crowded with long-delayed items. Indeed, with the Congress scheduled to recess on October 3rd, in mid-September the list of unfinished business seemed overwhelming, including securing passage of a budget bill; 13 appropriations bills; a highway bill; handgun deregulation legislation; 5 major environmental bills including the Superfund, Safe Drinking Water, and FIFRA, an historic tax reform bill; and an override attempt of the president's veto of South Africa sanctions legislation. In addition, the Senate was scheduled to carry out the impeachment trial of Judge Harry Claiborne, the first impeachment trial in 50 years. While the time available for debate was thus extremely short, any attempt at OIRA reauthorization virtually guaranteed a protracted floor battle—perhaps led by Senator Robert Stafford (R-VT), chairman of the Environment and Public Works Committee. A second reason was that OMB, itself, was extremely reluctant to subject the reauthorization bill to a full floor debate apparently because support for OIRA—even among Government Affairs members—was fairly weak. Thus, OMB could not find enough strong-willed champions to carry its concerns in a legislative floor fight. Moreover, apparently OMB—or perhaps the White House—was unwilling or unable to call on the Senate Majority Leader, Robert Dole (R-KN), to enter the fray.

Stymied in its efforts to pass reauthorization legislation in the full Senate, the administration shifted its lobbying efforts to the Senate Appropriations Committee in an attempt to persuade this committee to fund at least the regulatory review office. In the Appropriations Committee opposition to OIRA was less marked, due in part simply to the administration's own good luck. The composition of the Appropriations Committee was such that there were few Republican members who had strong negative feelings about OIRA. Moreover, while some Democratic members might have wanted to spearhead a partisan defunding effort similar to that which occurred earlier in the House, such efforts were discouraged by the presence of the principle author of the Paperwork

Act on the committee, a Democrat. This was Senator Lawton Chiles of Florida, who, as the ranking member on the prestigious Budget Committee, held considerable sway over matters important to these other members. When Chiles made clear his intention to use the appropriations process to reauthorize and fully fund OIRA, other Democrats on the committee deferred to his interests. It is interesting to note that Chiles' determination came not because he particularly supported OIRA's regulatory review activities, but because he did not want to see the Paperwork Act fall victim to a dispute over two executive orders. While the committee did not go along with Chiles' reauthorization effort, it eventually acceded to his request for a full OIRA appropriation, $5.4 million. Thus, the Senate appropriations bill reported by the Appropriations Committee contained the entire OIRA budget request, while the House version contained no funds. In the end both appropriations bills were rendered irrelevant as vehicles for compromising OIRA funding when the House and Senate determined to pass a single, government-wide appropriations bill.

The story of congressional attempts to derail the administration's centralized regulatory review procedures by defunding OIRA took an unexpected twist in October, 1986. When the Congress failed to pass any appropriations bills by September, appropriations were rolled into a single continuing resolution to fund the government referred to earlier. Eventually, such a resolution would be voted on by both the House and Senate as an "all or nothing" proposition, and presented to the president. At this time, with Congress anxious to recess, the administration intensified its campaign to have OIRA funding continued by including this funding on a checklist of potentially veto-engendering congressional actions contained in the continuing resolution. The function of this unprecedented list was to give Congress advance warning that if any of the items on OMB's seven-item "A" list were not included (or in some cases if they were) in the continuing resolution, that the president would refuse to sign the bill. It is interesting to note that another flash point of congressional resistance to administration regulatory actions—the question of defunding the Reagan appointee–dominated Civil Rights Commission—also appeared on the list of veto bait.

In the end, the question of OIRA's funding and the related matter of OIRA regulatory review activities was only partially resolved through actions on the continuing resolution. After a protracted battle among Senate members, House members, and OMB staff, the office was reauthorized. A line-item OIRA account was put into the continuing resolution and OIRA was precluded from using any of these funds to review rules, unless such rules were contained in or related to an information collection request. It is doubtful that this kind of congressional warning will have a significant impact on OIRA activities. Nonetheless, even in this incomplete form, it well illustrates the intensity of the struggle between the administration and Congress over control of regulatory administration and the unrelenting nature of congressional attempts to constrain administration efforts to implement its management strategy of regulatory reform.

The most visible—and perhaps most damaging—evidence of the negative consequences of the administration strategy of using management techniques to bypass Congress and implement the president's regulatory policies by administrative fiat is that—with almost no participation by the administration—the Ninety-ninth Congress ended a five-year regulatory legislation drought. In the second session—for the most part even as Congress was engaged in budgetary skirmishing with OMB over OIRA—it passed and sent to the president no less than four major environmental statutes overdue for reauthorization. These were the Clean Water Act, the Safe Drinking Water Act, the Water Resources Act, and the Superfund program. According to congressional aides close to the legislative process for these programs, "The White House stood on the sidelines. The occasional deputy under-secretary would call to quibble over this or that, but overall there was no policy leadership or guidance coming from the Administration." Indeed, so remarkable was this legislative feat that—in addition to being remembered for passing an historic tax bill—some on Capitol Hill believe that the Ninety-ninth Congress will be remembered as the "Environmental Congress." If this prediction is fulfilled, it would indicate that to an important extent the regulatory management strategy may well prove to have been eclipsed by congressional regulatory activism during the Reagan administration, at least insofar as environmental policy is concerned. It is important to note that these statutes continued the pattern of increasingly more detailed and prescriptive regulatory statutes, a tactic that Congress is apparently using to reduce the latitude of executive branch discretion.

Overall, legislative actions such as these might be considered as lying within the realm of traditional checks and balances when a relatively liberal Congress faces off against a relatively conservative president. More important for the focus of this study, however, Congress also showed itself capable of mounting some more untraditional resistance to a set of actions that might appear to lie entirely within the province of the executive branch—those actions we have termed Reagan's management strategy toward achieving regulatory reform. Taken together, recent legislative initiatives and congressional oversight have proved to be a significant constraint on the success of the management strategy.

OTHER INSTITUTIONAL CONSTRAINTS

While Congress has been the most obvious factor circumscribing the management strategy's success, legislative action has often been precipitated by forces outside government. Typically, the compelling influence of organized lobbying, media, and litigation by interest groups prodded Congress into action.

The president's regulatory strategy was in part predicated on an organizational assumption that regulatory administration was hierarchical and insulated, thus susceptible to new, ideologically oriented leadership. Indeed, to a surprising extent, as we have seen, the administration was able to inculcate the regulatory bureaucracy with the president's values, a remarkable accomplishment in itself. It soon became apparent to White House strategists, however, that agency administrators who disregard the outside political forces that comprise the agency's main constituency risk a great deal. The decline of the EPA and Interior Department during the respective tenures of Gorsuch and Watt illustrates what happens to agencies when their leadership rejects natural agency constituencies, discounts the media, and disregards public opinion. As Norton Long wrote,

There is no more forlorn spectacle in the administrative world than an agency and a program possessed of statutory life, armed with executive orders, sustained in the courts, yet stricken with paralysis and deprived of power . . . an object of contempt to its enemies and of despair to its friends. . . . It is clear that the American political system of politics does not generate enough power at any focal point of leadership to provide the conditions for an even partially successful divorce of politics and administration. Subordinates cannot depend on the formal chain of command to deliver enough political power to permit them to do their jobs. Accordingly, they must supplement the resources available through the hierarchy with sources they can muster on their own. . . . (Stillman 1984, p. 95)

Because public support for environmental regulation in particular and social regulation in general remained strong throughout the Reagan years, the attempts of Gorsuch, Watt, and other top administration officials to portray organized interest groups as left-wing radicals, out of touch with public sentiment, largely backfired. Many of these groups turned populist administration rhetoric back upon itself through highly successful grass roots campaigns to build memberships and increase donations. For example, Sierra Club membership doubled between 1980 and 1983, growth unrivaled in the club's history except during the Earth Day boom years. The administration has also failed in some of its attempts to undercut advocacy groups by changing the rules of the game by which these groups obtain resources from the government to carry out litigation. For example, the EPA moved to eliminate federal subsidies for attorney's fees in class action suits. However, in Sierra Club v. Gorsuch, the court found that these fees were payable under the Clean Air Act, even when plaintiffs lost their cases. The administration made a similar attempt to defund intervenor groups that participated in the nuclear plan licensing hearing process, with similar, negative results.

All during the Reagan years, interest group opposition ran the gamut of tactical maneuvers, including direct mail drives, testifying at hearings, leaking material to an information-hungry press, and litigation. Litigation has concerned both the regulatory administrative process—notably OMB review activities—and the results of Reagan's management initiatives in the regulatory arena. Judicial review of agency decisions is grounded in requirements for due process and reasoned decision making as set forth in the Administrative Procedure Act of 1942 and as continuously modified by a series of court precedents since then. The drafters of the APA envisioned judicial review of agency regulatory actions as a safeguard against overzealous agency administrators and arbitrary rule-making activity. For decades, the primary function of the courts was to restrain the tendency of regulatory agencies to engage in regulatory activities that were considered excessive, unrealistic, or unfair by some of the parties involved. But, the Reagan regulatory initiatives presented the judicial community with a set of novel problems. As Judge Wald commented,

As a result [of deregulation], the kinds of cases coming to the courts for review have changed. . . . Instead of arguing that a regulatory agency is overzealous, the new appellants are often challenging an agency's inertia in applying a regulatory program. Instead of alleging that an agency has deprived a particular individual of a fair and adequate opportunity to present her case or to participate in a benefits program, appellants may now be challenging the elimination of an entire program. . . . These new types of challenges put the courts in a difficult position. It is one thing to tell an agency that it has gone too far, but another to tell it that it has not gone far enough. (Wald 1983, pp. 44–5)

The number of lawsuits brought against regulatory agencies by public interest groups rose dramatically in response to the Reagan initiatives. Chapters 4, 5, and 6 report many instances that occurred in which the courts chastised agencies for failing to regulate and then remanded rule-making actions back to them for further consideration. Early interest group victories overturned the Transportation Department's rescission of a Carter administration rule that required autos be equipped with air bags and the Labor Department's more flexible rule implementing the Davis Bacon Act governing wage scales in federal and federally aided construction projects. In addition, the courts rejected the failure of the Interior Department to enforce its surface mining regulations and EPA's 1981 attempt to expand the definition of pollution sources to include an entire plant rather than individual pieces of machinery.

More recently, the Supreme Court ruled against the Justice Department in several civil rights cases dealing with employment discrimination.

The Justice Department, acting as point man for the White House, has made several policy changes than in effect push toward deregulation in the employment rights arena. The Reagan Justice Department reversed federal practice by throwing out minority hiring quotas. The no-quota policy led at the federal level to widespread reversals of existing administrative practices, ranging from personnel to contracts. At the local level, the administration attempted to force local governments to abandon their existing affirmative actions hiring plans (including some based on consent decrees) and to stop the practice of routinely setting aside a share of federally aided construction projects for minority contractors. The Justice Department also fostered a new test for discrimination in hiring: suits had to prove that specific individuals rather than classes of people had been harmed by past practices. The effect of this policy has been to dramatically reduce the number of hiring discrimination cases filed by the Justice Department.

In 1986, the administration's deregulation policy in the civil rights area was seriously set back when the Supreme Court endorsed the use of affirmative action as a means to redress past discrimination in hiring, rejecting the Justice Department argument that remedies must always be limited to identifiable victims of abuse (Witt 1986). In July, 1986, in two separate cases—*Local #28 of the Sheet Metal Worker's International* v. *Equal Employment Opportunity Commission*, and *Local #93 of the International Association of Firefighters* v. *the City of Cleveland and Cleveland Vanguards*— the Court ruled that neither court-ordered minority quotas for union admission nor race-based job promotion quotas violated Title VII of the Civil Rights Act of 1964. In May, 1986, the Court refused to declare affirmative action inherently unconstitutional. While the Court declared it unconstitutional for the Jackson, Michigan School Board to lay off white teachers in order to preserve the jobs of black teachers with less seniority, it also stated: "[I]n order to remedy the effects of prior discrimination, it may be necessary to take race into account." Justice O'Connor explicitly noted, "The Court is in agreement [that] remedying past or present racial discrimination by a state actor is a sufficiently weighty state interest to warrant the remedial use of a carefully constructed affirmative action program" (Witt 1986).

Individual states also have sued the federal government when federal regulatory policy became too lax. For example, when the Interior Department proposed to expand offshore leasing on the coast of California beginning in 1981, the state sued, sued, and sued again. In the end, California succeeded in overturning the Interior Department policy.

These victories for the opposition notwithstanding, judicial review of agency decisions has become more circumscribed in the 1980s. A number of scholars have pointed out that in two recent decisions—*Chevron, U.S.A.* v. *Natural Resources Defense Council, Inc.* (104 S.Ct. 2778 [1984]) and

Heckler v. *Chaney* (105 S.Ct. 1649 [1985])—the Supreme Court first narrowed the range of judicially reviewable regulatory issues to ones where Congress clearly intended there to be such review, and then accorded agencies unprecedented discretion to interpret statutes by applying a standard of reasonableness to agency interpretations. The courts have also recently become concerned with whether deregulatory actions are not arbitrary or capricious. In *Motor Vehicle Manufacturers' Association of the United States, Inc. et al.* v. *State Farm Mutual Automobile Insurance Co.* (463 U.S. 29 [1983]) the Court ruled that "[A]n agency changing its course by rescinding a rule is obligated to supply a reasoned analysis for the change beyond that which may be required when an agency does not act in the first instance." In 1986, citing the State Farm precedent, the District of Columbia Court of Appeals ruled against OSHA in the case mentioned earlier involving the short-term exposure of hospital workers to the toxin ethylene oxide. The court decided that OSHA had failed to consider relevant scientific evidence and remanded the issue back to the agency for further consideration.

These examples convey a rather mixed pattern of court action on the substantive elements of Reagan regulatory actions—some decisions favoring the administration, some not. It is clear that the courts continue to pay deference to agency expertise when exercising their judicial review responsibilities; it is equally clear, however, that the courts do not hesitate to act when agencies substantially disregard their responsibilities under statute. Overall, judicial review of agency decisions during the Reagan administration has served as a reminder that the reach of the administrative strategy is confined by existing regulatory statutes. And, as we have seen, the trend is toward quite specific regulatory statutes.

In addition to filing suits on substantive regulatory matters, interest groups also sued in opposition to centralized review procedures that increased the influence of OIRA and OMB over agency rule making. In one case, *The Environmental Defense Fund* v. *Thomas and Miller*, the environmental group charged that OMB had illegally delayed EPA rules on underground toxic storage tanks. The court rejected the Justice Department's argument that OMB had the right to delay agency regulations when it was "reasonable" or "justifiable." Instead, it ruled that OMB had no authority to delay rules beyond statutory deadlines. In the OSHA case already mentioned, the court failed to rule on the constitutional issue of OMB's involvement in the ethylene oxide rule making. Under the assumption that "courts do not reach out to decide such [difficult constitutional] questions," Judge White stated, "Since we have determined that OSHA's decision on the STEL [short term exposure limit] cannot withstand our statutory review, we have no occasion to reach the difficult constitutional questions posed by OMB's participation in this episode" (U.S. District Court of Appeals 1986, pp. 57–58). On the other hand, Judge White was critical of OMB's contribution to OSHA's decision process and expressed strong dissatisfaction with OSHA's failure to exercise its scientific expertise in regards to the health effects of short-term exposure to ethylene oxide. "While we acknowledge our deference to the agency's expertise in most cases, we cannot defer when the agency simply has not exercised its expertise" (p. 53).

Interest groups have made the most of their opportunities to advance their concerns by presenting testimony before Congress and garnering media coverage. Advocacy groups have regularly appeared before congressional subcommittees to complain about administration regulatory practices. Often, these congressional appearances, together with the verbal fireworks that they generated, were successfully linked to media stories of administration abuses. Over the past six years, most major newspapers including the New York *Times* and the *Wall Street Journal*, but especially The Washington *Post*, have carried stories about OMB's failure to meet regulatory responsibilities.

Congress has sometimes been moved to act based upon what it has read. For example, The Washington *Post*'s persistent coverage of OMB's actions blocking HUD efforts to collect data needed to regulate minority contracting practices led the Senate Governmental Affairs Committee to commission a GAO investigation in 1985. Certainly, media coverage of Gorsuch and Watt contributed significantly to building congressional pressure, calling for their resignations.

In some ways, the federal system itself imposed some constraints on the efficacy of the management strategy. As mentioned earlier, the states themselves became litigants against the Reagan-dominated federal regulatory agencies, either to block actions they opposed or to push federal agencies to regulate strictly. And in spite of the fact that the states and localities in many cases desired more regulatory administrative freedom, state and local officials soon became suspicious of the administration's agenda for intergovernment regulatory reform, believing that almost any administration proposal would involve substantial cuts in federal grants to state and local governments.

Because of these factors, state and local governments never became willing partners with the administration's campaign to push for regulatory relief or intergovernmental regulatory reform. Furthermore, with the states, as with Congress, the administration's most radical deregulation efforts backfired to some extent. In cases where the political leadership of states disapproved of administration deregulation policy, state and local governments continued to operate programs according to old federal regulations, or instituted new, perhaps even stricter, regulatory policies of their own. For example, when some members of the House—with the administration's silent approval—tried to reverse traditional patterns of regulation in the area of pesticides, by proposing to limit state pesticide standards to ones no more (rather than the traditional no less) stringent than those of the federal government, state lobbyists and some members of the Senate reacted negatively, passing an amendment to reverse the House action, returning once more to traditional regulatory practice in this area.

EVALUATING THE MANAGEMENT STRATEGY

The Reagan administration was remarkably successful in turning around a sprawling, entrenched regulatory bureaucracy and getting it to march to the new drumbeat of regulatory relief and centralized regulatory planning. But, as we have seen, the administration faced many institutional constraints outside the regulatory bureaucracy, and was not very successful in getting these outside forces to follow its lead on regulatory reform. Looking past the administration's immediate successes, it seems that the actions of outside institutions—such as Congress, public opinion, interest groups, the courts, and the media—imposed considerable constraints on Reagan's deregulation and devolution objectives. And, it appears that—as a result of the regulatory relief strategies that the administration chose, the way they implemented those strategies, and the guerrilla warfare–like conflicts that erupted over how much regulation was appropriate or desirable—the goal of achieving true regulatory reform received some setbacks.

Why Reagan Adopted the Management Strategy

Both the successes and the failures of Reagan's regulatory reform efforts spring in large part from a set of administrative actions that have been the main focus of this book—what we have termed the administration's management strategy. The administration chose the management strategy over a strategy of statutory reform—changing statutes that govern regulation. The management strategy consisted of a mandated slowdown in agency rules; the appointment of politically loyal, pro-business department and agency heads as well as subcabinet-level staff; the centralization of regulatory planning and review functions in OMB; reduced regulatory enforcement by federal agencies; and intergovernmental program budget cuts.

The administration chose to go this uncharted route on the reasonable assumption that advancing regulatory reform initiatives in Congress would clutter the legislative agenda with controversial issues and dilute administration resources on Capitol Hill. The White House, therefore, focused congressional attention on the president's two highest priorities, budget and tax policy, rather than on items in a regulatory reform agenda. Early in the transition, Reagan advisors made a calculated decision not to support a program of. modest, incremental reform of the major social regulatory programs or of the intergovernmental system, but instead to push for radical change—a choice that left little room for negotiating with Congress, state and local governments, or interest groups.

Given this situation, the management strategy emerged as a promising approach. It seemed promising because it offered a way to avoid the difficulty of carrying out the complex negotiations necessary to gain needed support from organized groups or the general public. It could be accomplished with little publicity since administrative actions would be diffused throughout the bureaucracy. And, it promised to circumvent congressional opponents of regulatory relief.

Administration Assumptions about the Management Strategy

The success of the management strategy rested on the truth of two assumptions, one political, the other organizational. First, the president could dominate regulatory administration if opponents of regulatory change were unaware of administration actions or unorganized in their responses. In short, the strategy could succeed in a political vacuum. Reagan's initial success is consistent with this explanation: Our case studies on intergovernmental relations, environmental protection, and nuclear licensing show that most opposition forces were either already battling the administration or preparing for it by the end of 1982. Thus, our analysis indicates that this kind of political advantage offered only temporary success to the management strategy.

Alternatively, a strategy that focused on regulatory administration might work if outside interference could be minimized. Once the political advantage of surprise was gone, success turned on the organizational assumption that regulation could be administered hierarchically, with little outside influence.

One of the important findings of this book is that the executive office of the president was remarkably successful in its efforts to redirect federal agency regulatory policy formulation and administration. To do so, Reagan melded some time-tested methods for controlling the bureaucracy into his overall management strategy: the appointment of political loyalists, informal White House monitoring of agency activities, and the creation of agency oversight structures in the executive office of the president.

Reagan's efforts paid some handsome dividends, as Chapter 3 shows. Within agencies, the management strategy and the Reagan regulatory goals it was intended to advance were well institutionalized by the time we carried out our survey in 1984–85. These goals were identified principally as economic ones—deregulatory and devolutionary—a perception that is confirmed by our detailed analyses of intergovernmental relations, environmental protection, and nuclear licensing. Insofar as executive branch agencies are concerned, according to those we surveyed, OMB emerged as the major influential actor in both setting and carrying out agency regulatory policies, with political appointees turning in a more mixed performance. Insofar as independent agencies are concerned, OMB played a less influential role. In these agencies regulatory reform policies were more often internally determined, according to our survey respondents. All of these findings parallel those from our case analyses. Also as we expected—based on our in-depth research in specific policy areas—individual elements of the management strategy were applied to varying degrees across the different types of agencies, although a few elements—notably the reexamination of existing regulations and reductions in agency operating budgets—were ranked as important by the large majority of respondents.

While the survey and case study results paint similar pictures of the Reagan regulatory reform initiatives in terms of what elements were applied, who applied them, and with what results, we found one important difference. Agency personnel we surveyed regarded the budget cuts as only marginally effective mechanisms for achieving the Reagan regulatory goals. However, our case studies suggest that they have been effective in the short run and that they may leave an even greater deregulatory and devolutionary legacy in years to come.

We count two related reasons for this apparent discrepancy. The first, and most important, follows from the unavoidable negative impact of budget cuts on agency day-to-day operations. While the immediate effect of the budget cuts is to make it more difficult for agencies to carry out their existing regulatory responsibilities, the long-term effect may be that agencies will have fewer new responsibilities to fulfill. We regard this outcome as wholly consistent with Reagan regulatory policies, but it is a connection that bureaucrats—themselves negatively affected by budget cutting—likely find hard to draw. For example, agency staff we interviewed at EPA—an agency already under-funded in relation to its ever-expanding regulatory responsibilities—rightly perceived budget cuts as immediately debilitating. These staff members recognized that it takes funds to regulate less as well as to regulate more. Few of those we interviewed were ready to admit, however, that sustained budget cutting would eventually be effective—effective, that is, if the goal is to *not* regulate. A related point is that we found a tendency among those we interviewed to take the short-term view of budget cuts. If this perception was also present among those we surveyed, then our survey results likely understate the effect of budget cutting on agencies' abilities to fulfill their missions over time. As the environmental protection case study demonstrated, the long-term effect of the budget cuts—that fell heavily on EPA's research and development offices and bureaus—will mean that EPA will be less able to identify and study environmental problems. This, in turn, plays into the hand of those who believe the federal government is already too much involved in the affairs of business, industry, and state and local governments.

In sum, our survey findings suggest that—to a surprising extent—the Reagan management strategy maximized the president's ability to manage the sprawling regulatory bureaucracy from the top down. To be sure, federal regulatory agencies differed in this respect with the chief distinction coming between independent and executive branch agencies. Nor do we wish to convey the impression that sailing was always smooth for the president. Nonetheless, insofar as the assumption of hierarchy is concerned, the president showed that the executive branch is far from being the unmanageable place that many students of the presidency had believed it to be during the 1970s.

However, as our examination of the congressional and other institutional responses to the management strategy and the White House and federal agency regulatory policy proposals has shown, there exist substantial outside influences on regulatory administration and the regulatory bureaucracy itself that need to be taken into account to effect lasting change.

Whatever Happened to Regulatory Reform?

Our research indicates that the administration made considerable headway toward its objective of reducing the federal regulatory role in state, local, and private-sector activities. If success is defined by whether the management strategy reduced regulatory burdens on these groups, then the answer to the question, "Was the management strategy a success," is a qualified, "yes." But, if success is defined in terms of achieving authentic regulatory reform—that is, putting in place a more rational regulatory policy, one that balances competing interests and values, and that offers promise of regulatory stability for the future—the answer is "generally no."

Let us now evaluate the success of Reagan's management strategy for achieving regulatory reform within the three major policy areas investigated in our research: intergovernmental relations, nuclear licensing, and environmental protection.

Intergovernmental Regulatory Reform. Over the past six years, as Chapter 4 shows, the budget reductions in intergovernmental grant and regulatory programs have advanced the president's agenda by placing more and more responsibilities onto the states. However, the extent to which these federal reductions have actually lowered state and local regulatory burdens is a mixed picture.

For the most part, the administration attempted to link budget cuts to greater regulatory flexibility by relaxing standards and reducing federal oversight in programs ranging from surface mining to maternal and child health. In surface mining, there is abundant evidence that coal-producing states are much less likely than their federal counterparts to enforce regulations strictly. But, in many policy areas states did not always pass this regulatory relief onto local governments or the private sector. For example, to the dismay of local officials, states continued to operate the OBRA-passed block grants with the same regulatory strictness as federal agencies had in the past. And, in affirmative action and professional licensing regulation, there is evidence that states and localities are inclined to regulate more aggressively than the administration would prefer. The federal system, itself, constrained the administration. Chapter 3 showed that the White House has been able to administer regulatory programs from the top down within the executive branch to a remarkable extent, but Chapter 4 showed that there is nothing hierarchical about the relationship between the nation and the states. When the administration failed to consider the connection between federal and state regulation, its deregulatory efforts were often frustrated. Time and again, state and local interest groups allied themselves with other interest groups and congressional supporters to force the administration to modify or withdraw its regulatory relief proposals. In a few cases, cities and states successfully sued the administration to block actions they opposed or to get federal agencies to regulate more aggressively.

Moreover, the onslaught of administration intergovernmental program budget cuts in its first year and OMB's insistence on linking regulatory changes to further budget cuts reduced prospects for reform later. Once states and localities became convinced that regulatory reform was a Trojan horse, containing an army of sharp-weaponed budget cutters, they withdrew support for it. A similar dynamic cooled the state and local reception of the New Federalism of 1982. Overall, the Administration did not progress farther because it was unable to force its agenda on hesitant partners, and because it was unwilling to make adjustments to meet state and local objectives.

Environmental Protection Reform. The case study on environmental protection policy, presented in Chapter 5, offers some of the best examples of the management strategy's successes, as well as some of its negative consequences. Here, the administration harnessed each element of the strategy: political appointments; budget cuts (especially in research, development, and enforcement); reduced federal oversight; a rescission of existing rules; and OMB review of rules. In the first years of the Reagan term, the EPA under Burford and the Interior Department under Watt instigated major reductions in agency enforcement, research and development, and oversight of state-run environmental programs. After the departures of these two officials, EPA and Interior Department policies were moderated, but OMB continued to bring the full force of its enhanced powers down on EPA.

The price has been high, however. EPA's integrity has been seriously damaged by the Superfund scandal. Evidence mounted that OMB's review of EPA rules served not to refine them but, rather devitalize them. The substitution of OMB for EPA regulatory decisions further eroded the relationship between Congress, the interest groups that comprise EPA's traditional constituency, and the agency itself. The emasculation of EPA's research capacity has made it difficult for the agency to manage yet-unknown environmental risks effectively and to fulfill its statutory missions. Consequently, there are clear signs that Congress is acting to displace agency decision making by legislating ever-more detailed restrictions and deadlines. So onerous are some of these recent provisions that they have been nicknamed "hammers": In the absence of agency action, they pound down on a date specified in statute. Congress has also acted to circumvent EPA. The Senate's 1986 answer to EPA's failure to regulate contaminants in drinking water was to mandate the states to do it. For example, whereas it took EPA three years to identify and regulate fewer than ten contaminants, the Senate-passed version of the Safe Drinking Water Amendments requires the states to identify and regulate 77 such contaminants in three years. These new requirements, with their ambitious timetables, however, may take the country even further from the goal of achieving a rational regulatory system in the environmental protection area. There is evidence that these kinds of hastily conceived provisions often prove impossible for states to comply with. Moreover, municipal storm water system provisions contained in this same Act require local governments to sample water from thousands of storm water dispatch points in the nation's largest cities for toxic substances. While the EPA worked out a compromise agreeable to local government lobbyists that would greatly reduce these costs, the agreement was unsatisfactory to both the Senate and the House, in part, because, as congressional staff report the situation, neither body trusts EPA enough to give the agency the degree of discretion called for in the compromise.

Most observers agree that U.S. industry has benefited from deregulation due to reduced enforcement and relaxed rules. But, without statutory reform, these gains may be lost when Reagan leaves office. And, as we have seen, the congressional backlash is already being felt in surface mining, toxic waste, and wastewater treatment. Many industry experts believe that the mishandling of congressional relations by Reagan appointees has poisoned the well for future progress, and they worry also about regulatory balkanization. In the words of one industry spokesman, "We may have more to fear from 50 state standards than a single federal one."

Nuclear Licensing Reform. Chapter 6 demonstrated that having failed to enact nuclear regulatory licensing reform through the legislative process, Reagan appointees moved with some success to streamline the process administratively. By management action, the NRC modified its hearing procedures, closed its meetings to the public, and relaxed backfitting rules. There is no doubt that in making these changes the administration benefited from careful political appointments and closing off public access to NRC deliberations, but other elements of the management strategy played little, if any, role in the NRC's management of its regulatory programs, demonstrating an important difference between independent and executive branch agencies.

These accomplishments notwithstanding, the Commission's regulatory relief efforts were also checked by outside, opposing forces. Overall, negative public opinion, intervenor group objections and litigation, and the media coverage of the partial meltdown at the nuclear power plant at Chernobyl in the Soviet Union more than offset the modest achievements of administrative action.

The nuclear power industry, itself, was not an enthusiastic adherent of the management strategy. Our research indicates that administrative changes were considered insufficiently thoroughgoing and stable in an industry where plant construction might span two or more presidential administrations. Thus, even from an industry point of view, the Reagan administration's management strategy could not be considered as having successfully achieved authentic regulatory reform. Thus, throughout the Reagan administration, the political forces that lowered demand for nuclear power in the past continued to hinder growth and to block real regulatory reform in this area.

Despite efforts of Congress, interest groups, and state and local governments to preserve and enhance the federal role in a number of popular regulatory programs, there is little doubt that Reagan has moved regulatory policy back from the extreme activism that characterized the 1960s and 1970s. But, regulatory policies are by no means dismantled, and there are clear signs that new environmental protection statutes will further restrict the scope of presidential administrative discretion in the future.

Our research thus suggests that management can be an effective tool to advance regulatory reform; but it also suggests that both the degree and duration of its success decline before growing opposition. Part of the explanation for this conclusion lies in the task the administration set out to accomplish by its strategy. From the beginning, regulatory management was regarded as a way of attaining the president's agenda without the sacrifices that compromise entails, of settling for no less than radical regulatory relief, of winning without expending effort on assembling a winning legislative coalition. Had the administration followed a more modest policy course—one of incremental change rather than radical deregulation and devolution—it might have enjoyed more continued success beyond the first years. Certainly, this was the lesson of our environmental and intergovernmental case studies: The administration made substantial headway when it worked within the framework of existing consensus, making changes at the margins.

In its determination to reduce regulatory costs, the administration thus relied too heavily on the administrative process to bypass legitimate interests. Regulatory relief was, after all, a cornerstone of the president's economic recovery program. Throughout the two terms, from the initial "hit lists" to OMB's persistent effort to alter agency regulations, the administration has held unswervingly to the idea that economic costs of regulation should be reduced to the maximum extent possible to improve the nation's economic performance.

The White House has consistently gauged success in regulatory reform in terms of diminution: less burden from existing regulations, fewer pages of the *Federal Register*, and fewer rules promulgated. In these terms, the administration may be judged to have enjoyed some success. But, in terms of the broader question of whether true regulatory reform has been achieved, we must conclude that the Reagan administration has largely failed.

REAGAN, THE ADMINISTRATIVE PRESIDENCY AND THE MANAGEMENT STRATEGY

Reagan and the Administrative Presidency

In the late 1970s, the cumulative wisdom of students of the presidency was that we had reached the end of the presidential era in U.S. politics (Cronin 1980; Huntington 1981; Salamon 1981, p. 287). Heclo and Salamon (1981, p. 1) called presidential government a "grand illusion," something to mislead presidents no less than the public. Paul Light (1982) suggested that chief executives were shackled to an outdated institution, one which he characterized as the "no-win presidency." Domestic policy was singled out as particularly problematic by scholars such as Wildavsky (1966b), Shull and LeLoup (1979), and Cronin (1980), who argued that Congress, the courts, and state and local governments coalesce against radical change. Overall, Neustadt (1980, p. 241) captured the general sentiment when, reflecting on Carter's performance, he asked, "Is the presidency possible? Even in the humble sense of keeping the game going, handing on the office reasonably intact."

If Ronald Reagan was familiar with this summary wisdom, he was undaunted by it. Riding a wave of popular support, he achieved a number of highly visible, nonincremental successes by 1982, including an unprecedented tax cut and a substantial reordering of federal budget priorities. Added to these were changes in key social regulatory policies which, unlike the administration's tax and budget initiatives, were the product of administration, not legislation.

The impressive list of accomplishments left students of the presidency perplexed. The institution so recently dispatched for burial was not only alive and well, but the oldest president ever was enjoying an exceptionally robust term of office. Few observers discounted the contribution of Reagan the man to this resurrection. However, most credited administrative style as well as presidential charisma, including Reagan's careful use of appointments to ensure ideological conservatism and political loyalty; politicalization of the senior executive service; strengthening other executive office staff at the expense of the cabinet secretaries; and elevation of OMB's role in legislative clearance, paper work, regulatory implementation, and congressional budget negotiations (Newland 1983). Nathan (1983, p. 93) returned to the term that he had coined in the past for Nixon, the "administrative presidency"—only this time he used it to describe the singularly effective style that Ronald Reagan employed to accomplish so much of his agenda within the sometimes perplexing contemporary policy process.

What Can We Learn from the Reagan Regulatory Experience?

These assessments notwithstanding, the findings in this book underscore a basic truth about public administration in general and public management in particular. In the federal system, the administrative process—like the legislative process—is essentially an open system where those who are willing to invest the necessary time and effort can participate. Unquestionably, administrative fiat can preempt outsiders and government institutions, a task perhaps made somewhat easier when the president sets out to restrain rather than enlarge government. But the gains accompanying a management strategy designed to circumvent the legitimate claims of Congress and the public are likely to be short-lived. Without a political consensus, gains will be blocked by Congress, overturned in court, exposed through a combination of interest group and media pressure, or undone by subsequent statutory or administrative means. Once mobilized, Congress, interest groups, the media, and public opinion are powerful forces for moderation which no management strategy could avoid indefinitely.

The management strategy succeeded, in many instances despite the objections of Congress and interested outsiders, in achieving the administration's short-term deregulatory and devolutionary objectives. But Reagan was not very successful in terms of how the actions of his administration contributed to the broader objective of improving the efficiency and effectiveness of regulatory policies and of the policy system in which they are embedded. We are forced to conclude that in the regulatory reform arena, short-term success does not necessarily translate into effectiveness. Ronald Reagan's philosophy of government regulation and the strategies he adopted to achieve regulatory relief have been quite controversial. On the extremes, detractors have charged the Reagan administration with dismantling America while supporters have applauded him for getting Washington off the country's back. As we have seen, many thoughtful people have had serious concerns about the appropriateness of administration actions, such as, pushing regulatory agencies in directions apparently contrary to their legislated missions; centralizing regulatory administration in OMB; making the possession of a correct ideology an apparent prerequisite of staff appointments within regulatory agencies; and generally attempting to make regulatory policy in isolation from Congress, other concerned institutions, even the public. There seems little doubt, on the down side, that the Reagan strategy has undermined public confidence in regulatory institutions. It has politicized regulatory administration; undercut the relationship between Congress, agencies, and the executive office in regulatory policy-making and implementation; debilitated regulatory agency management capacities and research capabilities; increased tension in the intergovernmental system; and produced a legislative backlash that has foreclosed prospects for reforming a number of important regulatory statutes in the future and is already leading to more stringent detailed regulation.

It is our conclusion that if the race is to the swift, Reagan should have been declared the winner in 1982. However, the ultimate race for both better and less regulation will go to the constant, long-distance runner, working steadily for change within a pluralistic system that demands, but also rewards, compromise.

APPENDIX

RESEARCH METHODOLOGY

Since the main objective of our survey of regulatory agencies was to provide as systematic and complete a picture of bureaucratic attitudes and behavior as possible, we needed to cast the net widely. Thus, from a total of 91 agencies listed in the Directory of Federal Regulatory Agencies (DFRA) cross-checked against the Federal Regulatory Directory (FRD) and the academic literature, we selected 55 agencies, subdivided into 19 independent regulatory commissions and 36 executive branch agencies. When we selected agencies to survey, we eliminated agencies whose regulatory responsibilities we regarded as either insignificant in the eyes of the administration or irrelevant for the purposes of our research, such as the Packers and Stockyards Administration, the Saint Lawrence Seaway Development Corporation, the U.S. Parole Commission, and the New Community Development Corporation. The sample included agencies with direct and indirect regulatory responsibilities. For example, an agency that plays an indirect—but important—role in transportation regulation is the National Transportation Safety Board (NTSB). While this board does not administer regulatory policies, it investigates transportation accidents and makes recommendations to agencies that do regulate transportation. Thus, we included NTSB and other agencies with similar oversight responsibilities.

Of the 55 agencies surveyed, 40 responded for a total of 171 surveys returned. This figure includes 14 independent regulatory commissions and 26 executive branch agencies. We also collected information from both federal and regional level staff. We considered this information important for two reasons: first, it enabled us to tell whether federal and regional staffers shared similar views, goals, and commitments (overwhelmingly they did); and second, it helped us to focus not only on the formulation of regulatory initiatives in central offices but also on their impact and effectiveness at the local level where implementation occurs (Pressman and Wildavsky, 1979). Of those we surveyed, 122 federal level officials and 49 district or regional level officials responded.

We also collected data from a cross-section of policymakers. We obtained a well balanced set of responses not only from mid-level staff but also from chairmen, vice-chairmen and commissioners of the independent regulatory agencies, division directors and regional directors, chief administrators and administrative law judges, executive directors of regulatory reform task forces in agencies and general counsels.

The regulatory reform survey consisted of three sets of questions: one on the formulation of regulatory reforms within the agency, with particular attention to the major goals of their regulatory reform effort, the main impetus for regulatory changes, actors directly or indirectly involved in the formulation process, and linkages with other agencies; a second set examining the type of approaches agencies used to formulate their initiatives and the justification for them; and a third set was devoted to data on the respondent, including his or her agency affiliation, position, title, tenure and so forth.

In addition to the survey, data for our analysis of the bureaucratic response to Reagan's regulatory policies and administration were collected from two other sources: we personally interviewed agency officials (n = 54), career and political staff at OMB (n = 8), congressmen and their staff (n = 14), and representatives from interest groups (n = 17). These interviews, conducted during 1984–86, provided much of the data used in the case studies (Chapters 4–6), and therefore were principally concerned with regulatory activity in the intergovernmental, environmental and nuclear policy areas. Many of the participants who were most directly involved in regulatory reform activities (for example, NRC commissioners, chairmen of Regulatory Reform Task Forces), were interviewed several times at critical points in the formulation process. Questions in the field instrument were identical to those in the survey questionnaire. Finally, we drew upon numerous relevant public and congressional documents and internal executive department memoranda that were made available to us.

BIBLIOGRAPHY

Advisory Commission on Intergovernmental Relations. 1984. *Regulatory Federalism: Policy, Process, Impact and Reform.* A–95. February. Washington, D.C.: Government Printing Office.

———. 1984. *Changing Public Attitudes on Governments and Taxes.* S–13. Washington, D.C.: Government Printing Office.

———. 1981. *An Agenda for American Federalism: Restoring Confidence and Competence.* A–86. Washington, D.C.: Government Printing Office, 1981.

———. 1980. *A Crisis of Confidence and Competence.* Washington, D.C.: U.S. Government Printing Office.

———. 1977. *Improving Federal Grants Management.* A–95. 'Washington, D.C.: Government Printing Office.

Alliance for Justice. 1983. *Contempt for Law: Excluding the Public from the Rulemaking Process.* Washington, D.C.: Alliance for Justice.

American Nuclear Energy Council. 1985. *Report To Members.* January 21. Washington, D.C.: American Nuclear Energy Council.

Asselstine, James K. 1986. *Separate Views.* Document submitted to the House Committee on Appropriations, Subcommittee on Energy and Water Development. March 4. Washington, D.C.: Nuclear Regulatory Commission.

Atomic Industrial Forum. 1982. *Analysis of the Proposed Legislation.* January 15. Washington, D.C.: U.S. Government Printing Office.

Baker, Stewart A. 1981. "The Deregulation That Wasn't." Washington *Post.* July 19. p. C2.

Ball, H. 1984. *Controlling Regulatory Sprawl: Presidential Strategies from Nixon to Reagan.* Westport, Ct.: Greenwood Press.

Bardach, E., and Kagan, R. A. 1982. *Going by the Book: The Problem of Regulatory Unreasonableness.* Philadelphia: Temple University Press.

Beam, David. 1983. "From Law to Rule: Exploring the Maze of Intergovernmental Regulation." *Intergovernmental Perspective* 9 Spring, pp. 7–22.

———. 1981. "Washington's Regulation of States and Localities." *Intergovernmental Perspective*. Summer, pp. 8–18.

Bernstein, J. Z. 1982. "The Presidential Role in Administrative Rulemaking: Improving Policy Directives: One Vote for Not Tying the President's Hands." *Tulane Law Review* 56, pp. 818–829.

Bernstein, M. H. 1955. *Regulating Business by Independent Commission*. Princeton: Princeton University Press.

Brigman, W. E. 1981. "The Executive Branch and the Independent Regulatory Agencies." *Presidential Studies Quarterly* 11, pp. 244–261.

Bruff, H. H. 1979. "Presidential Power and Administrative Rulemaking." *The Yale Law Journal* 88, pp. 451–508.

Burford, Anne M. with John Greenya. 1986. *Are You Tough Enough*. New York: McGraw-Hill.

Bush, G. H. 1985. "Test of statement given by Vice President George Bush at a press conference on release of the first annual Regulatory Program of the United States Government." August 8. Washington, D.C.: The White House.

Carson, Rachel. 1962. *Silent Spring*. Boston: Houghton Mifflin.

CBS News, New York *Times*. 1981. *National Surveys, 1981*. Ann Arbor: Inter-university Consortium for Political and Social Research.

———. 1983. *National Surveys, 1983*. Ann Arbor: Inter-university Consortium for Political and Social Research.

Center for the Study of Government Regulation. 1982. *Major Regulatory Initiatives During 1982*. Washington, D.C.: American Enterprise Institute for Public Policy Research.

Chemical Week. 1981. "We Need a Credible EPA." *Chemical Week*. October 21. p. 3.

Civiak, Robert. 1983. *Nuclear Power Plant Safety and Licensing*. Report No. IB80081. Washington, D.C.: Congressional Research Service.

Clark, Timothy B. 1981. "Do the Benefits Justify the Costs? Prove It, Says the Administration." *National Journal*. August 1, pp. 1382–1386.

———. 1981. "Substance Over Process." *National Journal* 13, pp. 2–8.

Coad, Gail B. 1984. "Letter to Ms. Patricia Norry, Director, Office of Administration, U.S. Nuclear Regulatory Commission." September 27, Washington, D.C.: Executive Office of the President.

———. 1982. "Remarks before the Intergovernmental Roundtable of the American Society of Public Administration, National Capital Area Chapter." Washington, D.C., March 21.

Commission on Organization of the Executive Branch of the Government. 1949. *Task Force Report on Regulatory Commissions, A Report with Recommendations, Appendix N*. Washington, D.C.: Government Printing Office.

———. 1949. *The Independent Regulatory Commissions. A Report to the Congress*. March. Washington, D.C.: Government Printing Office.

Congressional Budget Office. 1986. *Budget Memorandum to the Senate Government Affairs Committee*. September 15. Washington, D.C.: Congressional Budget Office.

———. 1984. *The Budget of the Environmental Protection Agency: An Overview of*

Selected Proposals for 1985. April 1984. Washington, D.C.: Congressional Budget Office.

"Congressional Democratic Policy Statement on Regulatory Reform." 1975. *Paul C. Leach Papers*. Box 26. June 25. Gerald R. Ford Library. Cited in Martha Derthick and Paul Quirk, *The Politics of Deregulation*. 1985. Washington, D.C.: The Brookings Institution.

Congressional Quarterly. 1982. "EPA and Congress at Odds Over Budget, Policy Issues." *Congressional Quarterly Weekly Report*, July 31, pp. 1827–1829. Washington, D.C.: Congressional Quarterly Inc.

———. 1981. *Energy Policy*. Washington, D.C.: Congressional Quarterly.

———. 1981. *Congressional Quarterly Almanac—1981*. Washington, D.C.: Congressional Quarterly Press.

———. 1979. *Energy Politics*. Washington, D.C.: Congressional Quarterly.

Conlan, Timothy J. 1985. "Federalism and Competing Values in the Reagan Administration." In *American Intergovernmental Relations—Foundations, Perspectives, and Issues*, edited by Lawrence J. O'Toole, Jr., pp. 265–280. Washington, D.C.: Congressional Quarterly.

———., and Steven Abrams. 1981. "Federal Intergovernmental Regulation: Symbolic Politics in the New Congress." *Intergovernmental Perspective*. Summer, pp. 19–26.

Cordia, Louis J. 1981. "Environmental Protection Agency." In *Mandate for Leadership: Policy Management in a Conservative Administration*, edited by Charles L. Heatherly, pp. 969–1038. Washington, D.C.: Heritage Foundation.

Council on Environmental Quality. 1983. *Environmental Quality 1983: 14th Annual Report of the Council on Environmental Quality*. Washington, D.C.: Council on Environmental Quality.

———. 1970. *Environmental Quality: The First Annual Report of the Council on Environmental Quality*. Washington, D.C.: U.S. Government Printing Office.

Cronin, Thomas E. 1980. *The State of the Presidency*. Boston: Little, Brown.

Cushman, R. E. 1949. *The Independent Regulatory Commissions*. New York: Oxford University Press.

Cutler, L. N. 1982. "The Case for Presidential Intervention in Regulatory Rulemaking by the Executive Branch." *Tulane Law Review* 56, pp. 830–848.

Davies III, J. Clarence. 1970. *The Politics of Pollution*. New York: Pegasus.

Davis, Albert J., and Howard, S. Kenneth. 1982. "Perspectives on a 'New Day' for Federalism." *Intergovernmental Perspective*, Vol. 8 No. 2. pp. 9–22. Washington, D.C.: Advisory Commission on Intergovernmental Relations.

Davis, K. C. 1982. "Presidential Control of Rulemaking." *Tulane Law Review* 56, pp. 849–862.

DeMuth, Christopher C. 1983. "A Strategy for Regulatory Reform." *Regulation*, Vol. 7. March/April, pp. 25–30.

———. 1982. "Viewpoint: A Strong Beginning on Reform." *Regulation*, Vol. 6. January/February, pp. 15–18.

———. 1981. "Letter to Nunzio J. Palladino, Chairman NRC." October 30. Washington, D.C.: Executive Office of the President.

Derthick, Martha, and Quirk, Paul. 1985. *The Politics of Deregulation*. Washington, D.C.: The Brookings Institution.

Dingell, John. 1981. "Testimony in hearings before the U.S. Congress, House, Subcommittee on Oversight and Investigations of the Committee on Energy and Commerce." *The Role of OMB in Regulation: Hearing*. 97th Cong., 1st sess., June 18. Serial no. 97–70.

———. 1986. *Press release*. June 20. Washington, D.C.: U.S. Congress.

Dodd, Lawrence C., and Oppenheimer, Bruce I., eds. 1977. *Congress Reconsidered*. New York: Praeger.

Domenici, Peter V. 1982. "Emissions Trading: The Subtle Heresy." *The Environmental Forum*. December. pp. 18–24.

Dommel, Paul R.; Rich, Michael J.; and Rubinowitz, Leonard S. 1983. *Deregulating Community Development*. Report on the Cleveland State University Field Study of the Community Development Block Grant Program. May. Washington, D.C.: U.S. Department of Housing and Urban Development, Office of Policy Development and Research.

———. *Block Grants for Community Development*. 1980. Washington, D.C.: The Brookings Institution.

Doniger, David D. 1986. "The Bubble on the Cusp." *The Environmental Forum*. March, pp. 29–33.

Downs, Anthony. 1967. *Inside Bureaucracy*. Boston: Little Brown.

Doyle, Denis P., and Hartle, Terry W. 1986. "De Facto New Federalism." *State Legislatures*. 12, pp. 21–24.

Eads, George. 1981. "Harnessing Regulation: The Evolving Role of White House Oversight." *Regulation*. May/June. pp. 19–26.

Eads, G. C., and Fix, M. 1984. *Relief or Reform? Reagan's Regulatory Dilemma*. Washington, D.C.: The Urban Institute Press.

———, eds. 1984. *The Reagan Regulatory Strategy: An Assessment*. Washington, D.C.: The Urban Institute Press.

Eidenberg, Eugene. 1982. "Federalism: A Democratic View." *A New Partnership for the Republic*, edited by Robert B. Hawkins. San Francisco: Institute for Contemporary Studies.

Environment Reporter. 1984. "OMB Official Favors Minimizing Effects of Environmental Rules on Business, Having EPA rules As Last Resort After State, Local Action." *Environment Reporter*. December 14, pp. 1387–1389.

———. 1982a. *Environmental Regulation of The Automobile*. Monograph No. 31. Volume 13. Washington, D.C.: The Bureau of National Affairs.

———. 1982b. "EPA's First Year Under Reagan Marked By Friction With Congress, Criticism over Budget, New Direction." *Environment Reporter*. January 29, pp. 1272–1276.

Ferry, Steven E. 1978. "Carter's Unstated Energy Plan." *The Nation*. March 18.

Fisher, L. 1981. *The Politics of Shared Power: Congress and the Executive*. Washington, D.C.: Congressional Quarterly Press.

Foote, Susan B. 1984. "Administrative Preemption: An Experiment in Regulatory Federalism." *Virginia Law Review*. 70, pp. 1429–1466.

Ginzberg, D. 1985. "Remarks at a Press Conference at the Old Executive Office Building." Washington, D.C., August 11.

Glendenning, Paris, and Reeves, Mavis M. 1984. *Pragmatic Federalism*. Pacific
    Palisades, CA: Palisades Publishers.
Godfrey, Hodgson. 1980. *All Things to All Men: The False Promise of the American
    Presidency*. New York: Simon and Schuster.
Gottlieb, Daniel W. 1982. "Business Mobilizes as States Begin to Move into the
    Regulatory Vacuum." *National Journal* 14, pp. 1340–1343.
Gray, B. 1981. "Testimony in hearings before the U.S. Congress, House, Sub-
    committee on Oversight and Investigations of the Committee on Energy
    and Commerce." *The Role of OMB in Regulation: Hearing*. 97th Cong., 1st
    sess., June 18. Serial no. 97–70. Washington, D.C.: U.S. Government
    Printing Office.
Greider, William. 1982. *The Education of David Stockman and Other Americans*. E.P.
    Dutton: New York.
Grubb, W. Norton., Dale Whittington, and Michael Humphries. 1984. "The
    Ambiguities of Benefit-Cost Analysis: An Evaluation of Regulatory Impact
    Analyses under Executive Order 12291." In *Environmental Policy under
    Reagan's Executive Order*, edited by V. Kerry Smith, pp. 121–164. Chapel
    Hill: The University of North Carolina Press.
Hall, H. M. 1961. "Responsibility of President and Congress for Regulatory
    Policy Development." *Law and Contemporary Problems* 26, pp. 261–282.
Halperin, Samuel. 1976. "Federal Takeover, State Default, or a Family Prob-
    lem?" In *Federalism at the Crossroads: Improving Educational Policymaking*,
    edited by Samuel Halperin, p. 19. Washington, D.C.: Institute for Edu-
    cational Leadership, The George Washington University, 1976.
Hamilton, Martha M. 1982. "Nuclear Power Industry Runs Out of Steam." The
    Washington *Post*. April 2, p. 22.
Harris, Carolyn. 1972. *In Productive Harmony*. Washington, D.C.: Environmental
    Protection Agency.
Haveman, Judy. "OIRA Clashes with Hill." The Washington *Post*. July 12, 1986.
    p. A–22.
Heatherly, Charles L. 1981. Editor. *Mandate for Leadership: Policy Management in
    a Conservative Administration*. Washington, D.C.: Heritage Foundation.
Heclo, Hugh, and Lester M. Salamon, eds. 1981. *The Illusion of Presidential Gov-
    ernment*. Boulder, Col.: Westview Press.
Hellman, Caroline J. C., and Hellman, Richard. 1983. "The Lousy Economics
    of Nuclear Power." *The Wall Street Journal*. August 2. Vol. CCII, No. 22,
    p. 28.
Heritage Foundation. 1982. *Agenda: 1983*. Washington, D.C.: The Heritage
    Foundation.
Hibbing, J. R. 1985. "The Independent Regulatory Commissions Fifty Years
    After." *Congress & the Presidency* 12, pp. 57–68.
Huntington, S. 1981. *American Politics: The Promise of Disharmony*. Cambridge,
    Mass.: Belknap Press.
Joskow, Paul, and Noll, Roger. 1981. "Regulation in Theory and Practice: An
    Overview." In *Studies in Public Regulation*, edited by Gary Fromm. pp. 1–
    77. Cambridge, Mass.: MIT Press.
Kelman, Steven. 1980. "Occupational Safety and Health Administration." In *The

Politics of Regulation, edited by James Q. Wilson, pp. 236–266. New York: Basic Books.

Kettl, Donald F. 1983. *The Regulation of American Federalism*. Baton Rouge: Louisiana State University Press.

———. 1981. "The Uncertain Bribes: Regulatory Reform in Reagan's New Federalism." In *Publius, Annual Review of American Federalism*, edited by Stephen L. Schechter, pp. 19–34. Philadelphia: Center for the Study of Federalism, Temple University.

Kirschten, D. 1982. "Government of Men." *National Journal* 14, p. 340.

Kneese, Allen V. and Charles L. Schultze. 1975. *Pollution, Prices, and Public Policy*. Washington, D.C.: The Brookings Institution.

Koch, Edward. 1980. "The Mandate Milestone." *The Public Interest*. Vol. 61, p. 6.

Landis, J. M. 1960. *Report on Regulatory Agencies to the President-Elect*. Processed, Washington, D.C.

Large, Arlen J. 1982. "Ills of Nuclear Power Aren't Likely to End with Faster Licensing." *Wall Street Journal*. August 30, p. 1, 8.

———. 1980. "Nuclear-Power Industry Pins Hopes for Survival on Reagan Presidency." *Wall Street Journal*. December 15, p. 27.

Levin, Michael H. 1986. "The Clean Air Act Needs Sensible Emissions Trading." *The Environmental Forum*. March, pp. 29–34.

———. 1985. "Building a Better Bubble at EPA." *Regulation*. March/April, pp. 33–42.

Light, Paul C. 1982. *The President's Agenda: Domestic Policy Choice from Kennedy to Carter*. Baltimore: John Hopkins University Press.

———. 1982. "Presidents as Domestic Policymakers," in *Rethinking the Presidency*, ed. Thomas E. Cronin. Boston: Little, Brown.

Liroff, Richard A. 1986. "The Bubble: Will It Float Free...Or Deflate?" *The Environmental Forum*. March, pp. 28–30.

Litan, R. E., and Nordhaus, W. D. 1983. *Reforming Federal Regulation*. New Haven: Yale University Press.

Lovell, Catherine. 1983. "Effects of Regulatory Changes on States and Localities." In *The Consequence of Cuts*, edited by Richard P. Nathan, et al., Princeton, NJ: Princeton Urban and Regional Research Center.

Malbin, Michael J. 1981. "Delegation, Deliberation, and the New Role of Congressional Staff." In *The New Congress*, edited by Thomas E. Mann and Norman J. Ornstein, pp. 134–177. Washington, D.C.: American Enterprise Institute for Public Policy Research.

Mann, Thomas E., and Ornstein, Norman J., eds. 1981. *The New Congress*. Washington, D.C.: American Enterprise Institute for Public Policy Research, 1981.

Marshall, Eliot. 1983. "Hit List Claims a Victim at EPA." *Science*. April 1, p. 38.

McCraw, Thomas. 1980. "Regulatory Change, 1960–79, in Historical Perspective." In *Government Regulation: Achieving Social and Economic Balance*. Vol. 5, Special Study on Economic Change, Joint Committee Print, U.S. Congress, Joint Economic Committee, 96th Cong., 2nd sess. Washington, D.C.: Government Printing Office.

McDowell, Bruce D. 1982. "Forum—Deregulation: Effects on State and Local Governments." *The Bureaucrat* 11, pp. 22–31.

McGraw-Hill. 1981. "The Pitfalls of 'Defederalization.' " *Chemical Week*, June, pp. 54–58.

Meese, Edwin III. 1983. "The Institutional Presidency." *Presidential Studies Quarterly*. 13, pp. 191–4.

Meier, K. J. 1985. *Regulation: Politics, Bureaucracy, and Economics*. New York: St. Martin's Press.

Metz, William D. 1977. "Nuclear Licensing: Promised Reform Miffs All Sides of Nuclear Debate." *Science*, November 11. Vol. 198, No. 4317.

Miller, J. 1981. "Testimony in hearings before the U.S. Congress, House, Subcommittee on Oversight and Investigations of the Committee on Energy and Commerce." *The Role of OMB in Regulation: Hearing*. 97th Cong., 1st sess., June 18. Serial no. 97–70.

Mitnick, B. M. 1980. *The Political Economy of Regulation: Creating, Designing, and Removing Regulatory Forms*. New York: Columbia University Press.

Morrison, Alan B. 1982. "New Federalism Holes," New York *Times*, November 1, p. E14.

Mosher, Lawrence. 1986. "Environmental Quality Council Trims Its Sails in Stormy Budget Weather." *National Journal*. July 24, pp. 1306–1307.

———. 1982. "More Cuts in EPA Research Threaten Its Regulatory Goals, Critics Warn." *National Journal*. April 10, pp. 635–639.

———. 1980. "Talking Clean on the Hustings." *National Journal*, November 1. p. 1850.

Murley, Thomas. 1983. Memorandum to Victor Stello, Jr. *Summary and Asessment of CRGR Activities to Date*. February 28. Washington, D.C.: Nuclear Regulatory Commission.

Myers, Richard. 1983. "Doing It Right in the Nuclear Business." *Energy Daily*, Vol. 11, No. 14. January 20. p. 4.

Nadel, Mark V. 1971. *The Politics of Consumer Protection*. Indianapolis: Bobbs-Merrill.

Nader, Ralph. 1965. *Unsafe at Any Speed*. New York: Grossman.

Nathan, R. P. 1983. *The Administrative Presidency*. New York: Wiley.

National Academy of Sciences. 1977. *Research and Development in EPA*. Washington, D.C.: National Academy of Sciences.

National Commission on Air Quality. 1981. *To Breathe Clean Air*. Washington, D.C.: U.S. Government Printing Office.

National Governor's Association. 1982. *The State of the States: Management of Environmental Programs in the 1980's*. Washington, D.C.: National Governor's Association.

NBC News/Associated Press. 1981. *Poll #72*. New York: NBC News.

Neustadt, Richard E. 1980. *Presidential Power: The Politics of Leadership from FDR to Carter*. New York: John Wiley.

Newland, Chester. 1983. "A Mid-term Appraisal—The Reagan Presidency: Limited Government and Political Administration." *Public Administration Review*. January/February, pp. 1–21.

Nixon, Richard M. 1973. "President's Message to Congress." *Congressional Record*. April 18. p. S7692.

Norton, Clark. 1981. *Congressional Veto Provisions and Amendments: 96th Congress,*

Report 80–86. Washington, D.C.: Congressional Research Service, Library of Congress.

"Nuclear Commission Votes to Close Talks to the Public." 1985. New York *Times.* May 17. Vol.46. Section II, p. 11.

Ogul, M. S. 1976. *Congress Oversees the Bureaucracy: Studies in Legislative Supervision.* Pittsburgh: University of Pittsburgh Press.

Office of Management and Budget. 1985. "Bulletin 85–9: Agency Guidance For Preparing Regulatory Programs." Washington, D.C.: Office of Management and Budget.

OMB Watch. 1985. *OMB Control of Rulemaking: The End of Public Access.* Washington, D.C.: OMB Watch.

Ottinger, Richard L. 1982. "Letter to NRC Chairman Nunzio Palladino." April 9. Washington, D.C.: Nuclear Regulatory Commission.

Palladino, Nunzio J. 1983. "Letter to President of the Senate, George Bush." February 21. Washington, D.C.: Nuclear Regulatory Commission.

Palmer, John L., and Sawhill, Isabel V., eds. 1984. *The Reagan Record: An Assessment of America's Changing Domestic Priorities.* Cambridge, Mass.: Ballinger Publishing Company.

Patterson, Samuel C. 1978. "The Semi-Sovereign Congress." In *The New American Political System,* edited by Anthony King, pp. 125–177. Washington, D.C.: American Enterprise Institute for Public Policy Research, 1978.

Penoyer, Ronald. 1981. *Directory of Federal Regulatory Agencies.* 3rd ed. St. Louis: Center for the Study of American Business.

Peterson, Cass. 1985. "Rare Criticism of OMB Draws Some Attention." The Washington *Post.* July 18, p. A21.

Presidential Task Force on Regulatory Relief. 1983. *Reagan Administration Regulatory Achievements.* The White House, August. Washington, D.C.: Executive Office of the President.

———. 1982. *Reagan Administration Achievements in Regulatory Relief for State and Local Government, A Progress Report,* August. Washington, D.C.: Executive Office of the President.

———. 1982. *Reagan Administration Achievements in Regulatory Relief, A Progress Report.* August. Washington, D.C.: Executive Office of the President.

Pressman, Jeffrey L. and Aaron Wildavsky. 1979. *Implementation.* Berkeley: University of California Press.

Rausch, R. 1981. "Congress Adopts Some Reagan Block Grants." *Congressional Quarterly Almanac.* Volume XXX. Washington, D.C.: Congressional Quarterly Inc.

Reagan, Ronald W. 1982. "State of the Union Address." *Weekly Compilation of Presidential Documents.* January 26. Washington, D.C.: U.S. Government Printing Office.

———. 1981. "President Reagan's Inaugural Address." *Congressional Quarterly Almanac.* Volume XXX, p. 11-E. Washington, D.C.: Congressional Quarterly Inc.

———. 1981. "Policy Statement on Nuclear Power." *Congressional Quarterly Almanac.* p. 24-E. Washington, D.C.: Congressional Quarterly Press.

Redford, E. S. 1965. "The President and the Regulatory Commissions." Texas Law Review 44, pp. 288–321.

————. 1952. *Administration of National Economic Control.* New York: Macmillan.

"Regulation and the 1986 Budget." 1985. *Regulation* March/April pp. 9–11.

Reiber, M., and Halcrow, R. 1974. *Nuclear Power to 1985.* Washington, D.C.: Center for Advanced Computation.

Ribicoff, Abraham. 1974. "Remarks in the Congressional Record—Senate". *Congressional Record,* August 13, p. S14869.

Ripley, Randall B. and Grace A. Franklin. 1984. *Congress, the Bureaucracy and Public Policy.* Homewood: Dorsey Press.

Robinson, Glen O. 1978. "The Federal Communications Commission: An Essay on Regulatory Watchdogs." *Virginia Law Review* 64, March, pp. 169–262.

————. 1971. "Reorganizing the Independent Regulatory Agencies." *Virginia Law Review,* Vol. 57, No. 6. September. pp. 947–995.

Rolph, Elisabeth. 1979. *Nuclear Power and the Public Safety: A Study In Regulation.* Lexington, Mass.: Lexington Books.

Rosenbaum, Walter A. 1977. *The Politics of Environmental Concern.* New York: Praeger.

Rothenberg, Irene Fraser. 1984. "Regional Coordination of Federal Programs: Has the Difficult Grown Impossible?" *Journal of Policy Analysis and Management* 4, pp. 1–14.

————. and George J. Gordon. 1984. "Intergovernmental Review under the New Federalism: The First Year." Unpublished Paper delivered at the Annual Meeting of the American Political Science Association, 30 August to 2 September. Washington, D.C.

Runkle, John. 1986. "Letter to the Secretary of the Nuclear Regulatory Commission." August 15. Chapel Hill: The Conservation Council of North Carolina.

Russakoff, Dale. 1984. "Early Vision Dimmed for A-Industry: Retiring NRC Official Sees Lax Regulation." The Washington *Post,* Vol. 107, July 2, p. 10.

Salamon, Lester M. 1981. "The Presidency and Domestic Policy Formulation." In *The Illusion of Presidential Government,* by Lester M. Salamon and Hugh Heclo, pp. 177–201. Denver: Westview Press.

Salamon, Lester M., and Abramson, Alan J. 1984. "Governance: The Politics of Retrenchment." In *The Reagan Record: An Assessment of America's Changing Domestic Priorities,* pp. 31–68. Cambridge, Mass.: Ballinger Publishing Company.

Scalia, Anthony. 1979. "The Legislative Veto: A False Remedy for System Overload." *Regulation,* November, pp. 19–26.

Seidman, H. 1980. *Politics, Position, and Power: The Dynamics of Federal Organization.* 3rd ed. New York: Oxford University Press.

Shafer, William, and Thurber, James. 1981. "The Legislative Veto and the Paradox of Congressional Oversight." Paper presented at the Annual Meeting of the American Political Science Association, New York, September 3–6.

Shapar, Howard K., and Malsch, Martin G. 1974. "Proposed Changes in the Nuclear Power Plant Licensing Process: The Choice of Putting a Finger in the Dike or Building a New Dike." *William and Mary Law Review* 15, pp. 539–555.

Shull, Steven A. and Lance T. LeLoup. 1979. "Presidential Impact: Foreign Versus Domestic Policy," in *The Presidency: Studies in Policy Making*, edited by Shull and LeLoup. Brunswick, OH.: King's Court Communication.

Smith, Terence. 1980. "Carter Softens His Criticism of Foe; Reagan Defends Record on Ecology." New York *Times*, October 10, pp. A1, D14.

Smith, V. Kerry. 1984. "Environmental Policy Making under Executive Order 12291: An Introduction." In *Environmental Policy under Reagan's Executive Order*, edited by V. Kerry Smith. Chapel Hill: The University of North Carolina Press. pp. 3–37.

Stanfield, Rochelle L. 1986a. "EPA Administrator Lee Thomas Is More a Manager than a Policy Maker." *National Journal*. February 15, pp. 391–395.

———. 1986b. "The Elusive Bubble." *National Journal*. April 5, pp. 820–822.

———. 1986c. "Nuclear Option." *National Journal*. July 5. No. 27. pp. 1646–1652.

———. 1984. "Ruckelshaus Casts EPA as 'Gorilla' in States' Enforcement Closet." *National Journal*. May 26, pp. 1034–1038.

Stillman, Richard J. II. 1984. *Public Administration: Concepts and Cases*. 3rd ed. Boston: Houghton Mifflin.

Stone, Alan. 1982. *Regulation and Its Alternatives*. Washington, D.C.: Congressional Quarterly Press.

Sundquist, James L. 1981. *The Decline and Resurgence of Congress*. Washington, D.C.: The Brookings Institution.

———. 1981. "Congress, the President, and the Crisis of Competence in Government," in *Congress Reconsidered*, edited by Lawrence C. Dodd and Bruce J. Oppenheimer. Washington, D.C.: Congressional Quarterly Press.

———. 1980. "The Crisis of Competence in Government." In *Setting National Priorities: Agenda for the Eighties*, edited by Joseph A. Pechman. Washington, D.C.: The Brookings Institution.

———. 1962. *Making Federalism Work*. Washington, D.C.: The Brookings Institution.

Sussman, Barry. 1986. "Seventy-Eight Percent of Americans Balk at New Nuclear Reactors." The Washington *Post*, May 24. p. A6.

Sweet, William. 1982. "Energy Policy: The New Administration." *Energy Issues: New Directions and Goals*. Washington, D.C.: Congressional Quarterly. pp. 3–6.

Synar, Mike. 1982. "Testimony in hearings before the U.S. Congress, House, Subcommittee on Oversight and Investigations of the Committee on Energy and Commerce." *The Role of OMB in Regulation: Hearing*. 97th Cong., 1st sess., June 18, 1981. p. 7. Serial no. 97–70.

Taylor, Stuart. 1983. "Ex-EPA Official Tells of 'Pro and Con' Lists." New York *Times*. March 17, p. B14.

Tether, Ivan. 1986. "Will a Final Policy Rejuvenate the Bubble?" *The Environmental Forum*. March, pp. 28, 31–32.

Thompson, F., and Jones, L. R. 1982. *Regulating Policy and Practices: Regulating Better and Regulating Less*. New York: Praeger.

Tietenberg, T. H. 1985. *Emissions Trading, an Exercise in Reforming Pollution Policy*. Washington, D.C.: Resources for the Future.

Tolchin, S. J., and Tolchin, M. 1985. *Dismantling America: The Rush to Deregulate.* New York: Oxford University Press.

Tourtellotte, James R. 1982. *Status Report on Legislation.* SECY–82–399. September 30. Washington, D.C.: NRC Regulatory Reform Task Force.

Trop, Cecile and Leslie Roos. 1971. "Public Opinion and the Environment." In *The Politics of Ecosuicide,* edited by Leslie Roos. New York: Holt, Rinehart, and Winston, Inc.

Tugwell, Rexford. 1974. "Bringing the President to Heel." In *The Presidency Reappraised,* edited by Thomas E. Cronin and Rexford Tugwell. pp. 302–321. New York: Praeger.

Union of Concerned Scientists. 1985. *Safety Second: A Critical Evaluation of the NRC's First Decade.* Washington, D.C.: Union of Concerned Scientists.

U.S., Congress. House. Committee on Banking, Finance and Urban Affairs, Subcommittee on Housing and Community Development. 1982. *Community Development Block Grant Entitlement Regulations.* Hearing, 97th Cong., 2d sess. December 7. Washington, D.C.: Government Printing Office.

———. House. Committee on Energy and Commerce, Subcommittee on Commerce, Transportation, and Tourism of the Committee on Energy and Commerce. 1984. *Hazards of Exposure to Asbestos: Hearing.* 98th Cong., 2d sess., September 26, hrg. no. 98–174.

———. House. Committee on Energy and Commerce, Subcommittee on Oversight and Investigations. 1982. *Role of OMB in Regulation.* 97th Congress, 1st Sess. June 18. Washington, D.C.: U.S. Government Printing Office.

———. House. Committee on Government Operations, Subcommittee on Environment, Energy and Natural Resources. 1982. *Lead in Gasoline: Public Health Dangers.* U.S. Congress: Government Printing Office. 97th Congress, 2d Session.

———. House. Committee on Government Operations, Subcommittee on Environment, Energy and Natural Resources. 1981. *EPA Regulatory Delay Impact on Industry and State Environmental Programs: Connecticut.* U.S. Congress: Government Printing Office. 97th Congress, 1st Session.

———. House. Committee on Interior and Insular Affairs, Subcommittee on Energy and Environment. 1978a. *Hearings On the Nuclear Siting and Licensing Act of 1978.* 95th Cong. 2d. Session. Washington, D.C.: U.S. Government Printing Office.

———. House. Committee on Interior and Insular Affairs, Subcommittee on Energy and Environment. 1978b. *Hearings on the Nuclear Siting and Licensing Act of 1978.* 95th Cong. 2d. Session. Part II. Washington, D.C.: U.S. Government Printing Office.

———. House. Committee on Interior and Insular Affairs, Subcommittee on Energy and Environment. 1978c. *Hearings on the Nuclear Siting and Licensing Act of 1978.* 95th Cong. 2d. Session. Part III. Washington, D.C.: U.S. Government Printing Office.

———. House. Committee on Interior and Insular Affairs, Subcommittee on Energy and Environment. 1983. *Hearings on Nuclear Licensing Legislation.* 98th Cong. 1st. Session. June 30. Washington, D.C.: U.S. Government Printing Office.

U.S. Congress. Senate. 1982. *Congressional Record*. 97th Cong., 2d sess., 128, pt. 30, p. S2575.

———. Senate. Committee on Governmental Affairs. 1986. *Office of Management and Budget: Evolving Roles and Future Issues*; S. Prt. 99–134. Congressional Research Service, Library of Congress, 99th Cong., 2d sess., February. Washington, D.C.: Government Printing Office.

———. Senate. Committee on Environment and Public Works. *Hearings on Nuclear Licensing Legislation*. May 25. Washington, D.C.: U.S. Government Printing Office.

———. Senate. Subcommittee on Intergovernmental Relations. *Hearing on Oversight of OMB Regulatory Review*. January 28, 1986.

U.S., Department of Energy. 1983. *Nuclear Plant Cancellations: Causes, Costs, and Consequences*. April. DOE/EIA–0392. Washington, D.C.: Department of Energy.

———. 1982a. *Proposed Costs of Electricity from Nuclear and Coal-Fired Power Plants*. DOE/EIA–0356/1. August. Washington, D.C.: Department of Energy.

———. 1982b. "Report of Department of Energy Task Force on Nuclear Licensing and Regulatory Reform." October 15. Washington, D.C.: Department of Energy.

———. 1982c. "Minutes of Department of Energy Nuclear Licensing Reform Task Force." March 14. Washington, D.C.: Department of Energy.

U.S., Department of Energy, Energy Information Administration. 1984. *Electric Power Annual 1983*. DOE/EIA–0348(83). July. Washington, D.C.: Department of Energy.

U.S., Environmental Protection Agency. Science Advisory Board. 1979. *Report of the Health-Effects Research Review Group*. Washington, D.C.: U.S. Government Printing Office.

U.S., General Accounting Office. 1979. *Improving the Scientific and Technical Information Available to the Environmental Protection Agency in the Decision-Making Process*. Washington, D.C.: U.S. Government Printing Office.

———. 1982. *Cleaning Up the Environment: Progress Achieved but Major Unresolved Issues Remain*. Washington, D.C.: U.S. Government Printing Office.

———. 1980. *Promising Changes Improve EPA's Extramural Research: More Change Needed*. Washington, D.C.: U.S. Government Printing Office.

U.S. General Accounting Office. Comptroller General of the United States. 1985. *Block Grants: Overview of Experience to Date and Emerging Issues*. April 3. Washington, D.C.: Government Printing Office.

U.S., Nuclear Regulatory Commission. 1983. "Transcript of NRC Meeting." January 27. Washington, D.C.: Nuclear Regulatory Commission.

———. 1982a. "Comments on Analysis of Proposed 'Nuclear Standardization Act of 1982.'" September 30, 1982. SECY–82–399. Washington, D.C.: Nuclear Regulatory Commission.

———. 1982b. "Minutes of October 7, 1982 Meeting." Washington, D.C.: Nuclear Regulatory Commission.

———. 1982c. "Minutes of December 20, 1982 Meeting." Washington, D.C.: Nuclear Regulatory Commission.

———. 1986. *NRC Initiatives to Control the Alteration of Safety Features on Licensed Facilities*. March 4. Washington, D.C.: Nuclear Regulatory Commission.

———. Ad Hoc Committee for Review of Nuclear Reactor Licensing Reform Proposals. 1982. "The Proposed Nuclear Licensing Reform Act of 1983." December 15. Washington, D.C.: Nuclear Regulatory Commission.

U.S., Office of Management and Budget. 1985. *Regulatory Program of the U.S. Government: April 1, 1985–March 31, 1986.* Washington, D.C.: Executive Office of the President.

———. Office of Technology Assessment. 1976. *EPA Environmental Research Outlook FY 1976 through 1980: A Review.* Washington, D.C.: Office of Technology Assessment.

U.S. President's Committee on Administrative Management. 1939. *Administrative Management in the Government of the United States.* Washington, D.C.: Government Printing Office.

Verkuil, P. R. 1982. "Symposium: Presidential Intervention in Administrative Rulemaking." *Tulane Law Review* 56, pp. 811–817.

Vig, N. J., and Kraft, M. E. 1984. *Environmental Policy in the 1980s: Reagan's New Agenda.* Washington, D.C.: Congressional Quarterly.

Wald, Matthew L. 1985. "Nuclear Panel Sees Deep '86 Cuts in Research." New York *Times.* April 18. Vol. 46, 383. Section I. p. 19.

Wald, Patricia, M. 1983. "Judicial Review of Economic Analysis." *Yale Journal of Regulation.* 1, pp. 43–62.

Waldo, D. 1948. *The Administrative State: A Study of the Political Theory of American Public Administration.* New York: Ronald Press, 1948.

Walker, David B. 1981. *Toward a Functioning Federalism.* Cambridge, Mass.: Winthrop.

Wayne, Stephen J. 1982. "Congressional Liaison in the Reagan White House: A Preliminary Assessment of the First Year." In *President and Congress: Assessing Reagan's First Year,* edited by Norman J. Ornstein. pp. 44–65. Washington, D.C. American Enterprise Institute.

Weidenbaum, Murray L. 1984. "Regulatory Reform under the Reagan Administration." In *The Reagan Regulatory Strategy: An Assessment,* edited by George C. Eads and Michael Fix. Washington, D.C.: The Urban Institute.

———. 1981. "Reagan Federalism." *Journal of Contemporary Studies* 4, pp. 71–77.

Weidenbaum, Murray L., and DeFina, R. 1978. *The Cost of Federal Regulation of Economic Activity.* Washington, D.C.: American Enterprise Institute for Public Policy Research.

Welborn, David, William Lyons and Larry Thomas. 1984. *Implementation and Effects of the Federal Government in the Sunshine Act.* Washington, D.C.: Administrative Conference of the United States.

Welborn, D. M. 1966. "Presidents, Regulatory Commissioners and Regulatory Policy." *Journal of Public Law* 15, pp. 3–29.

White, L. J. 1981. *Reforming Regulation: Processes and Problems.* Englewood Cliffs: Prentice-Hall.

White House. 1983. *Final Report of the President's Task Force on Regulatory Relief.* August. Washington, D.C.: White House.

———. 1981. "Regulation." February 19. Washington, D.C.: White House.

Wildavsky, Aaron. 1966a. *The Politics of the Budgetary Process.* Boston: Little, Brown.

———. 1966b. "Two Presidencies," *Transaction.* Vol. 4. December.

Wilson, James Q., ed. 1980. *The Politics of Regulation.* New York: Basic Books.

Wines, Michael. 1982. "Chemical Industry Fears Pendulum's Swing Back to the 50 States." *National Journal.* November 13, pp. 1927,1954.

Witt, Elder. 1986. "High Court Rules in Affirmative Action Cases." *Congressional Quarterly Weekly Reports.* Washington, D.C.: Congressional Quarterly, Inc.

Wrightson, Margaret. 1986. "From Cooperative to Regulatory Federalism?" *SIAM Intergovernmental News* 9, p. 1,4.

Yaffe, Elaine. 1981. "Ambiguous Laws Fuel Debate on Bilingual Education." *Phi Delta Kappa* 62, p. 741.

Zech, Lando W. Jr. 1986. "Prepared Testimony Concerning Licensing Reform and Other Matters Submitted by U.S. Nuclear Regulatory Commission, Before the Subcommittee on Energy and Environment, Committee on Interior and Insular Affairs." #860722. Washington, D.C.: Nuclear Regulatory Commission.

INDEX

ABOUT THE AUTHORS

MARSHALL R. GOODMAN is Assistant Professor of Government at Georgetown University, Washington, D.C.

Dr. Goodman has published widely in the areas of public policy, public–private partnership programs, and legislative behavior. His articles and reviews have appeared in edited books and journals, including *Polity*, *Policy Studies Review*, and *Administration and Society*.

Dr. Goodman holds a B.A. from DePaul University, which included course work at Oxford University, Oxford, England. He received his M.A. and Ph.D. from The Ohio State University, Columbus, Ohio.

MARGARET T. WRIGHTSON is Assistant Professor of Government at Georgetown University in Washington, D.C.. From 1985 to 1987, she served as Staff Director, Subcommittee on Intergovernmental Relations, Committee on Governmental Affairs, United States Senate.

Dr. Wrightson has published in the areas of intergovernmental relations, congressional behavior, and local government. Her articles and commentaries have appeared in edited books and government documents as well as in journals, including *Journal of Politics* and *Urban Affairs Quarterly*.

Dr. Wrightson holds a B.A. in Political Science from the University of California at Berkeley, an M.A. in Public Policy and Management from California State University at San Francisco, and a Ph.D. in Public Administration from the American University.